THE JAPANESE MISSION TO EUROPE, 1582–1590

THE FOUR SAMURAI BOYS

Sketches of the four Japanese made by Urbano Monte during their visit to Milan in July 1585. From Beniamino Gutierrez, *La Prima Ambascieria Giapponese in Italia*, Milan, 1938

The Japanese Mission to Europe, 1582–1590

THE JOURNEY OF FOUR SAMURAI BOYS THROUGH PORTUGAL, SPAIN AND ITALY

■

Michael Cooper

GLOBAL ORIENTAL

THE JAPANESE MISSION TO EUROPE, 1582–1590
THE JOURNEY OF FOUR SAMURAI BOYS THROUGH PORTUGAL, SPAIN AND ITALY

By Michael Cooper

First published 2005 by
GLOBAL ORIENTAL
PO Box 219
Folkestone
Kent CT20 2WP
UK

www.globaloriental.co.uk

© Michael Cooper 2005

All rights reserved. No part of this publication may be
Reproduced or transmitted in any form or by any electronic,
Mechanical, or other means, now known or hereafter
Invented, including photocopying and recording, or in
Any information storage or retrieval system, without prior
Permission in writing from the Publishers, except for the
Use of short extracts in criticism.

British Library Cataloguing in Publication Data
A CIP catalogue entry for this book is available
From the British Library

ISBN 1-901903-38-9

Set in Stone Serif 9.5 on 12pt by Servis Filmsetting Ltd, Manchester
Printed and bound in England by Antony Rowe Ltd, Chippenham, Wilts

Contents

Plate section faces pages 108

Preface	*ix*
Acknowledgements	*xi*
Maps	*xiii*
Chronology	*xvii*

Part 1. The Legation is Planned
1. Christianity in Japan   3
2. Preparing the Legation   12

Part 2. The Journey to Europe
3. Passage to India   25
4. From India to Europe   35

Part 3. Through Portugal and Spain
5. Portugal   45
6. Spain and 'the Most Potent Monarch'   53
7. From Alcalá to Alicante   69

Part 4: Rome and the Two Popes
8. The Road to Rome   77
9. The Papal Audience   86
10. The Stay in Rome   92
11. The New Pope   98

CONTENTS

Part 5. Further Travels in Europe
12. Bologna and Ferrara   107
13. Carnival of Venice   113
14. From Padua to Genoa   118
15. Spain and Portugal Revisited   130

Part 6. The Return to Japan
16. The Return Journey   141
17. Reception in Japan   152

Part 7. Summing Up
18. Assessment of the Enterprise   163

Appendices
Appendix 1. The Boys' Later Careers   180
Appendix 2. The Sources   193
Appendix 3. Azuchi Screens and Braun's Cities   203

Notes   *212*
Bibliography   *246*
Index   *254*

*In memory of the boys
who went to Rome –
Mancio, Michael, Martin and Julian*

Preface

Pope Gregory XIII died in Rome at three o'clock in the afternoon of 10 April 1585, at the age of eighty-three. The death of the elderly pontiff was not unexpected, and twelve days later the available cardinals assembled in conclave to elect his successor. On 24 April, Cardinal Felice Montalto received their unanimous vote, accepted the nomination, and adopted the name of Sixtus V.

The solemn coronation Mass was celebrated in St Peter's basilica on 1 May, with the great cathedral filled with nobility, senators, ambassadors and civil officials, as well as cardinals, archbishops, bishops, abbots and other senior members of the clergy. When the new pope made his entrance at the end of a long procession, he was flanked by eight men, four on either side, holding poles supporting a canopy over him. This escort consisted of the French and Venetian ambassadors, the Duke of Sora, the Marquis Altemps and the Marquis Riano.

The remaining canopy-bearers were three Japanese teenagers. During the celebration of Mass one of these boys entered the sanctuary and ceremoniously washed the pope's hands.

Europeans first reached Japan in 1543, and Christian missionaries had begun preaching there only thirty-six years before this ceremony at St Peter's. So what were these Japanese youths doing in Rome? And why had they been invited to take part in the ceremony? This book recounts why the boys left Japan, their long and hazardous sea voyages, their travels through Europe, their return home and their subsequent careers.

PREFACE

Concerning their travels, J. G. Scheuchzer noted in 1727, 'the Eyes of all Europe were then turned' upon the Japanese visitors, while a modern scholar writes, 'That the [boys] put Japan on the map for most Europeans is beyond doubt.'[1] This is the story of the first Japanese to visit Europe and return to their native country.

JAPANESE WORDS AND NAMES

Japanese words, such as *sake* and *wakizashi*, are printed in italics, although this does not apply to terms, such as daimyo and samurai, that have entered the English language. Long vowels, as in Itō and Ōtomo, are indicated by a macron.
Names are given according to Japanese usage, that is, family name followed by personal name, e.g. Konishi Yukinaga and Kuroda Nagamasa; when a Japanese has a Christian name, e.g. Martin Hara and Julian Nakaura, this order is reversed.

Acknowledgements

I owe a debt of gratitude to many people who have studied the first Japanese legation to Europe and have published their findings. Foremost among these accounts is the record compiled by the missionary Luis Fróis, S.J., 1532–97, who based his text on the notes written by the Japanese boys and their companions during their travels, as well as on printed sources. Fróis met the travellers on their return to Japan, and lost no time in producing a day-to-day account of their expedition. This invaluable Portuguese record was published as *La Première Ambassade du Japon en Europe*, Tokyo, 1942, a remarkable feat in wartime Japan. The text was transcribed and annotated by the international team of J. A. Abranches Pinto, Okamoto Yoshitomo and Henri Bernard, S.J. I am grateful for permission from the estates of these three editors to make free use of their impressive labours. The present book is a paraphrase of Fróis's text, omitting repetitious and minor details, and supplementing his account by material obtained from other sources.

Among other contemporaneous sources is a Latin work also based, at least partially, on the diaries and notes written by the travellers. This is the less detailed record compiled by Alessandro Valignano, S.J., 1539–1606, titled *De Missione Legatorum*, Macao, 1590. Here I must acknowledge my deep gratitude to Dr J. F. Moran, who with remarkable generosity made available to me his unpublished translation of this lengthy and difficult text.[1]

As mentioned above, the present work is a paraphrase of Fróis's and, to a less extent, Valignano's accounts, and to have provided hundreds of page references to these two works in footnotes would have been extremely tedious. I have therefore added page references only when direct quotations are made. Specialists wishing to study the original texts can do so in the pages of *La Première Ambassade* and *De Missione*.

As Professor Adriana Boscaro, University of Venice, has shown, a great deal of relevant unpublished material is held in the archives of the cities visited by the Japanese boys as they travelled through Portugal, Spain and Italy. To comb these collections would take a lifetime and would result in a multi-volume encyclopaedic treatise. The purpose of the present book is otherwise. Little exists in English about the boys' mission, and so I offer a general introductory account, leaving it to other researchers to supplement this work at a later date in more detailed monographs.

The story of the boys' travels through Europe understandably occupies most of this book, but their lives, once they returned to Japan, is not without interest. Here I must acknowledge the contribution of Yūki Ryōgo, S.J., Nagasaki, who, in addition to his research on the expedition to Europe, has made a study of the subsequent careers of the first Japanese legates who visited Europe and returned to their country to tell their tale.[2] Fr. Yūki has answered dozens of my queries with both patience and erudition, and I am truly grateful.

Finally, it is my pleasure to acknowledge with thanks my gratitude to Professor Beatrice M. Bodart-Bailey, Otsuma University, as always for her much-appreciated advice and suggestions; Dr Aileen Gatten, for her expert help regarding the preliminary copy of the boys' letter to Venice; Dr J. F. Moran, for sending me, chapter by chapter, his translation of *De Missione*; Professor Reinier H. Hesselink, University of Northern Iowa, for his help with Dutch materials; Professor David Waterhouse, University of Toronto, for information about musical instruments; Tokiko Yamamoto Bazzell, Japan specialist librarian at the University of Hawaii at Mānoa, for her valuable and cheerful help; Nina Raj, Tokyo, for negotiating copyright permissions; and Mari Anne Wohl, Copenhagen, for her expertise regarding European nobility.

Michael Cooper
Honolulu, 2005

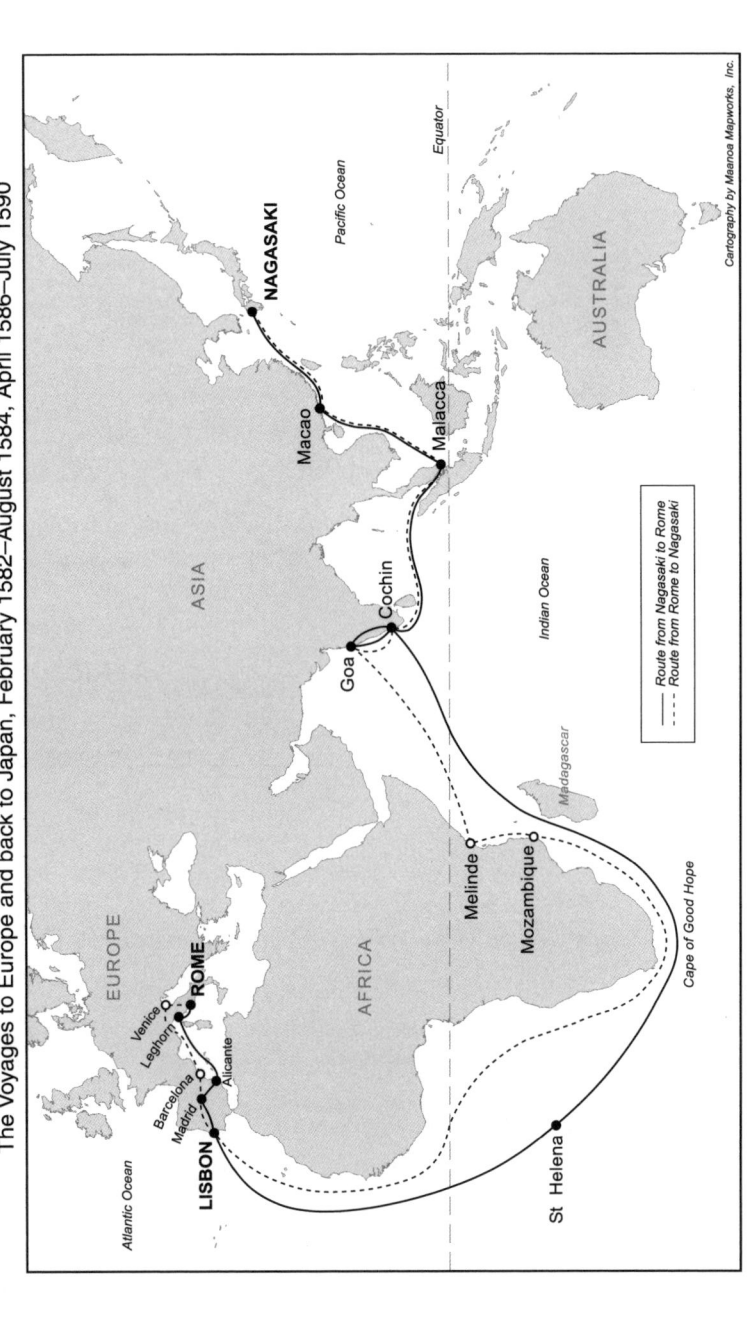

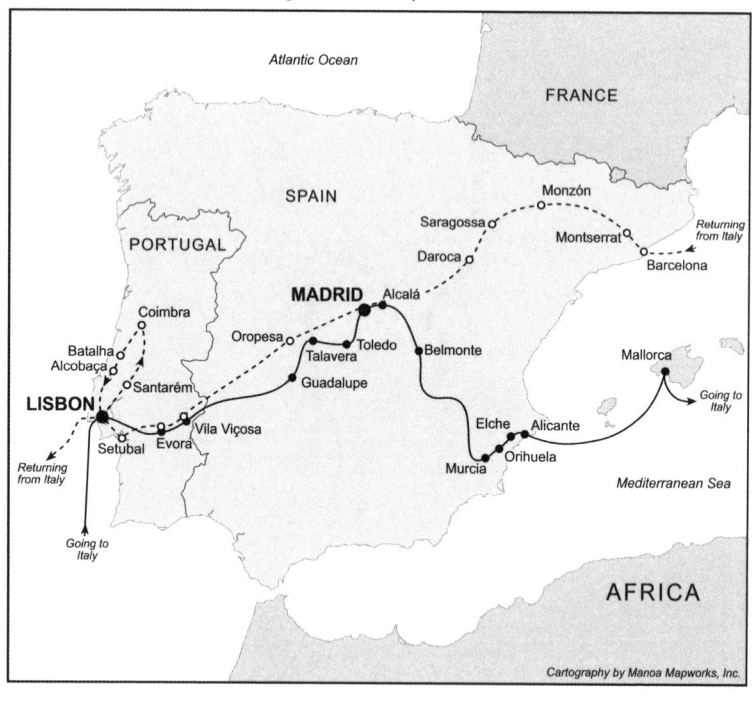

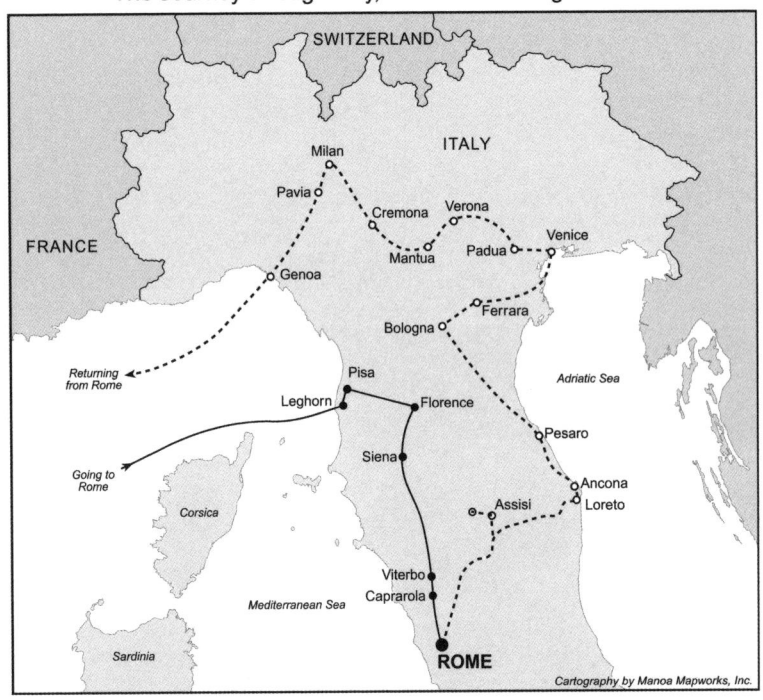
The Journey through Italy, March 1585–August 1585

Chronology

JAPAN
1581
December — Plan to send embassy to Rome
1582
February 20 — **Boys sail from Nagasaki**

MACAO
1582
March 9–December 31 — Macao
1583
January 27–February 4 — Malacca

INDIA
1583
March 31– — Overland trek across south India
April–October — Cochin
November 28–December — Goa; return to Cochin
1584
February 20 — Depart Cochin
May 27–June 6 — St Helena

PORTUGAL
1584
August 11–September 5 — **Lisbon**
September 8–15 — Evora
September 15–18 — Vila Viçosa

THE JAPANESE MISSION TO EUROPE, 1582–1590

SPAIN
1584
September 23–25	Guadalupe
September 29–October 19	Toledo
October 20–November 26	**Madrid**
November 11	Allegiance ceremony
November 14	**Audience with Philip II**
November 16–19	Escorial
November 26–29	Alcalá
December 10	Arrive Murcia

1585
January 3	Depart Murcia
January 5–February 7	Alicante
February 15–19	Mallorca

ITALY
1585
March 1	Leghorn
March 2–7	Pisa
March 7–13	Florence
March 14–17	Siena
March 22–June 3	**Rome**
March 23	**Solemn papal audience**
March 25	With pope to S. Maria sopra Minerva
April 10	Death of Gregory XIII
May 1	Coronation of Sixtus V
May 5	With pope to St John Lateran
May 27	With pope to St Mary Major
June 7	Assisi
June 19–22	Bologna
June 22–25	Ferrara
June 26–July 6	Venice
July 6	Padua
July 13–18	Mantua
July 25–August 3	Milan
August 6–8	Genoa

SPAIN
1585
August 16–	Barcelona, Montserrat
September 9	**Audience with Philip II at Monzón**
September	Saragossa, Alcalá, Madrid

xviii

CHRONOLOGY

PORTUGAL

1585	
October	Vila Viçosa
Early November–Nov.12	Evora
November	Lisbon
December 23	Arrive Coimbra
1586	
January 9	Depart Combra
	Lisbon
April 8	**Depart Lisbon**
August 31	Arrive Mozambique
1587	
March 15	Depart Mozambique

INDIA

1587	
May 29	Arrive Goa
1588	
April 22	Depart Goa

MACAO

1588	
August 17	Arrive Macao
1590	
June 23	Depart Macao

JAPAN

1590	
July 21	**Arrive Nagasaki**
1591	
March 3	**Audience with Hideyoshi in Kyoto**
July 25	Boys enter Jesuit novitiate

Part 1

The Legation is Planned

CHAPTER 1

Christianity in Japan

It was the Venetian traveller Marco Polo, c.1254–1324, who first introduced Japan to the West. He spent some seventeen years in China, and on his return to Europe he dictated his famous *Travels*, describing the many exotic cities he had visited in far-distant lands. Not content with recounting the places he had personally seen, Polo also mentions countries about which he had received only hearsay reports in the course of his travels. Among these is Japan, which he calls Zipangu, derived from the Chinese name for that country. He writes:

> I can tell you a wonderful thing about the Palace of the Lord of that Island. You must know that he hath a great Palace which is entirely roofed with fine gold, just as our churches are roofed with lead, insomuch that it would be scarcely possible to estimate its value. Moreover, all the pavements of the Palace, and the floors of its chambers, are entirely of gold, in plates like slabs of stone, a good two fingers thick; and the windows also are of gold, so that altogether the richness of his Palace is past all bounds and all belief.[1]

This colourful but erroneous reference to the abundance of gold in Zipangu not surprisingly aroused a good deal of interest in Europe, and for centuries mariners and merchants sought this mysterious island so rich in gold and other precious metals. Christopher Columbus, for example, had Zipangu much in mind during his voyages of exploration as evidenced by the marginal notes in his copy of the 1485 edition of Polo's *Travels*. He in fact believed he had located the island of so much gold and wealth in October 1492, but alas for Columbus's hopes, the explorer had reached Cuba, not Zipangu,[2] a striking example of mariners' inability to calculate distances of longitude in those days.

The first Europeans to set foot on Japanese soil arrived by accident in 1543, when a storm blew a Chinese junk carrying three Portuguese traders on to Tanegashima, a small island to the south of Kyushu, one of the main islands of Japan, and in this fortuitous way the century of European-Japanese relations began. Once news of Japan's 'discovery' spread, Portuguese merchant vessels began calling at ports in Kyushu, and a lucrative trade was soon established.

Missionary work in Japan was inaugurated by the arrival of the Jesuit priest Francis Xavier, 1506–52, and two companions in 1549. Xavier stayed in the country for less than three years before returning to India and then setting out on a fruitless attempt to enter China. In time reinforcements, mostly Spanish and Portuguese Jesuits, arrived in Japan and achieved remarkable success in their efforts to spread the Christian faith. Their main field of activity was Kyushu, and in due course Nagasaki, where the annual Portuguese ship docked from 1571, became for all intents and purposes a Christian city.

At the time no effective central authority existed in Japan, and the country was divided into dozens of fiefs ruled by regional daimyo, or barons. The missionaries were able to convert several lords in Kyushu, and this greatly helped their apostolate, for some of these rulers brought pressure on subjects to follow their example and embrace Christianity. Thus, by 1582, only thirty-three years after Xavier's arrival, the handful of missionaries (there were never more than fifty Jesuit priests in the country at any one time) had established a thriving Christian community said to number some 150,000 believers.[3]

Valignano

If Francis Xavier was the first founder of the Japanese mission, then the Italian Jesuit Alessandro Valignano, 1539–1606, can be considered the second. He entered the Society of Jesus in Rome in 1566, and his superiors were quick to recognize his exceptional administrative talents, for, when only thirty-four years of age, he was appointed the Visitor (or inspector) of the Jesuit missions in Asia. Valignano arrived in Japan in 1579 to begin the first of three extended visits to that country. He introduced far-sighted reforms in the mission, insisting, for example, that missionaries should make an adequate study of the Japanese language, and advocating cultural accommodation. In this Valignano was supported by Ōtomo Sōrin, daimyo of Bungo, who told him:

> The Fathers' customs are good in their own countries, but if they wish to convert Japan, they should study the language well and live in keeping with Japanese manners. . . . Foreigners who live in Japan in accordance with their own customs will be regarded as barbaric and vulgar people.[4]

This observation may express a self-evident truth in our own day, but was far from obvious to many missionaries in Valignano's time.

Valignano's campaign to promote acculturation achieved considerable success, and in 1596 a Spaniard visiting Japan remarked about the missionaries:

> They so imitate the Japanese that they wear their clothes, speak their language, eat like them on the floor without cloths, tables, or napkins. Nor do they use their hands but eat with a small stick, observing the same ceremonies as the Japanese do themselves.[5]

Valignano established two boarding schools, or *seminarios*, for Christian boys, one near Kyoto, the capital, and the other in Kyushu, where pupils studied not only the traditional subjects of Japanese letters and literature, but also Latin and Portuguese; the more talented were also instructed in European music, painting, and engraving. Emphasis was placed on daily exercises in Christian piety in the hope that students would later apply for the priesthood or enter religious life.[6]

Despite the mission's encouraging progress, various concerns occupied the Visitor's attention; some were of fundamental importance, others less so. But whatever their degree of urgency, Valignano, a man of determination and imagination, spared no effort to seek solutions to any obstacles threatening the well-being and future of the mission. Doubtless the church in Japan faced a variety of problems, but in Valignano's view, three issues were of the greatest importance.

Finance

Foremost among the problems facing the church in Japan from the beginning and a source of continual anxiety was the lack of adequate finance to sustain apostolic work and allow for further development. As Valignano explains in his copious writings, the mission could not be self-supporting. Christian daimyo appeared to be wealthy, but had little cash to spare to subsidize missionary activity, for, in accordance with the Japanese politico-economic system of those times, much of their income was used up in sustaining their many retainers.[7] Further, presenting costly gifts on each visit to these and other daimyo was a continual drain on mission resources.[8] Japan could hardly be more distant from Europe, and promised funds were often delayed en route or never arrived at all. In addition, missions in Asia and elsewhere were usually located in territories colonized by either Spain or Portugal, and as a result could expect funding from the Iberian governments and church.[9]

The situation in Japan, located off the eastern Asian landmass, was far different, for the country's size, remote location, and military strength precluded any possibility of European colonization. Financial aid coming from Europe and elsewhere was therefore inadequate and the resulting economic problems placed the future of the mission in jeopardy.

In a letter dated 17 December 1583, and sent from Goa to the outstanding benefactor of the Japanese mission, Theotonio de Brangaça, archbishop of Evora, who 'has always been the special protector and defender of this India and of Japan', Valignano goes into detail about the needs of the Japanese mission. He notes that there were about two hundred churches and more than 150,000 Christians in Japan ('this number is greatly increasing every day'), nearly twenty Jesuit residences, some eighty priests and Brothers, and two schools for boys; there was also the upkeep of servants looking after the churches. Valignano writes: 'Thus, we are supporting in Japan more or less five hundred people every year. As everything must be newly made . . . and we have no incoming rents, there is not enough to cover expenses.' For this reason, he adds, he was sending Fr Nuno Rodrigues to Rome to seek a remedy from the pope and Philip II.[10]

In a later letter to the same benefactor, dated 23 December 1585, Valignano puts forward the idea of inaugurating three Montes de Piedade, or charitable organizations, to lend money to poor Christians in Japan.[11] This plan would obviously require further capital, for each foundation would need at least 5,000 crowns to set up. He also raises the possibility of founding hospitals for Christian nobles and commoners, each of which would require 500 crowns a year. In this letter, Valignano repeats the figure of 'more than 150,000 Christians' in Japan, most of them living in southern Kyushu.

There could be no doubt about the mission's pressing financial needs that forced the Jesuits in 1578 to take part in the Portuguese silk trade with China. Canon law forbade clerics to engage in trade, for commercial and competitive transactions were considered unbecoming for the clergy. But the mission's financial problems obliged the Jesuits to seek and obtain special exemption from Rome for a limited participation in the silk trade. Nobody was happy about this arrangement, but the Jesuit superiors could find no other source of income to finance their work.[12]

Valignano believed that if only the mission were better known and publicized in Europe, some of the financial problems might be solved. Writing in 1583, he observes:

> ... until now there has not been in Europe a full and complete knowledge of the Japanese nation nor of the great things divine providence has wrought and daily deigns to perform in marvellous fashion through the religious of the Society [of Jesus] in this new Church. For lack of this knowledge this most noble province, among all those that have been recently converting to the faith of Jesus Christ our Lord, lacks the necessary means to sustain itself and progress. These would surely not be lacking if it were nearer to our Europe or if the Supreme Pontiff, vicar of Jesus Christ on earth, and other Christian princes and lords, both religious and lay, had a clearer and more complete knowledge of it.[13]

Time and again, Valignano deplored this lack of communication and the resulting dearth of income. At times his correspondence shows signs of desperation when he deals with the financial crisis of the Japanese mission. He writes:

> If Our Lord allows another ship to be lost, I can see no human remedy that can be applied, and when I see the great danger in Japan and how much fruit will be lost for lack of having anything to spend, I cannot live without great worry and anxiety. It seems to me impossible that if people in Europe knew what is really happening in Japan and the great danger resulting from this need, His Holiness, His Majesty, the cardinals and other Christian princes would not be moved to provide Japan with rents and substantial capital.[14]

Valignano was concerned about the needs of Japan to the very end. In his last testament, drawn up in his sick bed only three days before he died on 20 January 1606, in Macao at the age of sixty-seven, he once more discusses the financial crisis of the Japanese mission and makes various recommendations.[15]

Japanese Attitude

In addition to the lack of adequate funding for their work, the Jesuits faced a cultural problem in their dealings with the Japanese. This did not concern the need for missionaries to adapt to their way of life, but rather the Japanese attitude towards Europeans. In their reports, European observers time and again referred to the high esteem in which the Japanese held their own island country and culture. In this respect, the Japanese were, of course, not alone, for the Chinese regarded anyone who had the misfortune of being born outside their boundaries as barbarians.[16] For that matter, Westerners generally took for granted that Europe was the world centre of religion and culture. Although Xavier had described the Japanese as 'the best people so far met', he also noted they 'have a high opinion of themselves because they think that no other nation can compare with them as regards weapons and valour, and so they look down on all foreigners'.[17]

Xavier's observation was echoed by Luis Fróis, who wrote that the Japanese 'contemn all other nations in comparison with themselves, and standing in their own conceit do far prefer themselves before all other sorts of people in wisdom and policy'.[18]

Valignano himself comments on this problem, ruefully observing: 'Many people . . . believe we are poor men and impoverished in our own countries, and for this reason we have come to Japan to find some relief under the pretence of preaching the things of Heaven'.[19] He elsewhere makes this same point:

> When the Fathers were transmitting to their Japanese students all this information (and the like) [about Europe and its culture] together with the Christian law, they were hardly able to manage to imprint it deeply on their minds, and drive out entirely the false notions conceived about their own and our culture.[20]

Valignano was anxious that the glory and power of Renaissance Europe should be known and acknowledged in Japan through the medium of Japanese observers. As he notes elsewhere, the Japanese had such a high opinion of themselves and their country that European reports of their own countries were often regarded with doubt. If only some Japanese could provide eyewitness testimony about the splendours of Europe, then a more objective understanding of the West could be obtained.

Thus Valignano believed there was a pressing need not only to make Japan better known in Europe but also to make Europe better known and appreciated in Japan.

The Friars

In addition to these concerns, there was also a third issue facing Valignano, a matter that did not relate directly to the Japanese, but was extremely controversial and produced considerable bitterness and recrimination that were to last for years. The Christian mission in Japan had been inaugurated by Francis Xavier in 1549, and although he and his two companions were Spanish and Spanish Jesuits were labouring in Japan, the mission was considered very much a Portuguese project. Regardless of their nationality, missionaries were obliged to set out from Lisbon and sail in Portuguese ships; en route they called in at the Portuguese possessions of Goa and Macao. Ever since its inauguration, the Japanese mission had remained in Jesuit hands, and on their own frank admission the number of missionaries working in Japan was insufficient to meet the demands of the developing church, and reinforcements were sorely needed.

News of the successful apostolate and large number of conversions in Japan had been widely circulated abroad, and understandably other religious orders, for example, the Franciscans in the Philippines, wished to join the enterprise and help propagate the Christian message in Japan. Different religious orders worked side by side in other countries, although not always in complete harmony, and there appeared no need for Japan to be an exception in this regard. The mission's manpower shortage was well known, and it seemed reasonable for other religious orders, with their ample manpower, to enter the country and expand the Christian movement. This in fact was also the view of several Spanish Jesuits in Japan, who sent letters to the Philippines encouraging the friars to come and join in their work.[21]

This opinion certainly appeared persuasive and sensible, but Valignano adamantly opposed the introduction of other religious orders and strongly argued in favour of the Jesuit monopoly of mission work in Japan, fearing that the arrival of members of mendicant orders inexperienced in Japanese life and customs would set back his policy of cultural accommodation. Many of the friars, he believed, had worked in regions in South America or the Philippines where social and cultural development was low, and they might well introduce a conquistador attitude and policy, to be found elsewhere, with fatal results in the case of Japan. Further, the different customs of the Jesuits and friars might well confuse the minds of the newly-baptized faithful.[22]

Underlying much of the controversy was the rivalry existing between the venerable mendicant orders, founded by canonized saints centuries earlier, and the highly successful Jesuit order inaugurated within living memory. A further complication could be found in the mutual antagonism between Spaniards and Portuguese. This hostility had existed for years, but it was further aggravated in 1580 when Philip II of Spain, 1527–98, ascended the Portuguese throne as Philip I of Portugal, thus beginning what the Portuguese bitterly called their 'sixty-year captivity'.[23]

It is hardly necessary to state that the Franciscan friars in the Philippines disagreed with Valignano's position and resented their exclusion from the rich harvest field in Japan, a policy they found particularly galling and unreasonable.[24] This disagreement between Jesuits and friars would later give rise to unseemly quarrels between men of good will who had travelled around the world to spread the

Christian message of peace and love, but then, ironically and sadly, spent considerable time and labour in trading accusations and insults with fellow religious.

Thus Valignano was faced by these three problems in Japan – lack of finance, lack of Japanese knowledge and appreciation of Europe, and the retention of the Jesuit monopoly of missionary work despite the lack of adequate available manpower. Nobody could deny that the Visitor possessed both imagination and boldness in his policies and their implementation, and he used both qualities in a daring bid to settle the three issues.

Valignano hit upon a bold and imaginative plan to solve at least some of the problems facing the mission in Japan – he would organize and lead a Japanese legation to Europe. He explains:

> The purpose of the journey . . . to Portugal and to Rome is twofold. The first is to seek a remedy which, both spiritually and temporally, is needed in Japan. The second is to make known to the Japanese the glory and grandeur of the Christian religion, and the majesty of the princes and lords who have embraced this religion and the grandeur and wealth of our kingdoms and cities, and the honour and power our religion enjoys among them. Thus the Japanese . . . will later return to Japan and as eye-witnesses will be able to recount what they have seen, and in this way will give credit and authority in Japan that is fitting for our affairs. In this way people who have not seen these things and cannot at present believe them, will come to understand the reason why the missionaries decided to come to Japan . . . .[25]

Thus the first Japanese legation to Europe came into being.

■ CHAPTER 2

Preparing the Legation

In the usual sense of the term, an embassy represents the government of one country in its dealings with another. Valignano did not, of course, have the authority to organize a national embassy, and in any case Japan did not possess a central government at that time to be represented. Instead, he would settle for a less ambitious project and lead a small legation on behalf of the three Christian daimyo of Kyushu. The party would travel to Europe, deliver letters from these barons to the pope expressing respect and veneration, and visit some of the renowned cities of Catholic Europe. People in Europe had read a good deal about the far-off islands of Japan in published Jesuit reports, but had yet to personally meet and deal with the people of that country.[1] A small party of Japanese Christians under Jesuit auspices touring Portugal, Spain, and Italy would undoubtedly attract favourable attention and help solve some, if not all, of the mission's problems. On the legation's return, its members could then provide their fellow countrymen with first-hand reports about the splendid cathedrals, castles, and palaces of Renaissance Europe. It was a bold and imaginative plan, and quite in keeping with Valignano's forceful character.[2]

Valignano had arrived in Japan in July 1579 and was planning to return to India in the spring of 1582. When exactly his ambitious plan of leading a legation to Europe occurred to him is not known, but the decision appears to have been made in December 1581 or even as late as January 1582. This meant there was little time

PREPARING THE LEGATION

to organize the party and make arrangements for its long journey. To catch favourable winds, the annual Portuguese ship sailing from Japan back to India and Europe left in the spring on the first stage of its return voyage, and any undue delay in its departure from Nagasaki would risk losing a safe and swift passage to Macao. Thus, with little time at his disposal, Valignano was obliged to make hurried preparations for the expedition.

This haste limited the choice of delegates, who necessarily had to be living close to Nagasaki and readily available for imminent departure. The hurried departure also later caused problems for the party after its arrival in Europe, since there was insufficient time to assemble suitable gifts to present to their European hosts. Japanese were, and still are, punctilious regarding the exchange of gifts, and it must have been embarrassing later for the legates to be reduced to giving away their used Japanese robes for want of any other return present. They were able, however, to include in their luggage a pair of fine screens intended as a present for the pope, but nothing else of appreciable value was packed.

The three Christian daimyo whose representatives would travel to Europe were Ōtomo Sōrin of Bungo (baptized as Francis in 1578), Arima Harunobu of Arima (Protasius, 1579), and Ōmura Sumitada of Ōmura (Bartholomew, 1563). Of these three, the first-named was by far the most powerful, and he proposed as his representative his nephew Jerome Itō, the son of his sister and of the lord of the Hyūga region in east Kyushu. But Jerome was a pupil at the Jesuit school near Kyoto, and there was not sufficient time to notify him of his appointment and bring him down to Nagasaki before the ship sailed. His place in the legation was therefore taken by Mancio Itō, born in 1569, grandson of Itō Yoshisuke, lord of Hyūga, and indirectly related to Francis of Bungo. His personal Japanese name was Sukemasu.

The other two daimyo were to have a joint representative in Michael Chijiwa, born in Arima in 1567, nephew of Ōmura and second cousin of Arima. His personal Japanese name was Seizaimon. Captain-Major Miguel da Gama was Michael's godfather when Valignano baptized the boy, and this information sets the date of his baptism at 1580, and also offers an explanation for the choice of his Christian name.[3] So Michael did not receive baptism as an infant, and had in fact been a Christian for less than two years before his departure for Europe.

Two other Christian youngsters, Martin Hara and Julian Nakaura, were chosen to join the party as the legates' companions. The former, born in 1568, was related to the Ōmura family. Julian was born into a Christian family in 1568 in Nakaura, Ōmura, and his father had been the commander of a fortress in that fief. All four boys were pupils attending the Jesuit school in Kyushu.[4]

It is worth noting that, in his extensive writings, Valignano constantly refers to the legates and their companions as *os meninos, os moços, los niños* ('the boys') or *jovenes nobres* ('noble youths') in keeping with their youth. In Goa, when compiling at the end of 1583 instructions about how the boys should be treated in Europe, he still refers to them constantly as *meninos*.[5] In a letter sent from Nagasaki in 1582, the Jesuit Gaspar Coelho follows suit and calls them *meninos nobres*, or 'noble boys'.[6] In his day-by-day chronicle of the legation on which the present book is largely based, Luis Fróis, mindful that his text was destined for publication, usually refers to them as *senhores*, meaning either 'lords' or 'gentlemen'.

But by the time the boys were half-way through their European tour, some commentators in an excess of enthusiasm had promoted them to 'Japanese kings or princes', but neither Valignano nor the Jesuits in Japan were responsible for this startling and unjustified elevation in rank.[7] This is a point of some importance, because the Jesuits were later accused of advertising the youthful delegates as 'Japanese kings'. While it is true that some European observers were later to promote the legates' rank in such a dramatic fashion,[8] Valignano to the end refers to them as 'the boys'. He admits that in misguided zeal some Jesuits in Europe did in fact exaggerate the legates' ranks, but insists: 'If some called them kings and princes, we never called them anything else but boys and gentlemen.'[9] He goes into further detail to emphasize this point:

> As regards the way of sending these gentlemen, the [Jesuit] Fathers were far from giving them the title of Most Serene Princes and giving people to understand that they were the heirs of the said lords. . . . I myself wrote to His Majesty [Philip II] and His Holiness that although they were persons both noble and closely related to the said kings, they were the first fruits of the seminary in Japan, where they were brought up, and I never gave them the title of princes or heirs of the said kings.[10]

In an effort to discredit the legation, critics claimed that the party was made up of poor ragamuffins of no social rank. Such accusations are found in the writings of some of the Franciscan friars, who guessed that one of Valignano's purposes, although not publicized, for organizing the legation was to renew Rome's official approval of the Jesuit monopoly in the Japanese mission.[11] In his anti-Jesuit treatise, Fray Martín de la Ascensión waxes strong on this point, calling the delegates 'poor boys, sons of commoners, who would not have even a little rice to eat if they had not embraced the religious life. . . . , and they would wander around begging alms'.[12]

Valignano was well aware of these allegations and denied accusations that the Jesuit-sponsored legation to Europe was fraudulent.

> The friars are saying and publishing that the Japanese gentlemen who went to Rome are not the sons or relatives of great lords nor were they sent by them, but that all this is our invention with which we deceived His Holiness and His Majesty . . . His Holiness wished to receive them with public honour, but this was far from our intention . . . Far be it from me that I wished to make them princes and raise them up more than was fitting. I tried quite the contrary, writing . . . that they should not be given public receptions, though I certainly wanted them to be given every sign of love and welcome. . . .[13]

While the boys could not be described as Japanese 'kings', as appeared in some European accounts, they were certainly not, contrary to hostile rumours, commoners of base parentage. But the allegation about their 'base parentage' persisted for many years, and in a letter sent from Japan to Lord Salisbury in London and dated 10 December 1614, some thirty years after the legation set out, the English merchant Richard Cocks accuses the Jesuits of inflating the rank of the boys and deceiving their European hosts:

> [I]n anno 1584 the Jesuistes caried 3 Japans from hence w'th them into Spaine, geving it out they were sonns or nephews unto 3 kings, viz. of Bongo, Arima and Umbra. Whereupon the King of Spaine gave them the order of knighthood w'th many rich presentes, as other princes in Spaine and Italie did the lyke, amongst whome the Pope was not behindhand. But the truth is that these 3 Japans were neither kinges' sonns nor yet nobly borne, but of base parentage only sett on

(or subborned) by the foresaid Jesuistes, whoe receaved all the gifts and presentes w'ch were geven them for their owne private benefite or use.[14]

Another critic of the enterprise was somewhat surprisingly a Spanish Jesuit working in Japan. This was Pedro Ramón, who reached Japan in 1577 and was closely associated with Ōtomo Sōrin of Bungo. Writing to Rome on 15 October 1587, five years after the boys' departure, he not only downgrades their social status, but also reports that the daimyo of Bungo was unaware of the embassy to Europe before it sailed from Nagasaki. He therefore did not, Ramón asserts, write the letter presented to the pope at the solemn audience in March 1585.

While it is true that the original letter no longer exists (although Fróis provides its text in his account),[15] there is still preserved in the Jesuit archives in Rome another letter of the same date, from Ōtomo to the Jesuit General Superior, bearing the daimyo's *kaō*, or stylized signature, and specifically mentioning Mancio's role in the embassy to Rome.[16]

Further, Ramón's allegations go against the testimony of Valignano and other Jesuits in Japan. As Valignano himself points out, he could hardly have passed off commoners as princes during the long voyages to and from Europe and during their stay in Rome, even less on their return to Japan when they were received in audience by the virtual ruler of the country, Toyotomi Hideyoshi.[17]

From the very beginning Valignano visualized the legation being carried out on a low key:

> They went dressed as students, each one having only one page. This was seen there [in Japan] as a small train when they travelled in the name of the said princes, who themselves also had the same doubt for it seemed contrary to their honour to send the boys so unaccompanied. They, too, wished to send them in different fashion. But I disagreed with them about this, saying that as they were travelling so far, would be accompanied by our Fathers, and would always stay in our houses, it was not necessary to go with more people, for this would entail too much labour and expense. In the same way, I supplicated His Holiness and His Majesty to show them much affection and such kindness that they would return happy. I tried that they would not be received with public acclaim.[18]

Not only the daimyo but also the boys' families were unhappy about this arrangement. The boys' mothers proposed providing the party with sumptuous wardrobes in keeping with their status as representatives of lords, but Valignano limited each boy to two formal Japanese outfits, to be worn at the audiences with the pope and other dignitaries. For the rest of the trip they would wear ordinary European dress.[19] In accordance with this plan, the size of the legation was kept extremely small, especially when compared with the large and ostentatious retinues usually accompanying Japanese nobles on journeys. The problems that would arise in transporting to Europe a large number of attendants in the limited passenger accommodations on the ships may well have been a consideration, but most of all Valignano deliberately planned the embassy on a small and inconspicuous scale. As a result, the party would consist of less than a dozen men and boys. By no means could this small group be considered a grand and impressive embassy, although this lack of splendour would be compensated in other ways. For these Christian Asian boys came from Marco Polo's legendary and remote Zipangu, where according to Jesuit reports Christianity had met with remarkable success within a lifetime.

Valignano stressed repeatedly that the legation should be conducted on a low key. In letters to the pope, the Jesuit General, and King Philip II of Spain, he asked that the boys be received 'with few demonstrations of honour, but with many of affection'. They should not be housed in palaces or mansions, but in Jesuit residences. He laid down that solemn and public receptions should not be organized in their honour, and everything should be kept on a small and inconspicuous scale.[20] That these recommendations were later totally disregarded in Europe cannot be blamed on Valignano.

To return to the organization of the legation, only Mancio and Michael were the official legates of the daimyo, and on formal occasions it was they who took precedence, delivered speeches and presented letters from Japan. Of these two boys Mancio was considered the senior in rank as he represented the most powerful of the three daimyo. But in their everyday lives and activities, both on board ship during the long voyages and in their travels through Europe, little if any distinction seems to have been observed among the four. This lack of distinction is reflected in the contemporaneous accounts of the legation, for seldom is reference made to any one boy in particular, except to mention one of the party by name when he fell ill. As a result, no individual personalities emerge; instead, we generally read in some detail about what 'the young boys' or 'the Japanese gentlemen' saw and did as a group, with all four of them remaining in these accounts somewhat faceless and devoid of personality.

It was a prudent decision on Valignano's part to send companions with the legates, for two young Japanese boys travelling to and around Europe might well have felt lonely, but having others of their own age with them helped form a group and provided welcome company. Further, Valignano may well have included the two companions to act as substitute legates in the event of Mancio or Michael being disabled. As will be seen later, sickness prevented Julian from attending the papal consistory in Rome, the climax of the long journey from Japan. As he was only a companion, however, his absence did not unduly affect the formal event, but had Mancio or Michael fallen ill, a substitute would have been needed.

The boys were remarkably young to undertake such a venture.[21] The dates of their births are usually given as 'about 1570', although one scholar provides more specific details.[22] Martin appears to have been the oldest of the four. The Jesuit Gaspar Coelho was in Nagasaki at the time of their departure and in a good position to know the facts, and he reported: 'None of them is more than fourteen.'[23] This was an unusually tender age for representatives, and it is obvious that the boys' mission was intended as a pretext for publicizing the Japanese church and, on their return, impressing on their countrymen the high level of European civilization. Any serious negotiations regarding mission finances and the exclusion of friars would be made by Valignano himself, with the youthful Japanese party occupying centre stage in formal and social events.

Valignano was determined to send young legates to Europe, and explains in his writings that they had been chosen because their youthful age would enable them to endure the hardships of the lengthy voyages and adapt to European life and food. Then, on their return to their native country, they would, God willing, still have long lives ahead of them in which to recount their first-hand experience of what they had seen and done in Europe.

It is more than probable that there may have been yet another consideration, possibly a principal one, in mind: youngsters would be easier to supervise and shield from unseemly sights and events during their travels through Europe. Valignano was anxious that the legates should not be exposed to any religious divisions or untoward experiences during their visit to Europe, and escorting a quartet of teenagers, rather than mature adults, would make this task considerably easier. Further, the boys were of an impressionable age, and having viewed some of the splendours of Europe, they would report favourably and even enthusiastically about their experiences on their return to Japan.

Valignano hoped that the boys would be impressed by European cathedrals, palaces and castles, but at the same time he insisted they should not be allowed to view or learn anything that could give a contrary impression. He repeats that when visiting Rome and other cities the boys should be chaperoned so that they would see only the good and nothing of the bad. For this reason they must stay, whenever possible, in Jesuit residences. They should have no contact with anybody who might cause them scandal nor should they hear about any disorders in the court or church. For this reason they should not be allowed to extend their stay in Rome to study. Once they had accomplished their mission in Europe, they should return to Japan. After all, adds Valignano disingenuously, 'I promised their parents this'.[24]

Not without reason, the young boys' mothers expressed fears for their sons' safety during the long and dangerous voyages to and from Europe and their travelling through strange, distant lands. The parents initially gave their assent in the belief that the legation would never take place, but as preparations continued and the time for embarking approached, their anxiety about their safe return increased.[25] The mothers of Michael and Julian were widows and had no other sons,[26] and it took all of Valignano's considerable persuasive powers to obtain their reluctant permission for their boys to undertake the risky venture.[27] The mothers' fears were amply justified, and had they known of the future perils the party was to encounter at sea and on land, they would surely not have consented to their departure.[28]

Here we may briefly consider the moral responsibility that Valignano undertook in separating the boys from their families for eight years, although he had no way of knowing that the venture would be so protracted; even if all had gone well, it would not have been possible to complete the expedition in under five years. A more pressing consideration was the danger to which they would be inevitably exposed on their voyage to and from Europe. Sadly, shipwrecks were common at that time, to say nothing of illness and death on board caused by putrid food, foul drinking water and unhygienic conditions, and as a result the mortality rate among passengers and crew on many voyages was brutally high.[29] True, the boys usually received more comfortable quarters and better food on board than did other passengers, but no amount of favourable treatment could save them from the perils of storms, fire, pirates, shipwreck and sickness.[30] Scores of Jesuits had been lost at sea in the previous decades, but their deaths had been accepted with resignation as an inevitable consequence of their missionary vocation. But had any mishap befallen one or more of the youthful Japanese during their years of travel (and such an eventuality was not at all unlikely), Valignano in particular and the Jesuits in general would have been held accountable, and the legation, far from being a success and fulfilling the Visitor's objectives, would have brought the Christian church in Japan into disrepute.

To fill out the members of the legation, Valignano chose the 29-year-old Jesuit Diogo de Mesquita,[31] to accompany the boys as their guide, mentor, tutor, interpreter, and guardian. He had arrived in Japan in 1576 and had therefore only six years experience of Japanese life. As yet unordained, he would take the opportunity of receiving the priesthood from the local bishop during his stay in Macao. Valignano declared he had selected young boys for the legation as they could better withstand the hardships of the journey, and possibly he appointed the youthful Mesquita as their guide and mentor for the same reason.

Mesquita accompanied the boys on their voyage to Europe and during their travels through Portugal, Spain and Italy, acting as their interpreter in their audiences with two popes and a king. He then returned with them to Japan, thus becoming the first of only a few Jesuit missionaries to return to Europe and then make the long voyage back.[32] Of all the European Jesuits, Mesquita had the best opportunity to get to know all four boys in depth during their eight years of extensive journeying together on land and sea, and he kept in close touch with three of them after their return to Japan.

To show Europeans the high caliber of Japanese Jesuits, Brother George Loyola was chosen to accompany the boys to tutor them in Japanese language and literature during the long voyages; despite his name he was Japanese and had entered the Society of Jesus two years earlier. Two Japanese boys, Constantine Dourado,[33] aged fifteen, and Augustine, made up the remaining members of the legation as personal servants. It was indeed a small party making up the legation, but Valignano was determined to keep the embassy as simple as possible.

Four other Jesuits sailed on the same ship, but were not members of the legation. Fr Lourenço Mexia and Brother Oliverio Toscanello, who had been Valignano's personal assistants during his visit to Japan, accompanied the party as far as Macao, while Álvaro Dias and Cristóvão Moreira also set out for that port to receive priestly ordination from the resident bishop there.[34]

To keep a permanent record of the journey, the boys were instructed to take notes on the most memorable places and events they witnessed during their extensive travels. As the Jesuit Eduardo de Sande noted at the time:

> For this reason our Fathers never forgot one of the principal objectives of this embassy was that these high-born youths should bring back to their own country and impart to their compatriots full information about our things, and they reminded them insistently that they must not fail to observe, to note down, and to preserve in writing everything that they experienced throughout all the length of their pilgrimage. Admirable as they are in their character and in their obedience to the Fathers, they promptly recorded in their journal whatever things seemed to them notable and worth remembering . . . [35]

The extent to which these notes were compiled is unknown for they no longer exist, but there is no reason to believe that the boys and their companions were remiss in their duty of recording their experiences. The detail with which Fróis (who did not accompany the expedition) was able to compile his account of the legation on its return to Japan points to his reliance on the extensive notes taken by the Japanese during the course of their travels. At least some of these records were compiled in Portuguese, for in his account Fróis incorporates lengthy and detailed descriptions of Vila Viçosa, Toledo cathedral and the Escorial in excellent Portuguese, and these reports, as he specifically remarks, were taken verbatim from the notes written by one of the Japanese in the party. It is thanks to these notes that Fróis was able to compile an extensive account of the trip, providing a detailed coverage of where the boys went, whom they met, and what they saw, and thus pass down to modern readers a remarkably detailed account.

The party, with luggage, hastily assembled gifts, and the letters of the Christian daimyo addressed to the pope, the king of Spain and others, boarded Captain-Major Ignacio de Lima's ship at Nagasaki, and on 20 February 1582, set off on its long and arduous voyage to Europe. Thus began the mission that was to become known in Japanese history as *Tenshō Shōnen Shisetsu*, or the Tenshō Boys Embassy (Tenshō was the era name for the period 1573–91), or more formally *Tenshō Ken'ō Shisetsu*, or the Tenshō Embassy to Europe.[36]

Part 2

The Journey to Europe

■ CHAPTER 3

Passage to India

Sea voyages in the sixteenth century involved both danger and hardship. As regards the perils of the sea, violent storms sank an alarming number of ships. Portuguese merchant vessels, or carracks, had three or four decks and could hold a large amount of cargo, but they were clumsy to handle in a wind blowing from the side, and their high poop and forecastle added to their instability in rough weather. In addition, especially on their homeward voyage, they were often grossly overladen with cargo in the two lower decks and overcrowded with passengers and crew.[1] Another natural danger was the opposite when violent winds were replaced by no winds at all. Ships could remain becalmed and unmoving in the oppressive heat of the tropics for weeks on end, thus adding boredom and anxiety, as well as putrefaction of the food supplies. There was also the peril of fire on such occasions for the wooden vessels and their large sails, dried by the relentless sun in the intense heat, could easily catch fire, and equipment to douse the flames was primitive and often next to useless.

The art of navigation was still undeveloped and accurate maps were non-existent; instead ships relied mainly on *roteiros*, or rutters, that is, general accounts compiled by pilots on earlier voyages and describing their experiences, pointing out, for example, the changed colour of seaweed and movement of birds as indicators. These rutters had a large margin of error, and it happened only too often that ships ran aground in shallows when approaching land.[2] Although navigators were able to calculate their latitude with fair exactness, accurate readings of longitude were not possible until the eighteenth century, and as will be seen later, this inability nearly spelled disaster for the ship on which the four boys were travelling. Truly, voyages in the sixteenth century were no pleasure-cruise.

In addition to these mortal dangers were the living conditions on board. Quarters were cramped and crowded, and toilet facilities of even the most primitive kind were non-existent. Some twenty years later the French traveller François Pyrard observed from personal experience: 'These ships are mighty foul and stink withal; the most not troubling to go on deck for their necessities, which is in part the cause that so many die.'[3] Food supplies often rotted in the intense and muggy heat. Jan Linschoten, who reached Goa only two months before the boys' arrival, recounts that thirty men died on board during his voyage from Lisbon to Goa.

Lack of fresh fruit and vegetables caused beriberi, scurvy and dysentery, and medical facilities were totally inadequate to prevent and cure these often fatal ailments. As a result, the mortality rate among passengers and crew was at times high, as the boys were later to experience. Japanese screens depicting the arrival of the Portuguese carrack in Nagasaki invariably show a fine ship with billowing sails and flags flying, men performing acrobatics in the rigging, passengers and crew dressed in colourful robes. But on the hot, tropical stage of the voyage to India, conditions were often, sadly, far different.

But it should not be supposed that every ocean voyage was a nightmare of hardships and dangers, and it must be borne in mind that for many poor people life in the sixteenth century, both in Europe and Japan, was brief and brutish on land as well as at sea. As noted above, the boys received favoured treatment on board, but the possibility of disaster of some sort or other was inevitably present on ocean voyages.

As regards the first stage of the boys' voyage, the only ship at Nagasaki going to India that year was Ignacio de Lima's smallish vessel. A friend and admirer of Valignano, he was anxious for the Jesuit and his young charges to sail on his ship, and was even willing to surrender his own cabin to accommodate the boys, and his gracious offer was accepted.[4]

The Japanese set sail from Nagasaki on the long and eventful journey to Europe on 20 February in fine weather; they would not return to their country for more than eight years.[5]

The boys' religious duties and studies were not neglected on board as they settled into a regular routine. They continued their Latin lessons under Mesquita, while Brother George coached them in reading and writing Japanese. When weather permitted, Mass was said on Sundays and feast days. The boys recited daily the Litany of the Saints and other prayers, and Mesquita read to them the gospels. As far as possible their timetable followed that of their school in Kyushu so as to make the abrupt change in their routine less stressful. For relaxation, they enjoyed fishing from the ship's veranda, playing Japanese chess,[6] and practising on their European musical instruments. Meanwhile, the priests on board made their customary hour of prayer in the early morning and recited the divine office during the day. As the party was supplied with ample provisions, food was distributed to the sick and less fortunate passengers.[7]

This pious and pleasant routine was followed while the weather remained fair, but unfortunately it was not to last long. Within two or three days strong winds began to blow and waves pounded the ship like 'heavy shots of artillery', causing the boys to suffer severe bouts of sea-sickness. The experienced traveller Valignano both at this juncture and later tended the youthful travellers with much concern and kindness, but concern and kindness, however well intended, are not remedies for sea-sickness. Mancio was the least affected of the party and the dear boy sometimes joked at his companions' distress, although he, too, experienced some dizzy spells.

The weather further deteriorated and the boys experienced their first storm at sea, becoming apprehensive when the small boat roped to the stern disappeared under the waves only to bob up again. All the sails except one were furled, and only the upper part of that sail was left for the purpose of navigation. The stormy weather lasted five or six days, but then improved, much to the relief of the young travellers. It was with considerable joy that a little over two weeks after their departure from Nagasaki the boys sighted some Chinese islands.

The ship finally reached Macao, the first foreign city visited by the boys, on 9 March, seventeen days after leaving Japan. The Portuguese had established this commercial outpost at the southern tip of China in about 1555, and a diocese had been established there in 1576. Thanks to the lucrative trade in silk and silver the City of the Name of God, to give it its official name, had greatly flourished.

The Portuguese bought silk at the semi-annual fair at nearby Canton, carried it to Japan in their spacious cargo ships, and returned to Macao laden with Japanese silver. As Linschoten ably summed up this trade: 'The merchandise from Makau to Iapen, are silks, and from Iapen they return nothing but silver, whereby they doe greatly profit.'[8]

This trade brought prosperity to the settlement as a whole, for Macao citizens were able to participate in the profitable trade by buying shares in the commercial venture. The settlement was therefore prosperous, and accounts of a somewhat later date provide a colourful picture of its impressive buildings, churches and convents. The great stone facade of the Jesuit church, built twenty years after the boys' first visit, still remains as a moving testimony to the Macao of those prosperous times and gives some idea of the city's majestic buildings in its heyday.

The boys were welcomed by the governor, João de Almeida, and the local bishop, Leonardo de Sá, who had arrived in the previous year. In accordance with Valignano's wishes, the party stayed in the care of the local Jesuit community, the superior of which was Pedro Gómez, later to become the superior of the Jesuit mission for ten years. Although the voyage from Japan had taken less than three weeks, the party was obliged to remain in Macao for nearly ten months, the first of many protracted stopovers, for much of the two-year journey between Japan and Europe was in fact spent on land awaiting favourable winds.

During this enforced stay, the boys continued their studies under the supervision of Mesquita and Brother George; they also practised playing and singing European music. But their days were not all work and no play, and the Japanese were taken on sightseeing tours around the small town. Later in their travels they were to view far more impressive buildings, it is true, but Macao was their first stop outside Japan, and the sight of European buildings, churches and convents, to say nothing of hearing Portuguese and Chinese spoken around them, was a novel and unforgettable experience.

During the stopover in Macao several notable events occurred, although it is doubtful whether the boys recognised their full significance at the time. One was the arrival of Fr Matteo Ricci on 7 August, and the visitors were bound to have met the young priest. Ricci's remarkable erudition and affable spirit of adaptation in China were later to make him famous in the annals of missiology.

Another event had political significance that would affect the reception which the party later received in Europe. On 3 May the Spanish Jesuit Alonso Sánchez arrived from the Philippines, charged by the governor, Gonzalo Ronquillo de Peñalosa, with the delicate task of officially informing the Macao authorities that in April 1581 King Philip II of Spain had assumed the Portuguese throne with the title of Philip I of Portugal, thus initiating the joint administration of the two countries. This development presented the Macanese authorities with an awkward problem, because, to protect their commercial interests, they had repeatedly warned the Chinese about the Spanish presence in the Philippines and the growth of the Spanish empire through military conquest. Now they were faced with the unpleasant prospect of explaining that the same monarch ruled both Portugal and Spain.[9] The official proclamation announcing the amalgamation of the two thrones was not made in Macao until 18 December, when the governor swore allegiance to Philip at the hands of the bishop, shortly before the boys' departure. Two years later, the Japanese had the honour of being granted two audiences with Philip II and his family.

One further happening was to bring home to the boys in dramatic fashion the perils of sea travel. The carrack sailing from Goa that year was forced to return to port because of adverse weather conditions, and as a result there was no Portuguese vessel to carry Macao's rich cargo of silk and other merchandise to Japan. The city was therefore obliged to make use of two Chinese junks, which, duly laden, set sail for Nagasaki on 10 July. The smaller vessel ran into three great storms, but finally managed to reach Japan on 12 August with broken masts and in distressed condition. The larger vessel, carrying some two-hundred men on board, including the Jesuits returning to Japan after receiving ordination, and most of the merchandise from Macao, also set out on 10 July,[10] and this voyage was even less fortunate. Two days after departure the junk was hit by a violent storm and then ran aground off the coast of Formosa.

Personal accounts of the shipwreck provide a vivid picture of the disaster.[11] The crew and passengers remained in pitiful condition on an island for six weeks while building a skiff from the wreckage of their junk. To add to their misery, 'relations with the local headhunters were not exactly cordial'.[12] Setting sail on their make-shift craft, the exhausted survivors managed to traverse the 120 leagues back to Macao in early October after eight days of hazardous sailing. The news of the loss of life and rich cargo plunged the small settlement into deep distress. The Jesuit community was additionally saddened because the junk had carried a large amount of supplies to their confreres in Japan.

On their second attempt to reach Japan in the following year, the ordained Jesuits enjoyed a prosperous voyage of only twelve days, finally reaching Nagasaki on 25 July 1583. Thus the two ordinands had spent no less than seventeen months, at times in peril of their lives, to participate in a two-hour ordination ceremony in Macao. This pointed to the need for a bishop to be installed in Japan to eliminate the lengthy and wasteful time spent on the voyage. But somewhat surprisingly Valignano was opposed to such an appointment, fearing perhaps that it might cause a clash of authority between the bishop and the local Jesuit superior; also, the appointment of a bishop might well pave the way for allowing other religious orders to enter Japan.

In December the winds turned favourable and it was time for the boys to bid farewell to their hosts and resume their voyage to Europe. There were no less than three ships bound for India, two Portuguese (de Lima's ship and one other) and one Chinese. The captain of the second Portuguese ship urged Valignano to travel on his larger and stronger vessel, which in addition to greater safety offered more comfortable accommodation. Valignano hesitated about the choice, not wishing to hurt the feelings of his friend de Lima on whose ship he and the boys had sailed from Nagasaki. After considerable deliberation he decided to continue the voyage in de Lima's ship, but to appease the captain of the larger vessel, he arranged for two Jesuits to travel on his ship.

The party sailed from Macao on the last day of 1582. Some anxiety was felt as voyages for India usually began a month earlier, but weather conditions were good and a safe passage was predicted. The ship was laded with much, probably too much, cargo and, owing to its smaller size, had less sail to hoist than the other two vessels, which soon forged ahead and were lost to sight. Inevitably the weather deteriorated and the ship ran into a violent storm. One night waves smashed down the door of the boys' cabin, water poured in, and the youngsters had to be quickly evacuated to a higher place, while the crew hastily jettisoned cargo to stabilise the vessel. The rough weather lasted several days before the winds dropped, but further danger awaited them in the Gulf of Hainan, a region notoriously dangerous on account of winds and shallows. For a while an adverse wind blew the ship toward the shallows, but then it changed direction and bore the vessel away to safety.

But passengers and crew were disturbed by the ominous sight of cargo and clothing floating in the sea, and feared that pirates might have attacked the larger ships sailing ahead of them. Within thirty miles of Malacca, they sighted the Portuguese vessel, which had run aground in the shallows at the entrance of the Strait of Singapore, whose narrow width made it extremely difficult to navigate safely. Fortunately, the passengers and crew were safe, but the ship had lost its valuable cargo, some of which had been jettisoned and the rest looted by local brigands. As for the two Jesuits on board, both fell gravely ill on account of their physical sufferings, and one died on arrival in Malacca.

The boys' ship slowly negotiated its way through the strait, nearly coming to grief on some shallows while trying to avoid a whirlpool. But the passengers enjoyed some relief by watching local natives skilfully spearing fish from their small craft and selling their catch to passing ships. Finally, their 500-league voyage to Malacca was completed on 27 January 1583, and the Japanese were welcomed by Bishop João Ribeiro Gayo and the governor of the city. In contrast to their protracted stay in Macao, they spent only a week in Malacca before departing on 4 February in an effort to catch favourable winds.

As the ship approached the equator, the heat increased and the wind dropped leaving the vessel completely becalmed. Both Mesquita and Mancio fell seriously ill, the former remaining unwell for more than a month. Valignano tenderly cared for the sick boy, sitting by his bunk night and day, and persuading him to eat so as to recover his strength. The searing heat caused much suffering, and to add to their distress food supplies began to run short. To preserve the dwindling water supply, the captain himself doled out the small rations to passengers and crew. The relentless heat played havoc with the food and water supplies, and even when water was available, it was often in a foul condition. 'All the water in the ship stinketh, whereby men are forced to stop their noses when they drink,' as Linschoten graphically described similar conditions on a voyage at that time.[13]

Unable to stand the thirst, some men on board drank seawater in desperation and died as a result. All in all, it was a grim experience for the Japanese teenagers. Even if they did not have much contact with the crew, they are bound to have attended the burial service of the dead at sea.

The wind finally picked up and the ship could once more proceed. But unfortunately the pilot made a grievous error that nearly resulted in disaster and further added to the travellers' misfortunes. He believed the ship had rounded Cape Comorin, the southern tip of India, and was sailing north up the west coast of the continent, when in fact the vessel had not doubled the cape and was proceeding up the east coast – another example of navigators' inability to calculate longitude. From his past experience on his voyage to Japan in 1577, Valignano himself was not convinced that the ship had rounded the cape and implored the captain and pilot to take soundings, only to be greeted with laughter. But at his insistence (and the strong-willed Valignano's insistence was not easily dismissed) soundings were taken and to the consternation of all the sea was found to be only forty, then a mere fifteen fathoms deep, with the ship travelling at full sail toward rocky shallows. Land was then sighted which the sailors recognised as the Fishery Coast on the east coast of India. The wind and current made it impossible to reverse course immediately, so the ship dropped its anchors and managed to come to a halt.

Since the time of Xavier missionaries had been working in the region, and the Indian Christians were said to number about eighty thousand. Valignano sent a message announcing the ship's unscheduled arrival, and without delay the local Jesuits approached in small boats, bringing welcome supplies of fruit, rice and fresh water.

By then the boys were exhausted by the rigours of the voyage, and Valignano took his party off the ship to allow them to rest on land in a nearby village. On the following morning they were startled to see that overnight the currents had driven the ship a league toward the rocks; two of its anchor ropes had snapped, but a third held fast and saved the vessel from disaster.

The boys celebrated Easter on land on 31 March. In view of the danger involved in reversing the ship and again attempting to round Cape Comorin, Valignano decided to travel overland across the cape with the boys and attendants, a journey he had made in reverse direction back in 1577. They would then meet up with the ship at the port of Cochin on the west coast. Mesquita and some other members of the party, however, were too ill to move, so it was agreed that they would convalesce in the mission house at Tuticorin, and later join up with the main party when they had regained their strength.

There were no horses available to transport the party so they were carried in litters by teams of four natives, travelling eight to ten leagues by night to avoid the intense heat of the day until they reached the west coast. There they were fortunate to find a small boat that took them to the Portuguese settlement of Quilon where, as luck would have it, a ship was preparing to depart for Cochin, their destination, about a day's sailing away. But the party's troubles were not yet over. The ship was anchored some way off shore, and while Valignano and the boys were being rowed in a skiff to board it, two pirate vessels appeared and began bearing down on their small craft. The skiff was still a third of a league from the ship, and however hard the oarsmen rowed, they could not match the speed of the approaching galleys. Fortunately, the ship's crew saw their predicament and quickly raising sail brought their vessel to the rescue and the boys managed to board safely. After this frightening experience they set sail to Cochin, reaching the port within a day on 7 April.[14]

Cochin was an important link in the Portuguese chain of commercial stations in Asia. While Portuguese ships from Europe unladed their goods at Goa, they took on valuable cargoes of pepper, cloves, cinnamon and other Indian products at Cochin. As a centre of commerce, the city was second only to Goa in importance and possessed a number of impressive buildings.

Meanwhile, a recovered Mesquita was able to follow the same overland route to the west coast, but experienced some fearful moments. He and his guides misjudged the distance and as a result were obliged to spend a night in a deep forest where, he was told, many robbers lived. They ran into two armed natives, who shouted but made no attempt to harm them. Eventually, he and his companions reached Cochin where there was a joyful reunion with the boys.

The Japanese lodged in the Jesuit college, with its community of twenty-five men, and resumed their studies of Latin and Portuguese, while the organist of the local church coached them in Western music. The party made two attempts to set out for Goa, but both were unsuccessful because weather conditions were not favourable and the port at Cochin tended to silt up during the summer. During the enforced stay of eight months in Cochin, Valignano, never one to remain idle, finished in June the first part of his history of the Jesuits in India, and then completed on 28 October the text of his *Sumario de las Cosas de Japon*, his lengthy and detailed report on the Japanese mission, a work that provides so much information about Jesuit activity in that country.[15]

Valignano sent a messenger overland to Goa to announce the party's arrival in Cochin, and the Viceroy of India, Francisco de Mascarenhas, despatched a small, fast boat to welcome the travellers and order Portuguese officials posted along the coast to provide them with all necessary assistance and supplies as they passed. Finally, the Japanese were able to set sail and arrived in Goa about 28 November. This last stage of the voyage, in fact, took less time than the date of arrival would suggest, for two weeks before they reached Goa, the city authorities had adopted the new Gregorian calendar, promulgated in the previous year, and had deducted ten days from the month of November in order to align the local dating with the new system. In the following year the boys would meet the pope for whom this Gregorian calendar was named.[16]

■ CHAPTER 4

From India to Europe

In Goa the boys were lodged, in accordance with Valignano's wishes, at the fine Jesuit college of St Paul. Xavier had stopped in the city before setting out in mid-April 1552 on his fruitless voyage to China, where he had died at the end of that year at the age of only forty-six. The tomb containing his incorrupt body was located in the college chapel at the time, but was transferred to the church of Bom Jesus in 1613, where it is reverently preserved to this day.

Golden Goa, the headquarters, both political and religious, of Portuguese possessions in Asia, had been captured by Afonso de Albuquerque in 1510, and at the time of the boys' visit was at the height of its prosperity; such was its importance that its governor was titled Viceroy of India. François de Pyrard has left a first-hand description of the city, going into considerable detail when describing the grandeur of the viceroy. Like a king, he is escorted by many guards and 'is obeyed like the King of Spain'. On the day before he leaves the palace, drums and trumpets sound to summon the nobility to present themselves on the following day. But Pyrard does not gloss over the fact there were often greedy viceroys who used their appointment to enrich themselves. There were great misfortunes for the Portuguese in the Indies 'when they get a troublesome and choleric or vicious viceroy (as indeed is often the case)'.[1]

It was now time for Mancio and Michael to undertake their first ambassadorial duties. Dressed in Japanese robes,[2] they were escorted to the viceroy's great palace[3] and in their formal meeting with Dom

Francisco de Mascarenhas, Viceroy of India, the legates solemnly presented letters of greeting and friendship from the three Christian daimyo whom they represented, with Mesquita acting as interpreter. By this time the boys could speak Portuguese reasonably well, but understandably they preferred to use the services of an interpreter on special occasions when proceedings were conducted in formal and polite language. Remarking that he wished to present them with a souvenir of their visit, the viceroy fastened around the neck of each boy a gold chain from which hung a repository to carry relics. During their month's stay, the boys were also treated kindly by the archbishop, the Dominican friar Vicente de Fonseca.[4]

In addition to formal visits on important officials, there was plenty for the Japanese visitors to see and admire in Goa. Some years later, an English visitor, Peter Mundy, mentions the 'faire streetes, store of strong and faire buildings, many goodly Churches, Monasteries and colledges, as fair to see without as ritche and beautifully adorned within'.[5] François de Pyrard reached Goa in 1608 and mentions the viceroy's palace, the cathedral and archbishop's palace, the Franciscan church ('the handsomest and richest in the world'), the Jesuit church (built in 1560) and college, and the immense Dominican church (completed in 1564). He reckons there were about fifty churches and monasteries, concluding: 'The number of churches there is a marvel.'

Pyrard also describes the port facilities handling the large merchant ships, but reserves his most fulsome praise for the large Royal Hospital ('the finest in the world'), in which he had twice spent time as a patient. He marvelled at its fine facilities, the care of patients, the appetising food, the washing and toilet facilities, the cleanliness of the bed linen. Such medical facilities were necessary to treat passengers and crew after their exhausting voyage from Lisbon. Sometimes the arrival of a ship in distress would entail the admission of four hundred sick men, yet the Royal Hospital was able to cope with such emergencies. Pyrard also provides an account of the city's prisons (in which he spent some time), but with less enthusiasm.[6]

One further aspect of life in Goa would surely have impressed the Japanese coming from a monolingual country, and this was the remarkable mix of nationalities living within the city. According to Linschoten, there were Indians, Portuguese, Armenians, Gujurats, Bramens and others in Goa; most of them were engaged in trade.[7]

It was fortunate that the boys received such a warm reception in Goa for letters to Valignano from Rome, dated 4 January of that year and received in Cochin, caused an unwelcome change in plans that was to affect the legation profoundly. It had been Valignano's intention and wish that he himself would accompany the boys to Europe where he would lay before religious and secular authorities the needs of the Japanese mission and seek a solution to its problems. Valignano had spent two-and-a-half years in Japan on his tour of inspection and he, more than anyone else, was qualified to understand and explain how the church in that country could best be helped.

But the news from Rome would radically change his plans, for Valignano had been appointed Jesuit superior in India and in that capacity would have to remain on the continent, unable to accompany the boys any further on their journey to Europe.[8] Valignano was deeply disappointed by this change in plans and in a letter to Rome expressed his 'much confusion' and 'the many inconveniences there would occur in [the boys'] going without me'. He believed, with some justification, that he himself was the most suitable man to look after the boys' welfare and to present most effectively the needs of the Japanese mission to the pope and Philip II.[9] There was, however, no way he could continue his journey to Europe, and he was obliged to appoint Fr Nuno Rodrigues, the rector of the college in Goa, to take his place and accompany the party.[10]

Valignano was always inclined to spell out his orders in some detail, and on 12 December he compiled a list of fifty-five instructions for his replacement, leaving little or nothing to chance.[11] According to these directives, Rodrigues should take great care of the legates' baggage, especially the screens and other items destined to be presented as gifts to the more illustrious hosts in Europe; on arriving in Cochin, he should make a strict inventory of all the items. Due care should be taken that the boys are provided with nourishing food to preserve their health; Mesquita would be able to give good advice in this matter. Mesquita would continue to look after the boys on a daily basis, while, once arrived in Lisbon, Rodrigues would leave the party, and hurry ahead to Rome to attend the Procurators Congregation and deal with mission business.[12]

In Valignano's view, chaperoning the party from Lisbon to Rome by himself might well overtax the young Mesquita and so a Jesuit priest should be assigned in Portugal to help with the travel arrangements.[13] If Mesquita should die en route (which God forbid), then a prudent priest should be appointed to console the boys and accompany them to Rome. The boys should wear student dress, but in silk, on their journey through Europe, but should be clad in Japanese robes when they meet the king. If, however, they had grown out of their clothes, especially their trousers and shoulder *kataginu*, then satin replacements should be made in Portugal. When they visited the king, they should travel in a coach, or at least on horseback, as it was not fitting to walk through the streets of Madrid in their Japanese costume. When visiting other members of the royal family, it would be enough to wear student dress. The screens donated by the ruler Oda Nobunaga and the bamboo writing desk should always accompany the boys so that without fail these gifts could be presented to the pope and king.

To receive a good impression, the boys should be shown the riches of palaces, cathedrals and sacristies, and must be shielded from anything disedifying or upsetting.[14] Mesquita or another priest should always accompany them during their tours of cities. They should not be detained in Rome to study, but should return home as Valignano had promised their families; besides, a prolonged stay in Rome would undoubtedly expose them to less seemly aspects of life in Europe. So once they had presented the letters to the pope and visited some Italian cities, they should make preparations to return to Japan. It would be most helpful if the pope could donate screens and paintings depicting suitable themes to decorate Jesuit churches and residences in Japan.

Not content with these detailed instructions, the meticulous Valignano also sent ahead letters of recommendation to Europe. In one of these messages, dated 16 December and addressed to the Japanese mission's great benefactor, Dom Theotonio de Bragança, archbishop of Evora, he mentions the young legates and stresses: 'It is important that they be favoured and treated so well that they return to Japan happy and content.'[15]

The boys' month-long stay in Goa came to an end, and bidding Valignano an emotional farewell, for he had become a father figure and well-loved guardian during the hardships of their travels, they boarded the *Santiago* on 20 December 1583. As a final act of kindness, the viceroy donated 2,000 ducats for expenses incurred during the voyage and arranged for the captain's two cabins to be newly furnished and placed at their disposal.

The party was obliged to return to Cochin because ships sailing to Lisbon usually took on cargo at that port, and there they found five large ships docked. They sailed on the *Santiago* on 19/20 February 1584, leaving a little later than the other ships and therefore heavily laden. Preparations for the legates' official duties in Europe began, for once they arrived in Lisbon there would be little time to prepare formal speeches. Martin started work on an address in Latin to be delivered before the Jesuit General in Rome,[16] while Mancio labored at a shorter speech, later revised by a Jesuit in Evora, which he learned by heart and would give in their audience with the pope.

According to a letter written by Mesquita, the boys were all in good health, and distributed food from their ample supplies to the sick and needy on board. In addition to the time of prayer and study, they enjoyed ample relaxation, sitting on the poop chatting, practising on Western musical instruments, playing chess and fishing for bonito, tuna and catfish. In an hour on one particular morning they caught a dozen long-finned fish so large that one was enough to feed fifteen or twenty men.

For three or four days the ship enjoyed a favourable wind, but then began to take on so much water that the two available pumps were unable to cope. Believing that the leak was due to the blows that the barges had given the ship while taking on cargo, the crew laboriously moved the cargo and boxes, and discovered a large hole in the keel, which they managed to plug. The *Santiago* crossed the equator on 9 March, but then the wind dropped and the vessel remained becalmed for two weeks. This delay raised the possibility of being unable to round the Cape of Good Hope, in which case the ship would be forced to make a long stopover at fever-ridden Mozambique,[17] and would not reach Lisbon until the following year, 1585. But the wind finally turned favourable and the *Santiago* sailed cautiously through the dangerous straits of Madagascar. After some contrary winds blew the ship towards the south, the carrack successfully doubled the Cape of Good Hope in fine weather on 10 May amid much rejoicing on board, for sailors held, somewhat optimistically, that once that obstacle had been passed, the rest of the voyage would be prosperous.

On 27 May the *Santiago* reached the remote island of St Helena, a welcome and sometimes life-saving haven for Portuguese ships sailing from India to Lisbon, for here there were ample supplies of fresh food and water. According to tradition, the small island was discovered on 21 May, the feast of St Helena, in 1502 by João da Nova Castella on his voyage back from India. In his hearsay account, Arnoldus Montanus, 1625?–83, repeats the well-known version that the discoverer was

> ... a *Portuguese* merchant, who in the Year 1512 [sic] coming to Anchor here, and observing the pleasant Situation, and the solitariness thereof, which then agreed well with his disposition, being something inclin'd to Melancholly, and having been formerly much cross'd in his Fortunes, wearied with business, and the cunning practises of those he dealt withall, settled himself in this solitary Place, putting ashore those Sheep, Swine and Poultrey he had aboard, which increased in a short time to a Miracle ...[18]

Montanus continues his detailed account of the island with a lyrical description of its trees bearing oranges, lemons, figs and pomegranates, 'these trees always laden with ripe, green Fruits, and Blossoms'.[19] This pleasing account, often repeated in other sources, confirms that St Helena was an invaluable stopover for Portuguese shipping en route to Lisbon, in critical need of food and fresh water.

But the happiness at reaching the haven was considerably diminished on learning that the other four Portuguese vessels from Cochin had already left for Lisbon, for it was customary for ships to sail together in convoy from this point as a precaution against attacks from pirates based in the Azores. The *Santiago* remained at the island for ten or eleven days, giving passengers and crew a welcome chance to rest from the hardships and anxieties of the voyage. The boys occupied themselves in their favourite pastime of fishing from the ship's poop, using lines during the day and nets at night, and their plentiful catch lasted the party until the ship reached Lisbon.

The *Santiago* set sail again on 6 June, but not before the boys had fixed to the chapel walls written accounts of their travels. This was a custom of passengers and mariners of passing ships, and the English traveller Peter Mundy noted after his visit to the island in 1638: 'The Names of Divers shipps, principall Men, as allsoe of some women were Fairely written on boards and Nailed upp in the said Chappell.' So Mundy's crew recorded on a board the name of the ship's captain as well as 'the tyme off our arrivall and Departure hence . . . wee placed and Nayled itt Fast in the said Chappell by others thatt were there.'[20] But the boys' contribution was exceptional for they presumably wrote in Japanese. One wonders whether these records still existed when Napoleon Bonaparte, St Helena's most celebrated visitor, arrived on 15 October 1815 to spend the rest of his life in exile on the lonely island.

Sailing north towards Europe, the *Santiago* once more crossed the equator on 21 June. As the ship progressed northwards the temperature dropped abruptly causing widespread illness, especially chest ailments, and no less than thirty-two men died on board during this final stage of the voyage. Happily, the Japanese party was spared from sickness and remained in good health, although the deaths and burials at sea of so many men must have again been a traumatic experience for the youthful travellers.

Finally, on 10 August 1584, the *Santiago* reached Cascaes, the port of Lisbon, but waited until the following day to enter. The Japanese boys stared in wonder[21] at the hundreds of ships of different types and sizes and from so many countries docked in the busy port.[22] Among these were the ships they had seen in Cochin that had preceded them and had arrived only a week earlier. The grim news they had heard at St Helena was verified when they saw with their own eyes the *Salvador* with its bridge missing, torn away by a giant wave that had pounded the ship before it had rounded the Cape, drowning the captain and his nephew.

Skiffs carrying Jesuits came to greet the party and convey the passengers and their baggage to land at night so as not to attract undue and unwelcome attention. Nuno Rodrigues was the first to disembark and immediately set out for Rome to begin negotiations about mission business. After two-and-a-half years of travel the Japanese boys had at last reached Europe, and their important work as envoys would now begin. They were the first Japanese party to reach Europe.[23]

Part 3

Through Portugal and Spain

■ CHAPTER 5

Portugal

Lisbon, the boys' first port of call in Europe, offered the travellers an extensive introduction to European culture. Then at the height of its prosperity, the city could boast of fine palaces, cathedrals, monasteries and churches, many of which, despite the destructive earthquake in 1755, may still be visited and admired today. The grandeur and size of its huge buildings could hardly fail to impress the boys, while the genuine welcome extended to them must have added to their pleasure.

The boys were understandably tired after their long voyage and so after disembarking at night, they were taken to the Jesuit residence and church of St Roque, where they were cordially received by the community. After the Japanese had taken some rest, news of their arrival was sent to Cardinal Albert, 1559–1621, archduke of Austria, son of Emperor Maximilian, brother of Emperor Rudolph II, nephew of Charles V, nephew of Philip II, and the king's representative in Portugal. After the recent amalgamation of the Spanish and Portuguese thrones, the half-Portuguese Philip had spent two years in Lisbon to reassure the Portuguese their rights would be respected, and on his return to Madrid had appointed Cardinal Albert as his viceroy to govern Portugal in his name.

During their month's stay in Lisbon, the cardinal met the Japanese at least three times. On hearing of their arrival, he sent his coach and four white horses to convey Mesquita and the boys to his palace, where he received the party kindly. Mancio and Michael delivered in Japanese messages from the three daimyo, in which they asked the cardinal to favour the Japanese during their stay in Portugal. The legates then presented the cardinal with a cup made of rhinoceros horn, decorated with silver. Where they had obtained this unusual and most un-Japanese gift is not recorded, but their host graciously expressed his pleasure.[1] Then, with Mesquita acting as interpreter, Albert asked the boys at some length about their families, names, ages, health and other matters before the audience came to an end.

The arrival of the Japanese boys did not at first give rise to a great deal of public comment for Lisbon was an international port city and its citizens were accustomed to seeing people arriving from all parts of the world. Also, the heat in mid-August was intense and many people had left to spend their vacation in the countryside. The cardinal, in fact, set out for his country retreat in nearby Sintra on the day after the audience to obtain some respite from the oppressive weather, but left his carriage at the party's disposal.

Using this coach, the boys then went to pay their respects to Dom Jorge Almeida, archbishop of Lisbon, who also greeted them with warmth. Not content with welcoming his young visitors, he personally led them on a tour of his palace, showing them his library, study and other rooms. After bidding farewell to the archbishop, the Japanese went off on a tour of churches, among them being Nossa Senhora de Graça, which offered a fine view of the city. They also toured the large Royal Hospital and its many wards devoted to tending different illnesses; the expense of running this vast enterprise, they were told, was covered by financial grants left by kings John II and Manuel I.

On the following day, 14 August, the boys took the cardinal's carriage to visit the Jesuit college of St Antão and spent the whole day there in recreation. The Jesuits and students entertained them royally, and knowing that people wished to see their native dress, the boys put on their best Japanese robes. Doubtless Mesquita had guessed that these exotic garments would prove an attraction and would perhaps compensate for the visitors' lack of fluency in Portuguese, and so he had had the foresight to bring the robes in the coach. The Japanese then performed the rite of *sakazuki*, or the formal offering of *sake* wine to each other (presumably Portuguese wine was substituted for the occasion). This demonstration would have met with Valignano's approval for he had devoted an entire chapter to the subject in his treatise on Japanese etiquette, compiled in October 1581 during his first visit to Japan.[2]

Word of the exotic Japanese dress must have spread, for after a few days the cardinal sent a message to Mesquita that he, too, would like to see the boys in their robes, for during their first visit they had worn European costume. He sent a carriage in which they rode six leagues from Lisbon until reaching the monastery of Penha Longa near Sintra. Here they received by the Hieronymite community and ate with the friars in their refectory.[3] Then retiring into a private room, they changed into Japanese costume, and thus attired went by coach to the cardinal's palace. Albert greeted them with the same kindness as before, and greatly admired their dress. In accordance with their samurai rank the boys wore their decorated swords and short swords, which caused no little wonderment among the people present. The cardinal took one of their swords in his hands and examined it closely.

Later, when they were alone with the cardinal, the boys showed him the screens they had brought with them to Europe, and he questioned them closely about the paintings.[4] Cardinal Albert then sent his visitors back to the Penha Longa monastery, where they spent the night.

On the following day, the boys were taken at the cardinal's suggestion to see some of the fine palaces in Sintra and were much impressed by their paintings, decoration, and gardens. They were particularly intrigued by a 'house of water', where hidden pipes spouted jets of water in all directions on the unwary.[5] They next visited the Hieronymite monastery of Nossa Senhora de Pena, situated in a high mountain plain, to which they ascended on mules as the rough terrain made travel by coach impossible. They admired the wonderful view and the marble retablo showing Our Lady and scenes from the Passion.

On their return to the capital the Japanese visited more religious houses and received a particularly warm welcome in the Dominican monastery. Here they met one of the most celebrated authors and preachers of Christian devotion, the venerable Spaniard Fray Luis de Granada, 1504–88, to whom they showed 'his books translated into the language and letters of Japan', which pleased him greatly.[6]

The Japanese also went by coach on a pilgrimage to visit the church of Nossa Senhora da Luz. Then from Lisbon they proceeded by boat along the Tejo river to view the Belem fortress, and the Hieronymite church and monastery, with its beautiful cloister. This rich monument not surprisingly appears to have been the attraction that pleased them most in Lisbon. If they noticed the royal tombs and those of Vasco da Gama and Luis de Camões there, the record is silent. They then went on to see the São Julião de Barra fortress at the entrance of the harbour, where they were impressed by its mighty cannons guarding the port.

During their stay in the capital the Japanese paid visits on many bishops and nobles. They were entertained by the most skilful musicians and choirs of Lisbon and took special interest in their musical instruments. Shortly after their arrival Archbishop Theotonio de Bragança of Evora, friend of Valignano, sent word through one of his chaplains to bid the party welcome and invite them to visit him on their way to Spain.

The time came for the boys' departure from the capital on 5 September and they paid their third and last visit on the cardinal, who bade them farewell with every sign of friendship and affection. He donated three hundred crowns for their travel expenses and provided them with a passport that exempted the Japanese from taxes until they reached Madrid. To help with the travel arrangements, two local Jesuit priests accompanied the party as far as Evora.[7]

The boys set off on foot accompanied by a bevy of Jesuits and walked for a while before mounting the carriage that the archbishop of Evora had provided them; they would travel in this coach all the way to Madrid. On 7 September they arrived at the town of Montemor-o-novo, where they found that the archbishop had arranged luxurious accommodation for their stay. Before they retired for the night, a messenger arrived from Dom Theotonio welcoming them on his behalf. Such were the crowds assembled to see the travellers that the messenger experienced some difficulty in making his way through to deliver the greetings. Already Valignano's plan for a low-key legation was beginning to be disregarded.

On the following day the travellers arose early to attend Mass, and then set out for Evora; after covering five leagues, the party arrived at the beautiful city at 10 o'clock in the morning, and were greeted by the community of the Jesuit college, where they would be lodging. The archbishop wished them to stay in his palace, but the boys, doubtless supported by Mesquita, opted to board at the college in keeping with Valignano's instructions. This institution, like Coimbra, had been founded and endowed by King Henry, and was rather a university than a college for boys, as students came from all parts of Portugal to follow courses in philosophy and theology in its spacious halls. The Jesuit faculty numbered more than 120 members.

After lunch provided by the archbishop, their host arrived in person and embraced each of the boys, spending the afternoon in the college talking with and entertaining them before returning to his palace. Always mindful of the travellers' needs during their stay in his city, the prelate had ample food supplies delivered to them every day.

Shortly afterwards, the boys were taken by carriage to call on the archbishop, who emerged from his palace accompanied by his chaplains and staff, and formally welcomed the party to Evora. He then led his guests around the palace, showing them his library and the sacristy with its collection of relics, remarking that they could take anything they wished back to Japan when they passed through on their return journey. There followed a concert performed by choirboys singing motets and songs; this musical entertainment continued throughout supper, after which the boys returned to the college.

On 14 September, the feast of the Exaltation of the Holy Cross, the Japanese went back to the cathedral where they were again received by the archbishop, who celebrated a solemn Mass before a large congregation. In the procession the place of honour was accorded to the boys, who walked next to the prelate and in front of local dignitaries. In the sermon during Mass the preacher made complimentary references to the visitors, and praised them for coming such a distance through so many dangers in order to meet the pope. Afterwards, the archbishop took his guests back to his nearby palace and presented them with four tapestries woven of silk and gold with wonderful skill.[8] Dom Theotonio donated 250 crowns for travel expenses and promised a further thousand on their return journey to buy expensive gifts to take home for their families. He then led them into his dining hall, where he treated them to a banquet to the accompaniment of music. In keeping with the custom of the time, a dozen paupers sat at another table and enjoyed the same repast.

The boys were then taken to the choir of the cathedral where they admired the most beautiful organ they had ever seen. Although the church was packed because of the feast day, Mancio and Michael both played on the organ, much to the satisfaction of the archbishop and others who heard their performance.[9] It would be interesting to know more about their skill in this regard and how accomplished, in fact, the two boys had become by this time. Then followed yet another concert performed by a dozen choirboys.

Before the Japanese bade farewell to the archbishop and the college community, they expressed their gratitude to the prelate by inviting him alone to dinner to show him their Japanese robes, as well as some Japanese books and a short letter written by the ruler Oda Nobunaga to a Jesuit missionary in Japan. Dom Theotonio admired the boys' Latin handwriting, and was astonished to read a passage in Latin written by Brother George Loyola. He asked the Brother whether he understood the text and he replied that yes, he did. The text was closely examined and found to be perfectly correct in every detail. The boys offered the archbishop various gifts, but he would accept only one, a Japanese box which contained other boxes within, remarking presciently that they had a long way to travel and many people to meet, so they had better keep their gifts for later use.

Before the boys left Evora on 14 or 15 September, it was agreed that they would visit Vila Viçosa because the Duke of Bragança, the prelate's nephew, was anxious to meet them. The archbishop presented the Japanese with more tapestries marvellously woven and an additional two hundred crowns for their travel expenses.[10] He also proposed donating money to found a school in Japan, and sending oenologists to plant vines there so that the missionaries would not have to depend on India for Mass wine.

A league before the party reached Vila Viçosa, the country seat of the illustrious Bragança family, the carriage of Dona Caterina appeared and conveyed the boys for the rest of the journey. Despite a mishap on the part of Brother George, who nearly fell under the wheels of a moving coach, they arrived safely at their destination. Young Duke Teodósio, aged only sixteen, and his mother Dona Caterina, cousin of Philip II, received the Japanese in the Augustinian church, which contained the tombs of the Bragança family.[11] Also in the reception party were the duke's younger brothers, Duarte and Alexander, waiting for the visitors at the door of the church. After Mass he and his brothers left on horseback, while the Japanese rode in Dona Caterina's carriage. At the duchess' insistence, the boys were lodged in a richly decorated chamber in the Bragança palace.

Constantine, one of the Japanese attendants, was so impressed by all the wealth and luxury that he left a report written in excellent Portuguese, and Fróis includes his detailed account *ad literam* in his text. The description, written in the first-person singular, runs to 900 words. Constantine was overwhelmed by the lavish use of silver vessels, including 'a large bowl of twelve or thirteen spans in circumference for washing the feet'. He was greatly impressed by the many large tapestries. The stables housed fifty or sixty horses, the young duke explaining apologetically that they used to number two hundred but these had been lost in King Sebastian's expedition to Morocco, in which the duke himself had been captured and subsequently ransomed. Accompanied by a hundred men on horseback and foot, the duke led the visitors to a walled hunting reserve where some mountain boars were chased and killed. Finally, the party was treated to an equestrian tournament of *canas* with the riders using wooden lances.[12]

The duke and his younger brothers took all their meals with the Japanese and obviously enjoyed their company, for the visitors were about the same age as the duke.[13] As for their mother, Dona Caterina, she appears to have felt a particular affection for the Japanese, and sent them a dish of assorted sweetmeats every morning. During their stay in Vila Viçosa they visited her four or five times, on which occasions she had music sung and played for their pleasure. Learning of the boys' interest in music, the duke supplied them with instruments, and the visitors played on them and sang accompaniments. The duchess was much taken by the Japanese robes and the boys obligingly showed them off for her inspection. She was so impressed that she secretly had a similar set made up in rich material for her second son, Duarte, and then sent word to the visitors that they should return to her apartment as she wished to introduce them to a Japanese.

Somewhat puzzled by this invitation, the boys believed the duchess was referring to a Japanese brought to Europe on a Portuguese ship. But on arrival at her apartment, they found that the 'Japanese' was, in fact, her young son Duarte, clad in hurriedly-tailored Japanese dress. Apparently, he was not wearing the robes correctly, and so the Japanese put matters right and also showed him how to carry the sword.

The visitors were due to leave on 18 September, and went to bid farewell to Dona Caterina, thanking both her and the duke for the many favours received. The duke wished to accompany them by carriage as far as Elvas, and donated two hundred crowns for travel expenses. On reaching Elvas, they found a final gift from the family – a pack mule laden with ample provisions of food, a useful and thoughtful present for the region through which they were travelling was poorly provided with supplies.

CHAPTER 6

Spain and 'the Most Potent Monarch'

On leaving Elvas and entering Spain, the Japanese decided to make a pilgrimage to the shrine of Our Lady of Guadalupe, for the sanctuary was only a short way off their route. As usual, they were cordially welcomed and on the following day, 24 September, they attended Mass at the basilica, where they inspected a large collection of relics. They were shown around by the elderly Prior, and sat next to him at lunch in the refectory, after which they spent the afternoon touring the monastery. Next morning, they attended Mass celebrated at the high altar.

Here again in Fróis's text there are indications that the travellers carefully recorded their impressions for later use in Japan. There were so many things to be seen and admired in the great church that a person staying many years could not, it is said, describe all of them adequately. This was even more true of travellers spending only two days there, but the boys took notes as best they could so as not to forget some of the more memorable sights.

The church is very large, they observed, and at the high altar there is the famous black statue of Our Lady, in front of which burn some fifty silver lamps.[1] The walls and pillars are decorated with the iron chains of captives freed from the prisons of the Moors and Turks. There were also ex-vetoes left by people who had been cured of blindness and other afflictions through Our Lady's intercession.

When the boys departed on 25 September, they were presented with a handwritten book listing the miracles performed by Our Lady, as well as a plentiful supply of food for their journey. The next stop was Talavera, which had a Jesuit college founded only two years earlier by the Archbishop of Toledo. Rodrigues had already passed through en route to Madrid and Rome, and had told the community of the boys' approach. The Japanese did not intend to stop the night there, but the students had been busy preparing and rehearsing dances, plays and speeches, and the lengthy show they presented in the afternoon made an overnight stop inevitable.

On the following day, the Japanese set out for Toledo, the metropolitan seat of Spain, where they arrived late in the evening of the 29th. A coach with four horses was awaiting them outside the city to take them to their lodgings at the Jesuit residence, and many students from the college escorted them on horseback. So dense was the crowd awaiting them outside the college that the visitors could make their way into the building only with some difficulty. It was decided that on the following day, a Sunday, they should attend Mass in public in the main chapel so that the local people could get a glimpse of the travellers. They then went sightseeing through the ancient city. On 1 October, they visited the Jesuit college, where they looked in at some classes and attended a performance of speeches and recitals put on by the students in their honour.

Fróis here includes a first-person narrative composed by one of the party, possibly again Constantine, describing the grandeur of Toledo. He recounts in detail the city's religious houses, its layout, population, merchants and shops. They were shown around the massive cathedral by Juan de Mendoza, dean of the cathedral, younger brother of the duke of Infantado, and later to be raised to the cardinalate. The building, he declares, has eight doors; there are seventy-four beautifully carved wooden stalls in the choir, each worth a thousand crowns; as well as many silver lamps. Each nave has eleven arches or columns. The cathedral has twenty chapels, some of which are 50 by 30 paces large. Seven kings are buried in the Chapel of the Monarchs. Many relics are to be seen in the sacristy, as well as a large basin in which the archbishop washes the feet of a dozen poor people on Maundy Thursday. The tower has seven stories and eleven bells, one of which is 46 spans in circumference.[2] The Japanese attended a celebration in the cathedral to commemorate the memorable victory in the Battle of Lepanto, which had been fought on 7 October thirteen years earlier, and were provided special seats where they could view the canons vested in rich robes as well as the large choir of singers.

This long account is of no particular value in itself except to show again that at least one of the Japanese had a good command of Portuguese and that Valignano's instructions to the party to take notes on their travels were being observed with commendable zeal.

During their tour of Toledo, the boys were particularly impressed by the ingenious system of raising and distributing drinking water from the River Tagus to fountains up in the city. Even more, they were intrigued by a clock that told not only the time but also indicated the days, sun, moon, stars, planets and eclipses. Both mechanisms were devised by an elderly Italian, Gianello Turriano, who told them that it had taken him more than twenty years to devise and assemble the clock's intricate machinery.[3]

Since the end of September Michael had suffered from fever, and on 3 October, when the party was due to leave for Madrid, his ailment took a turn for the worse and chicken-pox developed, leaving his body covered with spots. There was no question of continuing the journey when the boy was so ill, and so only Perpinhão and a few servants set out to make arrangements in Madrid. Doctors followed the traditional European treatment for all illnesses, and poor Michael was bled twice. Mesquita was greatly worried as he was told two thousand children in Toledo had died of the disease, but happily Michael survived the two bleedings and recovered. Within two weeks he was judged sufficiently fit to resume the journey.

Once Michael was out of danger and on the way to recovery, his three companions were entertained royally, especially by Don Francisco de Mendoza, brother of the duke of Infantado.[4] The gentleman offered the party his coach to carry them to Madrid with an escort. Unfortunately, he was unexpectedly called away to visit his ailing brother, and was unable to follow up the offer. Dom João de Bragança, son of the Marquis of Ferreira and Tentugal, happened to be in Madrid at the time, and, hearing of this turn of events, sent his carriage to collect the Japanese party.[5] The cardinal was not in residence at the time and his place was taken by a venerable archdeacon, whom three of the boys visited to say goodbye, before the party set out from Toledo on 19 October.

Before reaching Madrid on the following day, the Japanese were met by a cavalcade of nobles in carriages and on horseback. Once suitable greetings had been exchanged, each of the boys rode in separate coaches drawn by four white horses, and were escorted to the Jesuit residence, where they were greeted by the community. It was now the turn of Martin to fall sick, with fever and a weak pulse. Four eminent doctors, including the king's personal physicians, tended him, and prescribed the inevitable treatment of bleeding the boy for three days, followed by a strong purge. Despite this treatment, Martin recovered after two weeks, while Michael finally regained his strength following his bout of smallpox.

Martin's illness delayed the party's progress, but it enabled the boys to witness a most solemn ceremony, for Philip II had summoned the leading nobles and officials of Castile to Madrid to swear allegiance and loyalty to his six-year-old son and heir, later Philip III, 1578–1621, of Spain. Fróis observes disarmingly that it would appear that God had sent Martin his illness and thus delayed the boys' journey so that the Japanese could attend the historic event of 11 November, the feast of St Martin. As a result of the forthcoming ceremony, many prelates and members of the aristocracy had gathered in the capital, and a bewildering array of dukes, counts, marquises, cardinals, archbishops and bishops called on the Japanese party, eager to meet the visitors who by now had acquired a widespread reputation.

At the time the king was residing in the Prado palace two leagues from Madrid, and on 8 November Mesquita and a Jesuit colleague went to confer with him and ask him when he wished to receive the Japanese in audience. After enquiring about the boys' health, Philip replied that he would be busy until the allegiance ceremony in three days time, but would be happy to meet them afterwards. Exercising some diplomacy, Mesquita asserted that the aim of the legation from such a distant country was primarily to meet the pope, but then the Japanese also wished to pay their respects to Christian kings and princes, among whom his majesty was the greatest. He went on to say the boys would be in the capital at the time of the allegiance ceremony, and wondered whether it would be possible for them to attend the event. Philip readily agreed, declaring that he, too, wished the visitors to be present and would order a place to be reserved for them. The ceremony would be held in the Hieronymite monastery, outside Madrid, because its great church was spacious and well equipped for the event.

Mesquita then presented to the king a letter from the archbishop of Goa, Vicente de Fonseca, which Philip immediately read, and also some chapters of a treatise written by Valignano on the government and customs of China.[6] Philip told him he would read the latter in his coach along the way, for he was about to set out. Speaking later with the court lady Doña Leonora de Mascarenhas, the king mentioned that the priest had presented him with a book about China and he had read it with interest.

On the day before the oath ceremony was due to take place, in characteristic fashion Philip himself went to the monastery church to view the preparations. With so much on his mind, he did not forget the Japanese delegation, and entering a tribunal, one of the most select places in the church to view the proceedings and large enough to accommodate twenty-five people, he declared, 'This is for the Japanese', although he was aware that the place had been reserved for a countess and other ladies.

On the following day, 11 November, the king sent a carriage to collect the boys, who were escorted to the great church by Philip's chief minister and confidante, Cristóbal de Moura, and other nobles.[7] On their arrival at the monastery, the visitors observed that the interior walls of the church had been covered with tapestries, the floor laid with rich carpets and the altar resplendent with a cloth of gold; extra vestments and decorations had been provided by the Escorial and Toledo. The Japanese, Moura and the nobles were ushered into the tribunal, where the boys sat in the front row together with Mesquita, who would explain to them what was taking place in the ceremony. As they had not yet been received in audience by the king, the Japanese could not appear in public at the event, and so a thin curtain was hung through which they could clearly view the proceedings but not be seen. This is an interesting fact, for it appears to show that the boys were recognized as true envoys from Japan, for until ambassadors present their credentials to the head of state, they have no official standing.

The king, his young heir, and his two daughters, accompanied by lords and ladies, entered the church in solemn procession at ten o'clock in the morning. Before them walked heralds bearing ceremonial maces and the royal coat-of-arms. Immediately in front of the king proceeded the Count of Oropesa carrying the unsheathed royal sword. King Philip sat on a throne, together with his son Philip, his younger sister (widow of the emperor),[8] and his daughters Isabella and Catarina, surrounded by pages and attendants. The tribunal in which the Japanese were placed was on the epistle side of the church, so close to where the members of the royal family were seated that the boys could not only see them clearly but also hear what they were saying to each other. Also present were the papal nuncio, the ambassadors of the Emperor and of Venice, eight bishops, and the presidents of the royal councils. Close to the high altar were the cardinal archbishop of Toledo and Philip's trusted adviser Cardinal Granvelle.[9] The vast interior of the church was filled with rows of nobles and officials.

Cardinal Quiroga, primate of Toledo, celebrated the sung Mass, while Cardinal Granvelle offered the kiss of peace to the king and Bishop Andre de Noronha of Placencia offered it to his family. But alas for the best-prepared liturgy, a slight mishap occurred, and Fróis here allows himself a little humour, noting: 'A funny thing happened in that most solemn Mass.' To save time because of the lengthy oath-taking ceremony to follow, the celebrant decided to quietly recite the Preface prayer instead of singing it as would be expected in a solemn Mass. But on hearing a bell rung, the choir at some distance in the great church misunderstood his intention and began singing the beginning of the Preface; the bell was rung a second time to correct this error, but this caused further misunderstanding and a good deal of mirth in the congregation. Finally, someone[10] managed to let the choir know of its mistake.

After the liturgy had been concluded, a table covered with precious cloth was set before the high altar, and on it were placed the Gospels and an ornate crucifix. The cardinal of Toledo then seated himself next to this table, while a magistrate read out the order of the ceremony, and a prefect of the royal council explained the form of the oath to be taken.

The empress took the oath first, with her brother and his daughters escorting her to the table as a mark of respect. She and the two princesses then swore allegiance, acknowledging the six-year-old boy as rightful heir to the throne. The empress tried to kiss the prince's hand, but he would not allow her to do so, and so aunt and nephew embraced. The prince also did not wish his sisters to kiss his hand, but at a sign from his father he finally allowed them to do so. Cardinal Granvelle then swore allegiance, followed by the bishops in due order with Andre de Noronha in first place. They were followed by the Spanish nobility led by the Admiral of Castile,[11] and then came government officials and finally representatives of cities. Those from Burgos were in the first place, followed by officials from other cities; the representatives of Toledo took the oath separately so that equal honour was accorded to Toledo and Burgos.[12]

In all, ninety-two persons took the oath of allegiance on that day and the ceremony lasted no less than five hours. It was a great honour for the Japanese to attend the event and view the proceedings at such close hand, but the boys would have needed all their samurai training to sit impassively through the lengthy proceedings.

At the time of the party's arrival in Madrid, Philip II was at the height of his power and was the 'most potent Monarch of Christendome'.[13] He had succeeded to the Spanish throne in 1556, and only four years before he had ascended the throne of Portugal, thus becoming sovereign of the vast overseas possessions of the two Iberian countries. In addition, he was king of Naples and Sicily as well as duke of Milan; he also ruled the Netherlands. He had spent more than two years in Lisbon in an effort to convince his new subjects that he would respect Portuguese interests, both at home and abroad. On becoming their king as Philip I, he had promised the Portuguese in November 1582 to respect their privileges, offices, language, coinage and judicial system; Portuguese commercial rights in Africa and Asia would be maintained (a proviso that had relevance to Macao's profitable silk trade with Japan). After twenty years of construction, the last stone of the Escorial, his austere palace-monastery-mausoleum, had been laid on 13 September 1584, just two months before the boys' visit. The defeat of his invincible armada was yet to come in 1588, some four years later.

On 12 November, the day following the oath-taking ceremony, the king sent his grand chamberlain, Cristóbal de Moura, to the Jesuit residence to discuss details of the royal audience, to be held two days later. Moura was Philip's right-hand man, and the fact that he personally arranged the meeting reflects the importance the king attached to the event. Moura told the party that a large entourage would not be necessary, a concession that would have pleased Valignano, who in his instructions had insisted on low-key receptions of the boys.[14]

On the same day two senior Jesuits went ahead to explain to the king the purpose of the Japanese legation to Europe – to pay homage to the pope, to meet Catholic kings and princes and to witness at first hand Christianity in Europe. On 14 November Philip ordered two richly-adorned carriages, accompanied by a military escort, to fetch the Japanese party, and the boys, dressed in Japanese robes and carrying their swords (*katana*) and short swords (*wakizashi*), set out at three o'clock in the afternoon.

An unidentified eye-witness who took special note of their Japanese apparel has left a detailed and fairly accurate description. They wore, he observed, an outer garment of white silk, decorated with various different colours and figures of birds, all of which made a most attractive show. The Japanese usually wore three robes of this material, one over the other, and these were open in front and long, almost touching the ground. The sleeves were ample and reached to just beyond the elbows. Although Japanese usually left the rest of the arm uncovered and bare, for the sake of modesty the boys wore underneath some vests of white silk. Their trousers were made of the same material, silk, and colour, and were long, rather like those worn by sailors. The robes had a piece of the same material, but most curiously worked, high on the shoulders, two spans wide and three long; its sole purpose was decoration. From both of its ends emerged a ribbon two fingers wide, which crossed over the chest from the shoulders, its purpose being to carry that piece of material and to encircle the body.[15]

The Japanese did not usually wear hats, the account continues, because they carried a shade against rain and sun, but to comply with European custom the boys carried hats or caps. Their socks (*tabi*) were like gloves, with the big toe of the foot separated from the others, which were placed together. They wore shoes like sandals, uncovered above and tied with a ribbon. All Japanese wore a sword and a dagger, made of very thin steel that can cut any armour, however strong it may be. The boys' scabbards were very rich and attractive. The larger one, made of a certain black material, was decorated with many pieces of mother-of-pearl of various colours. The smaller one was made of ground gold, and was just as smooth and attractive as the large one.[16]

An immense crowd filled the streets of the capital to witness the progress of the envoys and were doubtless not disappointed by their exotic costumes. It apparently was Philip's custom to view the people, especially nobles, entering and leaving his palace, without himself being seen, and noticing the arrival of the carriages, he exclaimed to the two Jesuits: 'They've arrived, they're getting out!' With this remark, he retired to another chamber. Such was the dense crowd that, on alighting from the carriages, the Japanese were unable to make any progress on foot, and more guards were quickly called to clear a path for them so as not to keep the king waiting unduly.

On finally entering the palace, the Japanese were led through twelve furnished halls, until they finally reached an inner chamber where the king and his children, the prince and the two princesses, were standing, awaiting their arrival.[17]

Bowing low, the Japanese approached the monarch to kiss his hand, first Mancio and Michael, and then the rest in due order. Philip, however, did not wish to offer his hand to be kissed, but smiling broadly he bade the two envoys and their companions to rise from their knees and then embraced them, including even the attendants Constantine and Augustine. The visitors also wanted to kiss the hands of the princesses, but following their father's example, they, too, embraced the boys. When the Japanese approached the prince, without hesitation he offered his hand to be kissed, because he had done this so often during the allegiance ceremony a few days earlier. At the end Mesquita went forward to kiss the prince's hand, but the king would not allow the priest to do so.

Philip then began the conversation, inquiring about the visitors' health, and showed interest in their dress, fingering Mancio's robe. Mesquita apologetically remarked that the garments were not in good condition on account of the long sea voyage, but Philip dismissed his excuse, declaring that the costumes were very fine. Mancio blushed with embarrassment as he tried to cover a part of his robe that was particularly faded. The king said he wished to examine a Japanese sandal and Mancio swiftly took one off for him to inspect. The king inquired what the sandal was called in Spanish. Mesquita replied that the boys did not know Spanish very well; they studied, he said, Latin, but they always spoke to him, Mesquita, in Japanese. Philip remarked that this was a good idea as in this way they would not forget their native language while travelling abroad. For the king's benefit, Mancio and Michael then spoke some words in Japanese. The king then asked many questions about Japan and their voyage to Europe.

When it came to present gifts to their royal host, Mesquita explained that the items were all they had to offer as they had left Japan in a hurry and had no opportunity to assemble worthy presents; the objects, he added, were only to allow His Majesty inspect some Japanese things as curiosities and were not real presents. Among the items offered were a bamboo writing desk with cleverly made compartments and drawers, a wooden bowl with gold decoration below its lacquer finish, and a box containing so many cunningly contrived compartments as to surprise the king. Finally, they presented a container skilfully lacquered both inside and out, and this item aroused the most admiration.

Philip took the gifts in his hands, examined them intently, and turned them over, observing that they were different from Chinese objects. On handling a jar, he asked Mesquita if the Japanese possessed a good liquor. The priest replied that they certainly did and that this container was intended for wine. The king had heard about tea and asked:

'But don't they drink hot water?'

Mesquita answered, 'Yes, they do, but they also make wine.'

'But do they drink hot water only in winter?'

The Jesuit told him that they drank it all year around, at which the king was not a little surprised.

Philip thanked his visitors for these gifts brought from so far away. He remembered to inquire about the two boys who had been ill, and asked whether they were fully recovered. Mancio and Michael then delivered their speeches in Japanese on behalf of the Kyushu daimyo they represented, and a Spanish translation was duly read aloud. The king replied he was happy to receive these messages and rejoiced that Christianity had spread to their country. They thanked him for his kindness. Placing the letters in the boxes in which they had come, each boy offered them to the king on his knees. Philip asked about the writing, and gave the documents to Brother George for him to read in Japanese. As he did so, Philip approached and asked where he had begun reading, marvelling that George read from top to bottom, and from the right, where Europeans ended their letters.[18]

The Japanese text of Ōtomo Sōrin's letter no longer exists, but a translation of the Portuguese version runs as follows:

> With the Lord's grace I write to Your Royal Majesty. Through the Fathers of the Society of Jesus, who teach the true doctrine in these kingdoms, I have often heard of Your Majesty's affairs and your

kingdoms. Because of navigation problems and the long route, I have not yet communicated with Your Majesty.

Father Visitor [Valignano] came to visit this Christian church of Japan and in the two years that he has spent here it is impossible to express the consolation we have received from his presence and good order. As for me, I cannot forget the great mercy that I received from the High God of Heaven, ruling that I receive His holy law and doctrine.

I decided to send my nephew, Lord Jerome of Hyūga, to kiss the foot of His Holiness, and also to visit Your Majesty. But this was not possible as he is in Kyoto, so I send my cousin, Lord Mancio of Hyūga. He travels in the company of Father Visitor. I beg Your Majesty that you may deign to favour him in everything, and also the Japanese church, and myself from now on.

Father Visitor and Lord Mancio will inform Your Majesty about the other things of these regions, and I beg Your Majesty to hear them with favour.

11 January 1582.

Francis of Bungo

The letters of Protasius Arima Harunobu, dated 8 February 1582, and Bartholomew Ōmura Sumitada, 27 day, First Month, 1582, are similar in style and content.[19]

The audience lasted about an hour and, as it was getting late, one of the Jesuits asked the king if he wished the boys to visit his sister, the empress. Philip agreed, but invited the visitors to first attend sung vespers and had the party conducted to his private chapel, where everyone was waiting for their arrival. The boys were shown to the front seats, next to the altar. The duchess of Veiro, her attendants, and other ladies were present, and the king himself later appeared. Vespers were accompanied by choir, organ and trumpets, and compline followed immediately afterwards. The boys then wished to visit the empress, but it was now almost evening, and she sent word that she would prefer to see them by day and invited them to return on the morrow.

In this way the boys' first audience with Philip II came to an end. Courtiers who had been present on the occasion, such as Cristóbal de Moura, Diego de Córdoba, and the Marquis of Dénia, assured the party that they had never seen the king pay such favours to his guests. These last remarks were borne out in a touching way.

A fifteen-year-old Chinese servant had joined the party in Cochin, and accompanied the boys to the royal palace, but not being Japanese, he had diffidently stayed outside the audience chamber.

When the party came out to attend vespers, Don Diego de Córdoba noticed the boy, and told him: 'You're the only one not to see the king.' So the courtier led him by the hand into Philip's presence, and the Chinese boy bowed to the monarch and his children, who asked his name and age. Mesquita was obliged to return and found the king and his children examining the gifts and admiring the ornate box containing the letters from Japan. The priest explained that the boy was Chinese and had come from India to serve the legates.

As the Japanese left the palace, the courtyard was again so crowded that guards had difficulty in making a way for them to enter their carriages. Even when they arrived back at their lodgings, they found the road outside the Jesuit residence packed with horses and coaches, while inside the church some noble ladies were awaiting their return. To satisfy these ladies' curiosity the Japanese made an appearance within the church, where they received greetings and good wishes. Back inside the college, they found two bishops and other gentlemen who had entered the residence from the church and had waited more than two hours for their return. They conversed with the Japanese for some time and then left late at night.

At one o'clock on the following day, 15 November, the boys went to visit the empress, and just before they set out, two of her coaches pulled up to convey them to her convent residence. As they were about to board, two more coaches arrived from the king, with the Head Coachman bearing orders to use them as they wished. To prevent causing any upset, they finally departed in all four coaches and arrived at the empress's convent, where she received them with the same kindness as had the king, her brother.

Both the empress and her companion, Doña Leonora de Mascarenhas, embraced the Japanese and curiously examined their robes. The empress took one of their swords in her hands, drew it out of its sheath, and examined the blade, expressing admiration for its beauty. The ladies asked to see some writings in Japanese as well as some in Latin letters, which the boys wrote and left there as a souvenir. The Japanese were thanked for this keepsake and then took their leave.

The legates also went to visit Don Juan de Borja,[20] the empress's senior chamberlain, who showed them many relics of saints, among which were twenty-eight heads of various saints encased in silver, as well as the six arms of other saints, one of whom was Mary Magdalen, and also a thorn from Christ's crown of thorns, and a cross carrying relics of the twelve apostles. After admiring this edifying collection, the boys returned to the college, where they found a message from the Cardinal Archbishop of Toledo,[21] Primate of Spain, to say he was waiting to converse with them, so they had no choice but to set out again and visit the primate in his palace.

The archbishop was happy to see the Japanese and they spent half an hour in his company. Two or three days before they departed from the capital, the cardinal hosted them to a banquet in his palace. The French ambassador also paid them a visit, extending an invitation from his king to visit his country. The boys replied tactfully that they were at present in a hurry to reach Rome, but would try to visit France on their return journey. This vague and diplomatic answer was not meant to be taken seriously, for France was never on their itinerary and a visit to that country would have unduly delayed their return to Japan.

When Mesquita had returned to the audience chamber to explain about the Chinese boy, he had taken the opportunity to ask the king whether he would allow the Japanese to be shown some of the royal treasures so that they could report on them when they returned to their homeland. Philip replied modestly that there was little to see, but he would be pleased to allow them inspect all he owned. Mesquita said they particularly wanted to visit the Escorial and the Royal Armoury, and also inspect the jewels in his treasury. The king readily agreed, and asked when they would go to the Escorial. Mesquita replied diplomatically whenever it pleased the king. Don Diego suggested the following day, but Philip remarked that they would then still be tired and it would be better to go two days later, that is, 16 November, for the Escorial was located some distance from Madrid.

The king ordered two ornate coaches to be provided for the expedition and sent two letters, one to Prior Miguel de Alaejos, asking him to receive the boys kindly at the Escorial, and the other to Sebastião de Santayo, his chamberlain, instructing him to prepare suitable accommodation near the monastery. Unfortunately, Martin was still too unwell to join the excursion, so the rest of the party set out to visit the immense monastery-palace, with its somewhat austere exterior but richly decorated interior. Following the wishes of his father, Emperor Charles V, Philip had begun construction in 1563 and took a personal interest in the project. The last stone had been laid in September 1584, only a month or so before the boys' visit, and it is hardly surprising that the king readily agreed for the Japanese to visit and admire the huge complex, which would eventually house the tombs of himself, his father, his son and other Spanish monarchs.

While being shown around the Escorial, the members of the party obviously took extensive notes, for in his account Fróis explicitly asserts that his description of their visit, written in the first-person plural, was compiled by the visitors. These notes were later sent to India and thence to Japan, so 'I shall use the words and form in which they wrote as follows'.[22] As regards the great Escorial, the party was understandably at a loss for words to describe its splendour:

> It is impossible to describe in writing its splendour, magnificence and great size, for even people skilled and learned in the language would hesitate and falter in many things. For truly they cannot be described to anyone who has not seen them. . . . It is not possible to descend into detail concerning these magnificent and spacious works, so we will deal briefly and succinctly about what we saw.[23]

Thus begins the detailed account of the great Monasterio de San Lorenzo el Real del El Escorial, the enormous but stern royal palace, monastery and mausoleum, staffed at that time by Hieronymite monks, with its 2,600 windows, 86 stairways and many miles of corridors. It had been built very much under the king's personal supervision, and Philip in fact had a room from which he could watch through a window the liturgy performed on the high altar in the great church. The vast complex was named after St Lawrence, on whose feast day, 10 August, in 1557 Spanish forces had overcome the French in the battle of St Quentin in Flanders. The overall design of the building is in the shape of a grid, representing the gridiron on which St Lawrence is said to have been martyred.

The Japanese dined on the first evening at the royal mansion, but on the following two days of their stay they took their meals with the monastery's prior, who showed them much kindness and personally conducted them around the massive building and its gardens. Some of the monks asked the boys what they thought of its grandeur and whether there was anything similar in their own country and in the countries through which they had passed, and the visitors admitted, probably in all sincerity, they had not seen anything comparable. The party was shown the sacristy of the great church and its rich collection of relics, including the heads of twenty-four of the eleven thousand virgins who suffered with St Ursula, nine thorns from Christ's crown of thorns, and many arms of saints, all encased in silver reliquaries.

Then on to the fine library, where the visitors admired richly bound books, two terrestrial globes, and precious missals and breviaries illuminated by hand, together with trophies captured from the Turks at the battle of Lepanto. The list of what the Japanese were shown stretches on interminably in Fróis's account: the infirmary, two dining-rooms, the great church with its sixty-four massive stone columns, fourteen cloisters, the nine towers with their twenty-four bells ('rung with hands and feet, rather like an organ'):

> We carried there Japanese paper and ink, and a book written in our letters and characters to show them our way of reading and writing. . . . In the library they showed us a book with letters belonging to various different nations, even Chinese letters. As there were no Japanese letters, they asked us to leave something in writing as a memento for that house and library.

So Brother George wrote on Japanese paper called *torinoko* the date of the Japanese gentlemen's visit, where, and for what purpose, as well as praise for His Majesty and the Escorial, with an accompanying Spanish translation. The chronicler Fray Juan de San Gerónimo was present and records that the boys were about fifteen or sixteen years old. He provides the Spanish text of Brother George's message, in which not only the boys and Mesquita, but also their attendants Constantine and Augustine, are mentioned by name:

> We came to see this house of San Lorenzo el Real del Escorial by order of the great Lord Don Philip, King of Spain, and we all greatly admire and are happy to see a work so magnificent. So far we have not seen or dreamed of seeing anything like this, and we consider the

hardships and perils that we have undergone in our journey of three years to have been well worthwhile for we have finally seen such a marvellous work.[24]

The prior also asked them to write some of the Commandments in Japanese letters, and said he would show them to the king, and in fact he later did so.[25]

After their return to Madrid, the boys went to inspect the Royal Armoury and duly admired the many suits of armour on display, including the armour of Charles V, as well as the extensive collections of lances, halberds, spears, large and small muskets, bows and arrows, and quivers; doubtless the rich collection would have been of more than passing interest to the young samurai. Next were the royal stables housing seventy fine horses, although they were assured that in Granada there was a stable with two hundred. When on another day they visited the Royal Treasury, they were overwhelmed by the display of gold and silver ornaments, as well as precious stones such as emeralds, diamonds and rubies. Inevitably, they were shown another set of relics enclosed in gold and silver cases encrusted with precious stones – a crucifix made by St Gregory, a part of Our Lady's cloak, a nail from the Crucifixion, and many others.

On another occasion during their stay in the capital the boys went to view an elephant and a rhinoceros, an outing that must have come as light relief after the lengthy ceremonial functions they had recently attended.[26]

CHAPTER 7

From Alcalá to Alicante

When the time for the boys' departure from Madrid came, the local Jesuits and some nobles considered it better not to bother Philip II with a formal visit; instead, Mesquita would go alone to court, and, on behalf of the Japanese party, thank him for his kindness and bid him farewell. The king was alone in his study and told the priest that he much liked the *Ecce Homo* painting the boys had presented to him. Did the Japanese paint such pictures by themselves or did the Jesuits instruct them? he inquired. Presumably Mesquita took this opportunity to talk about the two schools the missionaries had founded in Japan in which Western painting was taught.

Philip asked after the boys again, and donated 500 crowns for their travel expenses and an additional 200 to help the Jesuits' educational work in Japan. He also ordered a carriage to be provided for the boys and Mesquita, as well as a cart and mules to carry their baggage. To facilitate their progress, he issued a passport so that their luggage would not be inspected and taxed en route, and the royal coat of arms was to be featured prominently on their baggage as a safeguard.[1] He had already had instructions sent to officials on their route, commanding them to look after the travellers well and take care of all their needs. A letter was also sent to the Spanish ambassador in Rome, Enrique de Guzman, count of Olivares:[2]

> To the Count, member of our Council and our Ambassador. Together with some Fathers of the Society of Jesus, there have come from Japan

to these regions Don Mancio, nephew of the king of Hyūga, and Don Michael, cousin of the king of Arima, and also Don Julian and Don Martin. Having become Christians, they desired to come here and they will go to kiss the foot of His Holiness in the company of one of the aforementioned Fathers.

So that on their return to their country they may be able to praise the reception they have received and to move others to imitate their example, We charge you to help them in everything necessary, honouring and showing them favour so that they may thus receive all possible good treatment in that Court, for this is fitting on account of their quality and even more for the good choice they have made.

You will inform me about these matters, and the favour and kindness accorded them.

Madrid, 24 November 1584.

Small wonder that Mesquita returned to the Jesuit residence feeling much satisfied with the outcome of the visit to Madrid, little realizing that Philip was to make a final, and extremely dramatic, gesture of kindness to the boys.

Just as the party was about to set out in the early morning of 25 November and continue the journey to Rome, the king, the cardinal of Toledo and courtiers suddenly arrived at the college in their carriages to bid a final farewell. They suggested that it would perhaps be advisable not to leave on that day, a Sunday, but postpone their departure to the following day. If Fróis's account is accurate, this last meeting with the king was quite extraordinary, for here was Philip II, the most powerful monarch of Europe, to say nothing of the accompanying notables, hurrying to the Jesuit residence in their coaches that Sunday morning, to suggest the Japanese leave a day later.

Accordingly, the boys finally set out for Alcalá, six leagues distant, on 26 November. They had spent thirty-six busy days in the capital, during which time they had been received by the king, the primate of Spain and countless nobles and aristocrats, as well as attending the historic allegiance ceremony and touring the Escorial and Royal Armoury and Treasury. It had been a truly memorable visit.

In contrast, the initial reception at Alcalá was low-key, but through no fault of the local citizens. Students had gone out to greet the Japanese on the scheduled day of their arrival, but owing to the postponement of the party's departure from Madrid, they had returned home disappointed. In addition, the Japanese finally arrived late at night and in pouring rain. On the day after their arrival they visited the famous university and attended a theological debate in Latin. The event apparently lasted all day, but the boys probably did not sit for hours through a session conducted in Latin and in the form of syllogisms with the use of scholastic terms such as *nego minorem, stat difficultas,* and *distinguo minorem,* technical phrases that would have meant little or nothing to them. Speeches honouring the Japanese were also delivered at some length.

The Rector and senior university officials called to greet the Japanese, who duly returned their visits. They were taken to see the fine library and also the sacristy to inspect the rich collection of relics preserved there; more speeches were given in their honour before they left for the Jesuit residence, escorted by two professors from each faculty. The boys also visited the cathedral and solemnly processed with the canons to the main altar.

On 29 November the party left for Villarejo de Fuentes, nine leagues away. During the night the second coach carrying Augustine, Constantine, the Chinese boy and the luggage overturned. The carriage in which the boys and Mesquita were travelling was running ahead, but on hearing the commotion, Mesquita ordered the driver to stop and got out to investigate. Two of the four mules had broken loose, and the passengers were trapped in the overturned coach. Fortunately, they were soon released uninjured, although Augustine felt some pain for several days. Despite the accident, their luggage had suffered no harm. In the darkness and rain, friendly local peasants bearing torches came to their help. They explained that the party was on the wrong road and indicated the direction in which they should continue their journey.

The Japanese reached Villarejo de Fuentes on 1 December and were welcomed by the local Jesuit community. They stayed only one night as they had heard that there were four or five good ships available at the port of Alicante to carry them to Italy. On the following day they set out for Belmonte, only four leagues away. Doña Francisca Ponce de Leon, founder of the Jesuit college in Belmonte, sent staff and provisions to meet the boys two leagues from the city. Another league later the college Rector, Luis de Guzman, and other Jesuits were awaiting them; a little further along they were greeted by the prior of the cathedral escorted by nobles on horseback while fifteen men carried torches to illuminate the route for it was already night. Their entrance into the city was greeted by a cannon salute, followed by another salvo when they reached the main square. Students greeted them inside the church with music and then let off fireworks outside. On the following day, 3 December, they visited the Franciscan and Dominican monasteries, and then the canons of the cathedral showed them around the church to the accompaniment of organ music.

Large crowds had assembled by this time, with some people standing on steps, other climbing walls to gain a better view of the visitors from Japan. Two plays, one in Latin, the other in Spanish, were performed in their honour; the latter dealt with their journey from Asia and lasted two hours.

Doña Francisca appears to have been a lady of pious but strong character, and she took it on herself to arrange the party's reception. During their meeting, she showed them so much affection that she seemed like a mother, showering the boys with religious gifts – a missal, a breviary and a statue of St Francis receiving the stigmata. All these presents were later sent to Madrid for the party to pick up on the return journey, for it would be an unnecessary burden to carry them all the way to Italy and back. Both the Jesuits and Doña Francisca brought pressure to bear on the visitors to prolong their stay in Belmonte, but as they had heard a ship about to sail for Italy was awaiting them, they left the city on 5 December. As the area through which they would be passing was somewhat barren, Doña Francisca saw to it that the party was well supplied with ample provisions for their journey.

The brief stay at Belmonte is of some interest, as the Rector of the Jesuit college, Luis de Guzman, later wrote a two-volume history of the Jesuit missions in Asia, in which he includes a lengthy and detailed account of the Japanese legation, from the time it set out from Nagasaki in 1582 until its audience with the ruler Hideyoshi in Kyoto nine years later. On the whole Guzman's text (in Spanish) abridges Fróis's account (in Portuguese), but as Guzman actually met and spoke with the boys during their travels, he at times includes items of information unavailable elsewhere.

It is a pity that Guzman does not provide readers with personal information about the Japanese so that we could learn something about their individual personalities, but instead he merely offers a conventional account of their piety and virtue. They attended

Mass daily, and went to confession and received Communion every week, if not more often. Once when he suggested their attending a public Mass, they politely told him they preferred a private one so that they would not be distracted from their devotions. They met with students on the night before their departure and did not get back to their room until 11.00 p.m. When Guzman went to see them, he found the boys kneeling by their beds devoutly saying their night prayers despite the late hour and their early departure on the following morning. And once when a servant came to announce the midday meal was ready, Mancio replied on behalf of his companions that it was not necessary. But when he learned that Mesquita had said they should have something to eat, the boys obediently set off to the dining-room.[3]

After leaving Belmonte, the party spent five days on the road before finally reaching Murcia on 10 December. A messenger had been sent ahead to announce their imminent arrival and make the necessary arrangements for the voyage to Italy. He handed the king's letter to the governor, Don Luis Arteaga,[4] who immediately organized a reception party of more than a hundred men on horseback to escort the visitors into the city. An open litter was provided to carry Mancio and Julian; Michael, who was still convalescing, and Martin proceeded by carriage. Fanfares of trumpets and shawms greeted them as they slowly wended their way with some difficulty through the crowded streets. Some three or four hundred soldiers fired their muskets, while the artillery on the city walls thundered in salute. When they finally reached the Jesuit church, a short service of thanksgiving was held, and then the boys, doubtless fatigued by their long journey and noisy reception, were conducted to their rooms in the college.

After all their haste in recent days, the party was obliged to patiently wait almost three weeks in Murcia before a suitable ship entered the harbour at Alicante, but the stay there was spent pleasantly and profitably. The boys went to the Jesuit villa house in the countryside to enjoy a well-earned rest, and there they compiled letters to be sent to Portugal, India and Japan. They returned to the city on Christmas Eve to celebrate the festival with the community. A few days later, they went on horseback to visit the cathedral and other churches in the city. On New Year's Day, their hosts insisted they attend another *cañas* tournament, with the boys receiving the best seats to view the spectacle. Finally, on 3 January, they left

Murcia and made for Orihuela, about four leagues away, the first city of the Valencia region.

Half a league before reaching the city in the afternoon, the party met a large crowd of well-wishers, and on their arrival, the fortress began to fire its cannons in salute, discharging more than a hundred salvos. City officials and several thousand citizens greeted the Japanese and escorted them to the Dominican monastery, where they stayed the night as there was no Jesuit residence in the city. For their entertainment that evening the authorities organized a display of horsemen riding in formation and carrying lighted torches.

On 4 January the Japanese left for Elche, six leagues from Orihuela. The local authorities and others came out of the town to greet them although it was already night, with three to four hundred men in attendance. Once more the Japanese were treated to a military salute as the cannons of the fortress fired off a hundred salvos in their honour. Finally, on the following day, 5 January, the party set out for Alicante, five leagues distant. Again, the governor and city officials came out to greet the visitors and again, artillery fired off a salute. The Japanese lodged in the governor's mansion, and on the following day scores of gentlemen escorted them to attend Mass and once more cannons were fired. In the afternoon, races were held for their entertainment along the street in which they were lodged.

Fortunately, there was a first-rate ship of 5,000 tons, armed with thirty-four cannon and many soldiers, ready to sail to Italy. Thanks to the king's orders, the best cabins were readily made available to the boys and their luggage, and all their provisions on board were provided at the king's expense.

Part 4

Rome and the Two Popes

CHAPTER 8

The Road to Rome

Finally, on 18 January, the ship set sail for Italy, but had to return twice to port because of contrary winds. During their enforced stay at Alicante, the Japanese took the opportunity of writing letters to all the Jesuit residences and colleges at which they had stayed, thanking their hosts for their hospitality. Each boy received a personal letter from Theotonio de Bragança, urging them to hurry back to Evora.

The third attempt to sail was made on 7 February, and this was more successful, although not completely so as the ship was obliged to make an unscheduled stop at the island of Mallorca, and stay there for four days. The governor welcomed the party and provided an escort of four-hundred soldiers when they attended Sunday Mass. The Japanese put out to sea once more on 19 February, and this time enjoyed favourable weather until they finally arrived at the Italian port of Leghorn on 1 March. There they learned that their unsuccessful departures from Spain had in fact been a blessing as a pirate chief of Algiers had heard rumours that the Japanese party was carrying ten thousand crowns in gold and had sent a fleet to hunt them down. Nor had they run into a Turkish fleet which had just captured a large, well-armed ship.

The archduke of Tuscany's representative at Leghorn, Matteo Forsetani, extended much kindness to the travellers and despatched a messenger to his lord announcing their safe arrival.[1] Archduke Francesco promptly sent a member of his court, Antonio Inglese, to greet and escort them, together with two carriages and a luggage coach, to Pisa, where he was residing at the time. Although the party planned to press on to Rome without delay, they could hardly gainsay Francesco's request that they stay a few days in Pisa. For, indeed, he was an archduke, and the Japanese were told that his annual income exceeded four-hundred million ducats and his treasury was rumoured to contain eight thousand million. Enjoying such wealth and power, the archduke of Tuscany was a king in fact, if not in name.

The boys spent 1 March sightseeing at Leghorn, viewing the heavily fortified castle guarding the port and admiring the lofty lighthouse set half a league out to sea to guide mariners safely to port. On the following day, the party set out for Pisa in the duke's carriages and arrived at noon, escorted by nobles and university representatives who had come out from the city to greet them. In accordance with Valignano's instructions regarding accommodation, the Japanese had intended to stay at the Jesuit residence, but the archduke would not hear of it and insisted they stay at his fine palace, where, through his brother Pietro de' Medici,[2] he invited them to meet him. After a meal, the boys went to visit the Duomo, or cathedral, where they venerated relics with much devotion. Close to the cathedral stands, or rather leans, the famous tower, whose construction was begun in the twelfth century and was completed in the fourteenth. It was hardly possible for the visitors not to have at least seen, if not visit, the nearby *Torre Pendente*, a strange phenomenon unknown in Japan, but the records make no mention of the tower.[3]

In the evening the travellers went to call on Archduke Francesco. They had heard he wished to see their Japanese robes, and accordingly donned their native dress for the occasion. Francesco sent three carriages, with German guards and nobles bearing lighted torches to escort them to his palace. He himself came down to the middle of the steps to receive the visitors and embraced each of them, declaring that it was God's blessing that of all the princes in Italy, he was the first to welcome them into his house and state after their perilous journey from such a distant land. With Mesquita interpreting, the Japanese replied that for them it was no less a blessing that, on disembarking, they were received in the archduke's domains, for the missionaries had told them in their distant land the size and magnificence of his possessions.

Francesco then took Mancio by the hand, always offering him precedence as they passed through doors and other places, and led the party to the presence of the archduchess, who greeted and embraced the visitors. Francesco invited Mancio to be seated with them, while the other Japanese sat together with Pietro, his brother. The hosts spent much time asking about Japan, and finally, when bidding his guests farewell, Francesco escorted them to the door. There he asked them to stay to the first day of Lent, 6 March, and although the boys wanted to reach Rome as soon as possible, they agreed to do whatever he wished so as not to displease him. During their stay in Pisa, Francesco entertained his guests royally with a variety of entertainments, among which was a hawking hunt, a pastime the boys may well have experienced in their native country.

Another entertainment is particularly worthy of note. An evening banquet was held in honour of the visitors, with Mancio seated between the archduke and his wife while his companions again sat with Francesco's brother. After some ladies had begun dancing, the archduchess arose, tugged Mancio's sleeve, and invited him to dance with her. He hesitated as European dancing was so different from Japanese and presumably had not been on the curriculum at the Jesuit college in Japan, and so it would be easy for him to make mistakes and look foolish. In any case, would it be proper for him to accept a married lady's invitation?

So Mancio decided to consult his mentor Fr Mesquita about this tricky problem. The good Father pondered the matter, and finally gave his reluctant permission for four solid reasons. After all, the invitation to dance had come from a duchess, and she was their hostess that evening; it was also carnival time when everyone made merry, and Mesquita observed that the dancers did not make bodily contact with their partners. In view of these weighty considerations, Mancio was free to dance with the duchess.[4]

Thus far is Fróis's account of the dance in *Ambassade*, but *De Missione* casts aside all his hesitations and goes into considerable detail about this remarkable performance. Apparently, the archduchess had organized the ball and all the young ladies assembled were 'dressed and adorned with the utmost elegance'. The archduke's brother, Pietro, led the dance and then was free to invite the lady of his choice to join him, and he chose the archduchess, his sister-in-law.[5] It was now her turn to invite the man of her choice, and this was Mancio. Entering into the spirit of the occasion, Mancio then invited another lady to be his partner and she in turn invited Michael to dance. Afterwards came Martin, and then it was the turn of Julian (note that the boys' ranking was strictly observed even in a ball) to select a partner from among the assembled spectators. He approached a certain elderly lady, a choice that caused considerable amusement among the onlookers. In *De Missione* Julian is made to say somewhat ungallantly that he selected this partner so as to draw some of the attention away from himself. It is hard to imagine what sort of performance the Japanese boy and the elderly Italian lady put on, but the incident provides some light relief to the regular account of the boys' dignity, gravity and piety.[6]

On the morning of Ash Wednesday the Japanese were taken to the church of Santo Stefano dei Cavelieri, headquarters of the military order of Santo Stefano, inaugurated by Cosimo, Francesco's father, to defend the coast and its shipping from attack by pirates and marauders. The order possessed and kept in constant use armed and swift triremes to protect the region from this danger. In the decorated church the boys sat with the archduke himself before the high altar while the traditional liturgy was performed, with eighty knights, vested in their long white habits with a purple cross embroidered on the chest, in attendance.[7] The imposition of ashes on the forehead was performed, first for the archduke, then the Japanese visitors, and finally the knights. A solemn Mass was celebrated, and the guests then returned to the palace, the splendour of which moved the Japanese to declare that their host rightly possessed the title of archduke because of the grandeur and power he enjoyed. They thanked him for his kindness and for treating them with so much honour, and Francesco then gave them permission to proceed to Florence on the following day.

The party set out next day with a large military escort. Two miles before reaching Florence they were greeted by even more soldiers and nobles, among whom was Virginio Orsini,[8] Francesco's nephew, and the travellers were duly escorted to the Jesuit residence. But the archduke's representative would not allow the visitors to stay there, and insisted on their re-entering the coaches and riding to the ducal palace where sumptuous apartments had been prepared for their use. On the following day the Japanese went to visit the cardinal archbishop of Florence, Alessandro de' Medici. When they arrived at the cathedral, the prelate, dressed in rich vestments, greeted them cordially and presented them with gifts, including an ivory crucifix and a depiction of the Annunciation; the cardinal later returned their visit and spent some time talking to the boys.[9] Another prelate whom they met was the papal legate, Valerio da Corbara.

Again, Fróis interrupts his narrative to tell readers: 'I will say in this chapter what they noted in their memoirs so that they could later recount them to their fellow countrymen.'[10] The lengthy account that follows is given in the first-person plural. Thus: 'The archduke's palace in which we are staying . . .'

During their five days in Florence, the Japanese visited the city's many palaces, churches and gardens, always in the company of Virginio Orsini and other courtiers. The visitors were understandably impressed by the Villa Pratolino, located a league outside the city; it had two palaces, one of which consisted of five storeys, in each of which were fourteen rooms, richly decorated with tapestries, paintings and gold and silver ornaments. But what appear to have caused an even deeper impression were the dozens of ingenious fountains in the spacious grounds, with moving figures of Neptune, angels, nymphs, sea goddess and satyrs, some playing flutes or trumpets, and all driven by water power. A substantial section of the description of Florence in Fróis's account is devoted to this spectacle, with their hosts doing their best to explain the mechanism that produced such marvels. Yet another object causing admiration was a huge aviary filled with different kinds of birds.[11]

The report also has much to say about the Palazzo Vecchio, in which the party lodged.[12] They admired the fountain in which Neptune rides in a chariot drawn by four horses,[13] and made detailed reference to the palace's gardens and surroundings, mentioning some of the statues they had seen. On either side of a path there stood 'a big giant on a column, each having a club in his hands and threatening others under their feet'.[14] Nearby 'there are two other statues, one of a man and the other of a woman without arms, but we don't know what this means. These two figures or statues stand on two columns which hold a thick chain hanging across the entrance.'[15] With their musical experience, they were particularly intrigued by a remarkable musical instrument, six or seven spans in length and four in width, which could reproduce the different sounds of the organ, harp, lute, mandolin, and trumpet.[16]

The Japanese also visited the Duomo, or cathedral, the Pitti Palace, the Medici Library (Biblioteca Laurenziana),[17] many churches, the archduke's armoury which stored enough weapons to equip an army, and finally, as a relaxing entertainment, the zoo, where they admired ten lions, four tigers and four bears.[18]

Among the churches visited was the Santissima Annunziata which possessed a venerated mural painting of the Virgin of the Annunciation, shown to the public only once a year and on special occasions. According to tradition, a painter began work on this depiction of the Annunciation, but felt unworthy to portray the Virgin's face before prayer and receiving the sacraments. On the following morning he found that her face had been miraculously painted by angelic power. Naturally, the Japanese were anxious to view this sacred image, but the crowds flocking to see it were so dense and unruly (the guards used the poles of their halberds to keep them back) that the boys were twice unable to approach the sanctuary. On returning at dawn on 9 March, they finally obtained their wish and venerated the mural.[19]

During their stay in Florence, the archduchess invited the Japanese to inspect her collection of silver and gold ornaments, and many jewels. She offered to present them with the object that pleased them most, and Mancio, noticing a portrait of her, diplomatically declared that this was what he liked most. His decision understandably flattered the lady, and she told him that as the portrait was not completely finished, a copy would be immediately made and presented to the party.[20]

It is worth noting that while in Florence, the Japanese were always accompanied by thirty German halberdiers, who guarded the party both during their sightseeing tours and even within the palace in which they were staying. This service was also provided to a greater or less degree in other Italian cities. The military escort was laid on not only to add pomp and display but also to protect the visitors from any harm, for there was considerable social unrest and violence in Italy at the time, and the authorities would have been greatly embarrassed had any mishap befallen their honoured guests.[21]

The party left Florence on 13 March. Archduke Francesco promised to cover all travel expenses within his territory and arranged for the travellers to be escorted by many people in carriages and on horseback up to the border of the papal states. On the following morning the Japanese approached Siena and were met by a large crowd of nobles, officials, soldiers and the archbishop, Francesco Bandini, in whose carriage they rode into the city and were taken directly to the governor's palace. A banquet was held in their honour, where an observer noted that the boys had 'great fear' of the two priests who accompanied them. 'They dared not raise their eyes without asking their permission. They drank only water and no wine.'[22] In the afternoon the boys were taken to the cathedral, where they were greeted once more by the archbishop and given a conducted tour. They reached the Jesuit college in the evening, only to receive a message from the governor that the archduke had ordered the party to be lodged in his palace. In the next few days they visited various churches and venerated their collections of relics.

Before the Japanese left the city on 17 March to resume their journey, some excitement was caused when a wicked Spaniard stole one of their boxes containing valuables and fled in the direction of Florence, but the governor had the rogue pursued and brought him back to confinement in the city.[23]

News of the party's approach had reached Rome and Gregory XIII, aware of his failing health, was awaiting their arrival with growing impatience, and sending messages urging all speed.[24] The travellers crossed into the papal states and found three hundred musketeers awaiting their arrival, and, on the pope's orders, ready to escort them to Rome and protect them from bandits. Fearing that this escort was insufficient, Gregory ordered two companies of light cavalry to meet the travellers two days before they arrived in Rome;[25] one of these companies was despatched by the duke of Sora, General of the Holy Roman Church.[26] In addition to these troops, crowds of onlookers gathered along the route out of curiosity or devotion, and at times their number exceeded a thousand people. The pope had also ordered the governors of the papal states and Orazio Celso, his legate at Viterbo, to provide the travellers with everything needed at papal expense.

The party reached Viterbo on 18 March. During their one-day stay in this city they attended solemn Mass in the cathedral, were shown holy relics (including the jawbone of St John the Baptist and a thorn from Christ's crown of thorns), and prayed at the tomb of St Rose in a convent.[27] Then on to Caprarola where they were entertained by Cardinal Alessandro Farnese[28] in his palace, reputed to be one of the finest secular buildings in Italy. Five stories tall, it had some two hundred rooms, many of which were decorated with valuable paintings and gold ornaments. The gardens, with their nine beautiful fountains, were deservedly famous. The boys also inspected the underground wine cellar with its ninety-two enormous casks containing enough wine for only four months' needs, and then the stables housing a hundred and twenty horses.

Finally on 22 March 1585, the party reached the outskirts of Rome, the principal destination of their long and arduous journey. With pardonable exaggeration Fróis tells us in his usual enthusiastic style that their arrival was greeted with 'incredible joy and no less applause and happiness of everyone'. Some Jesuits, among whom was Nuno Rodrigues, who had travelled with them from India to Lisbon but had gone on ahead once the party reached Europe, met the travellers a mile outside the city. Also in this welcoming group were representatives of Philip II, who, it will be recalled, had ordered his ambassador to extend every courtesy to the Japanese and supply anything they might need. It was agreed that to avoid an unseemly commotion the Japanese would enter the city secretly by night.

That was the theory, but the plan was decidedly unsuccessful. The military escort refused to leave their charges unguarded and insisted on accompanying them through the city blowing their trumpets loudly, hardly conducive to a quiet and discreet arrival. As a result, large crowds of curious onlookers flocked to see the procession, filling the streets and impeding the progress of the coaches.

The weary travellers finally reached the Jesuit headquarters about midnight and there were greeted by the Superior General Acquaviva,[29] and some two hundred Jesuit priests and Brothers from the residence and the Roman College. In response to this welcome the boys politely told Acquaviva that their pleasure in meeting him amply compensated for all the hardships of their long journey. The party was led to the church, illuminated by torches and candles, where students from the German College led the congregation in singing the *Te Deum* in thanksgiving for their safe arrival. The Japanese were then taken to their rooms for some much-needed sleep.

No time was lost in holding the papal audience, for the ceremony was scheduled for the following day. But the reception was to be far different from the private meeting as envisaged by Valignano, for the pope had decided on a full-scale, public ceremony in the presence of dozens of cardinals and bishops in the Aula Regia, where kings and ambassadors were normally received. A solemn and public ceremony, the pope believed, 'redounded to the Honour of the Holy See, to the Edification of the Church of *Japan*, and confusion of Hereticks'.[30]

Acquaviva had been reluctant to agree to the change of plan, concerned that staging such a solemn spectacle for the Japanese might invite criticism of the Jesuits and give rise to controversy, but Gregory was adamant. In the words of the Jesuit historian Bartoli: 'Our Holy Father judged that the private sentiment of the Society ought not to be put before the public honour of the Church and, after praising the modesty of the Superior and his men, He said that, since we had well accomplished our religious duty, we should now allow him to fulfil his duty as Pope.'[31] Whether the Jesuits liked it or not, the reception was to be held in grand style, completely contrary to Valignano's plan.

■ CHAPTER 9

The Papal Audience

In the morning of Saturday, 23 March 1585, three years and one month after the boys had set out from Japan, the audience with Gregory XIII, the principal reason for their travelling to Europe, took place. Bearing in mind King Philip's instructions to help the Japanese in every way possible, the Spanish ambassador, the count of Olivares, sent a fine carriage to the Jesuit house to convey the party inconspicuously to Santa Maria del Populo, close to the Porta del Populo, the city's traditional northern entrance from which ambassadors and cardinals began their formal procession into Rome.

But poor Julian had suffered a continuous fever for nearly a week and had been told to stay at home and remain in bed. But in an uncharacteristic display of independence, he had insisted on accompanying the party, and permission had been granted in the belief that his deep disappointment at not meeting the pope might well aggravate his illness. But the boy was obviously too ill to attend the lengthy ceremony, so when his companions alighted at Santa Maria del Populo to make their formal entry, he remained in the carriage and Mons. Antonio Pinto escorted him to a private audience with the pope.

According to Fróis's account, Gregory received Julian kindly in his study, but told the boy he was far too ill to attend the audience and should return home; there would be, he assured him, other occasions when they would meet again.[1] And so the carriage took Julian back to the Jesuit residence. His disappointment was understandable, for the main purpose of the long journey to Europe was to present the daimyo's letters to the pope. Julian, however, was not one of the two official legates but only their companion, and so his absence from the ceremony, while regrettable, did not cause a major problem.

Back at Santa Maria del Populo, the three Japanese were greeted by the Master of the Papal Household, Bishop Alessandro Musotti, who welcomed them on behalf of the pope, who had, he declared, experienced much joy on hearing of their safe arrival. He and others of the papal household, he told them, had been sent by the pope to accompany them in procession through the streets of Rome to the papal consistory.

The procession to the palace was indeed an impressive sight. It was led by two companies of papal light cavalry and Swiss guards, dressed in colourful uniforms. Then came grooms riding on richly caparisoned mules and bearing the insignia of the various cardinals. Next, were the relatives of the cardinals and the families of the ambassadors of Spain, France and Venice. To add a festive note the procession also included musicians carrying trumpets on which they played fanfares from time to time. These were followed by the staff of the pope's household dressed in red, and then officials and clergy of the Sacred Palace. Next in the procession were the Roman Cavalry, followed by thirteen drummers, although the dense crowd of onlookers unfortunately disrupted their ranks and only nine were able to perform.

Then appeared the principal participants in the show, Mancio, Michael and Martin riding on fine horses led by pages; the horses had been provided by the duke of Sora and were decorated with black velvet cloth trimmed with gold reaching almost to the ground. The boys wore their Japanese robes, complete with the two swords; somewhat strangely, all three carried grey hats, each decorated with a white feather, obviously not a part of traditional Japanese garb. They were escorted by the papal guards. First rode Mancio, the senior legate, with an archbishop or bishop on either side, followed by Michael and Martin, both boys also accompanied by two bishops. Mesquita, who was to act as interpreter, followed them. The procession, estimated to be half a league in length, was concluded with many nobles on horseback. Dense crowds in the streets and women sitting in upper windows cheered and applauded the cavalcade as it wound its way through the streets of Rome.[2]

As the procession crossed over the Tiber by the bridge of Castel Sant'Angelo, the fortress's artillery, beginning with the smaller cannons and then followed by the biggest, thundered salutes in honour of the visitors. When the cavalcade entered St Peter's Square, it was the turn of the papal soldiers to fire their muskets in salute, and as the party reached the middle of the square, a dozen more small cannon were fired. All this noise made some of the horses shy, although the boys' well-trained mounts remained calm. At this point the crowd was so dense that it seemed impossible to proceed any further, for all of Rome appeared to have come to view the colourful spectacle.

The three boys dismounted in the Swiss Court, resting for a while in the apartments of Cardinal Savelli[3] and accepting some refreshment. The papal master of ceremonies then arrived to conduct them, each flanked by two bishops, and Mesquita to the audience chamber.[4] The Sala Regia was packed with prelates, including twenty-four or twenty-five cardinals, and nobles, and officials and ministers had experienced difficulty in making their way into the hall. When trying to enter the chamber, the pope is said to have remarked jocularly that there was no worry as the ceremony could not begin without him, and eventually all had managed to reach their assigned places.

A contemporaneous English translation of a Jesuit report vividly recalls the scene:

> Pope Gregorie the thirteenth, sitting in the Hall designed for entertaynment of Kings, and their Embassages on the three and twentieth of March, 1585, in the morning, in a most Ample Session of the Cardinals of the Holy Romane Church, and in a great assembly of Princes and Prelates with greatest industry, and most frequent attendance of all Orders: Mantius and Michael (who was also of the Prince of Omur) two Legates of Japonian Kings, were brought in, and one of the two Japonian companions of the same Embassage, of principall Nobilitie, to wit, Martine (for Julian the other of them was withholden by sicknesse).[5]

As soon as the Japanese appeared in the hall, the pope could not hold back his tears, and was obliged to wipe his eyes. Well coached beforehand, the boys knelt before the papal throne and bowed low. Then Mancio, followed by Michael and Martin, mounted the steps leading to the throne, approached the pope, and, following the traditional custom, kissed his foot and then his hand. As each boy rose to his feet, Gregory embraced him and kissed him on the cheek. Mancio and Michael then read to the pope the Japanese text of the letters from the three daimyo, with Mesquita briefly summarizing the contents in Italian. To this Gregory replied kindly, expressing his paternal benevolence towards the visitors, who spoke briefly to the pope, with Mesquita again acting as interpreter, recounting their journey to Europe and promising their obedience. A papal secretary later recalled that the pope had declared he had never before seen such modesty among boys that pleased him so much.

The master of ceremonies then led the boys to an elevated place in the hall so that they would be clearly visible to all present, and there they stood while the papal secretary solemnly read out the letters in Italian translation. Francis of Bungo's letter was dated 11 January 1582. Again, in an early (but reasonably accurate) English paraphrase, Francis

> professeth the Divine bountie in sending the Jesuites foure and thirtie yeeres before into these parts, whose seed had taken some rooting in his breast, which hee ascribes to the Popes prayers and merits. And had it not beene for his age, warres, and sicknesse, hee would have visited those holy places, and have kissed his holy feet, and set them on his head, and received his blessing, his breast crossed by his most holy hand: but so detayned, had thought to have sent his sisters sonne, the Lord Jerome, Sonne of the King of Fiunga his Embassadour, whose Cousin-german Mantius in his absence he now sent; thankes him for the Relikes sent him, &c.[6]

'Not much unlike was the tenour' of the other two letters, with Protasius lamenting he had been 'delayed by divers lets' and so had sent 'his Cousin-german in his roome'.

Then the Portuguese Jesuit Gaspar Gonçalves, a renowned scholar and humanist, delivered an eloquent speech in Latin lasting a little more than thirty minutes. The Portuguese translation takes up ten printed pages,[7] but we are told that the address did not seem long to anyone present, with the exception, perhaps, of the Japanese, whose grasp of Latin was not sufficiently advanced to understand much of the polished oratory.

Gonçalves noted that the Japanese islands were so far distant that nothing had been known about them in ancient times, but in fact the people there had so much natural talent and understanding, and also skill in military matters, that Europeans who had visited the country preferred it to every other country in Asia; indeed, in comparison with Europe, the Japanese lacked nothing but the Christian religion. But in recent times Christianity had been adopted not only by commoners but also by princes and nobles. This spread of the faith in such remote regions had to be a great consolation to His Holiness, for he had spared no effort to restore the Catholic religion in nearer countries where it had been destroyed by the machination of heretics.

Gonçalves went on to make specific mention of the British Isles that had now been replaced by the Japanese islands as regards the Catholic faith, 'thus compensating for that great loss with no less a gain'. Just as the British Isles had been converted under Pope Gregory the Great, so Japan was now embracing Christianity under another Pope Gregory.

The orator then aptly quoted Psalm 17: 45, 'A people whom I did not know will serve me; in golden hearing they will obey me,' and referred to Isaiah and Tobias in similar fashion. After making glowing references to Xavier, Gonçalves, obviously well prepared, mentioned by name Francis of Bungo, Protasius of Arima, and Bartholomew of Ōmura, and their ambassadors Mancio and Michael, with special reference to Bartholomew as the first Japanese noble to embrace the Christian faith. He concluded his speech by referring to the pope's generosity and zeal in providing the means to found seminaries in different countries to instruct boys in the faith. No sooner had the pope heard about the success of Christianity in Japan than he had ordered the foundation of seminaries there for selected pupils, and so the Christian nobles had sent their ambassadors to express their gratitude to the Holy See.

This fulsome oration is said to have renewed the tears of the pope and of everyone present in the hall. Whenever the speaker mentioned 'Holy Father', he bowed towards Gregory as custom required, and the boys followed suit. Then on behalf of the pope, Mons. Antonio Boccapaduli, secretary of Latin briefs, delivered a shorter welcome, beginning: 'O most noble youths, the Holy Father has ordered me to reply in this fashion to your speech.' He continued, in an early English translated version: 'That Francis King of Bungo, Protasius King of the Arimans, and Bartholomew his Uncle, Prince of Omur, hath sent you their kinsmen to him from the remote Japonian Ilands to the veneration of that power in presence, which by Gods bounty he holdeth, they have done godly and wisely'.[8]

The Japanese then approached the throne once more, and Gregory and the cardinals again spoke with them in the kindest terms. When the pope arose to withdraw from the hall, he indicated that Mancio and Michael should carry the train of his pontifical robes, a signal honour normally granted to the ambassadors of emperors, and thus the boys accompanied him out of the chamber.

From there Cardinal San Sisto[9] took the boys to a banquet, and other cardinals, as well as the duke of Sora, joined them in a fine lunch. When they had finished the meal, the pope summoned the party again for a meeting in his private chambers and spent time asking the Japanese about their voyage, the weather at sea, affairs of Japan, the conversion of gentiles, and number of churches. Then, after Gregory had recited a prayer, the boys took their leave and returned to the Jesuit residence in the coaches of Cardinal San Sisto and of the Spanish ambassador, accompanied by his retinue.

It had certainly been a memorable day for the Japanese boys.

■ CHAPTER 10

The Stay in Rome

Even before the party left the palace to return to the Jesuit residence, the pope sent word asking the boys to come to his private chapel on the following day, the third Sunday of Lent, but, on hearing of this invitation, Acquaviva begged leave for them to rest and Gregory agreed. The Jesuit General insisted the boys reside at the Jesuit Professed House, for if they stayed in the papal palace, as Gregory wished, they would have scant chance of relaxation.

But the legates were not to have a complete rest on that Sunday, for the pope sent around a tailor to take measurements and make suits in Italian fashion. Each boy would receive three rich outfits, one short and two long, of black velvet decorated with gold braid, the total cost coming to 3,500 crowns, to be paid from papal funds. The need for new clothes had been noticed, for their Japanese robes were becoming increasingly shabby and appear to have given rise to some ungracious comments when viewed in public. The pope's benevolence extended to the legates' attendants, who also received new clothing. In addition, Gregory promised that for Easter, which fell on 21 April, he would provide festival robes of gold cloth, because the black suits were for use only in Lent. And so a tailor delivered a large quantity of silk rolls of various colours from which the boys could choose their new wardrobe.

Determined to meet the Japanese as often as possible, the pope invited the boys to accompany him on Monday, the feast of the Annunciation, on a solemn outing to the Dominican church of Santa Maria sopra Minerva, where he was scheduled to distribute dowries to orphan girls, one of the notable annual events in the Roman calendar. So, wearing their Japanese robes, the boys rode with the pope on horseback to the church, where some 160 couples were to be joined in holy matrimony. On their arrival, Mancio and Michael bore the pope's train until they reached the chapel, and the pontiff had them stand on his right hand during solemn Mass, while Martin sat with Mesquita nearby.[1]

Unknown to the Japanese it was the custom to collect alms during the ceremony to add to the fund supplying the dowries, and unaware of this custom, the Japanese were not carrying any money on them. Observing their dilemma and to save them from embarrassment, the pope ordered some money be discreetly passed to the boys so that they, too, could contribute to the collection. At the end of the service Mancio and Michael once more carried the pope's train.[2]

From this time the Japanese began receiving visits from ambassadors, beginning with the emperor's representative, Frederico Madrucci, who was then followed by the French, Spanish and Venetian envoys.[3] On 1 April representatives of the Roman senate, dressed in colourful robes and preceded by twenty-four lictors bearing gilded staffs, set out in solemn procession to the Jesuit residence, accompanied by nobles, magistrates, and other officials of the Roman court. The purpose of their visit was to inform the Japanese that they would be granted the privilege of becoming Roman citizens and patricians, a high honour paid to only a few.

In addition, a number of cardinals appeared at the Jesuit house to talk with the boys, who in their turn left the residence and began paying return visits. Ambassadors plied the boys with invitations to banquets, at which they expressed the hope that the Japanese would pass through their countries, such as France and Savoy, after leaving Rome, but this would have meant a time-consuming detour on their return journey. However, as Venice was so close to Rome, the Japanese could hardly decline the invitation issued by the republic's ambassador, Lorenzo Priuli. Philip II's ambassador, the count of Olivares, went out of his way to entertain the visitors in every possible way, while Giacomo Boncompagni, duke of Sora, and Paolo Giordano Orsini, duke of Bracciano, paid visits and offered hospitality. Meanwhile, on hearing about these banquets, the pope expressed anxiety lest too much rich food might be harmful to the visitors' health and ruled that his permission should be obtained before accepting any more invitations.

Gregory's enthusiasm for the legation continued unabated, and he ruled that a commemorative medal be struck, bearing on one side his portrait and on the obverse the Latin inscription, '*Ab Regibus Iaponio[rum] Prima ad Roma[anum] Pont[ificem] legatio et obedientia, 1585.*'[4] Not content with this honour, on 29 March he ordered 1,000 crowns to be delivered to cover the party's expenses. Nearly every day he sent members of his household to call on the boys to see whether they were in any need, and he repeatedly told the Master of the Papal Household, Ludovico Bianchetti, to enquire after their well-being. Gregory himself often met the boys personally; appearing more like a father than a pope, he asked them countless questions, exhorted them to take care of their health and told them not to tire themselves by kneeling in his presence. News of his beneficence and favour spread widely and became the subject of much talk in Rome.

Neither did the pope forget Julian's illness and made frequent enquiries about his health, instructing the doctors to look after the boy well and visit him every day. On hearing that the patient had difficulty in swallowing medicines, he sent word that Julian should do his best to take them just to please him.[5] On Friday, 29 March, Gregory invited the other three boys to accompany him to St Peter's to gain the indulgences granted on that day, and clad in their new black velvet robes trimmed with gold, they duly processed to the basilica with the pontiff. Two days later, they attended sung Mass in Gregory's private chapel, with twenty-two cardinals present. This was on Rose Sunday when by tradition the pope blessed a golden rose to be sent as a gift to a Christian queen or princess. The new senior magistrate of Rome, together with other magistrates and officials, was also present and recited the oath of loyalty in the presence of the pope.

On 3 April, the boys were received in yet another private audience. The pope told Mancio and Michael to be seated while Martin remained standing, and then plied his visitors with questions about Japan. How many cities were there in the country? How many churches had been built? How many European missionaries were working there? What were the mission's prospects? It was then the time at this meeting for the Japanese to present the gifts that had happily survived the vicissitudes of their travels, the principal one being a fine pair of Japanese screens.[6] Gregory accepted the presents graciously and asked the boys further questions about their studies, recommending they learn about the church and its affairs. Mesquita remarked they had indeed studied this subject, and also others such as Latin, etc. Gregory went on to speak about the needs of the church in Japan, expressing his willingness to help not only in the spiritual domain but also in the temporal. He enquired what sort of gifts the boys would like to take back to their country, suggesting they draw up a list and promising to give them whatever they asked.

The pope then arose and personally led the visitors around the room, even showing them his bed; on entering his study, the Japanese admired the finely bound books on display, and Gregory pointed to a portrait of the late King Sebastian, explaining who he was. He then told Bianchetti to give the visitors a guided tour and show them the nearby Gallery with its fine paintings and rich decoration; it was here that the pontiff ordered the Azuchi screens to be placed to demonstrate his esteem for the gift. On their return to the study, the boys stayed talking to the pope until dusk, when Gregory bade them farewell and sent them back to the Jesuit residence.

On Passion Sunday the boys attended Mass in the pope's private chapel and, now happily recovered, Julian made his first excursion out of the Jesuit residence since his illness. On 9 April the Japanese wanted to visit the traditional seven churches of Rome, and hearing of their wish Gregory gave orders they were to be formally received at all the places they visited. In each church a procession of clergy greeted the visitors, the choir sang hymns, and organ music was played in their honour. Within the churches carpets had been replaced by brocaded rugs, and cushions were prepared for the boys to kneel on as they venerated the large collections of relics. Although these were private visits, word of the boys' coming had quickly spread and crowds gathered to catch a glimpse of the Japanese.[7]

But the boys' pleasant stay in Rome was soon to change abruptly as the elderly pope's health began to fail. On 5 April he suffered an attack of catarrh and felt indisposed, although three days later he was well enough to hold a meeting of cardinals and grant an audience to the count of Olivares. At 9.00 in the morning of 9 April officials gathered for the pope to sign documents, but on his doctors' advice Gregory sent word he could not attend and the signing would have to be postponed. This was the first public notice of his illness and the news spread quickly throughout Rome. On the following day Gregory felt somewhat rested, but then another attack of catarrh was so severe that his doctors advised him he should concentrate on spiritual matters as death was close.

To prepare for his end, the pope expressed the wish to make his confession and receive Communion, and his nephew, Cardinal San Sisto, administered the last rites to the dying man. During the day the duke of Sora[8] visited the pope, and on this occasion the pope again enquired about the welfare of the Japanese boys. Gregory XIII died peacefully at three o'clock in the afternoon; he was eighty-four years of age and had been pope for nearly thirteen years.[9]

The Japanese heard of the pope's death before they had learnt of his illness. A messenger sent by Cardinal San Sisto caught up with the boys as they were riding in a coach to complete their visits to the seven churches of Rome. On learning the news they abandoned their expedition, lowered the curtains of the carriage, and immediately returned to the Jesuit residence. Gregory's death came as an unexpected shock to the boys. Only eighteen days after they had first met him, they had lost their generous benefactor; indeed, he had shown them so much kindness, especially to the ailing Julian, that they regarded him as a father.

News of the pope's demise was immediately dispatched by express messengers to Spain, France, Germany and other countries, while in Rome an amnesty was declared and even desperate criminals were set free from prison. The pope was both a civil and an ecclesiastical ruler, consequently, in the interval between the death of one and the election of his successor, unrest and violence were liable to break out. Soldiers were posted at the city gates to prevent robbers from entering and taking advantage of the unrest occasioned by the crisis, while a thousand troops were stationed outside Rome in case any emergency arose; additional guards were mobilized to protect the mansions of cardinals and nobles, and some six thousand foreign mercenaries were said to be on the alert within the city. Elsewhere, Spanish troops were mustered in Milan and Naples in case of need. These precautions were justified, for on the death of the next pope five years later, mobs surged through the streets of Rome, looting and gleefully toppling a statue of the late pontiff.

Although busily occupied in funeral arrangements, the cardinals did not forget the Japanese and nominated Bishop Lucio Sasso[10] to visit the boys to assure them that whoever was elected as the new pope would treat them with the same kindness as Gregory had done.

On 11 April crowds flocked to the Pauline Chapel to view and venerate the pope's embalmed body. Accompanied by nine cardinals and a long procession of clerics bearing candles, the canons of St Peter's later carried the body to the Gregorian Chapel in the basilica. So many people came that in their enthusiasm they broke down the chapel door to view the body, which was then hastily removed elsewhere for the night. On the following day, the door was repaired and the body was returned for public veneration.

The pope's obsequies were held in the chapel of Pope Sixtus on 12 April, and then the available cardinals gathered to listen to an address in Spanish by Philip II's ambassador, who expressed his sympathy to the members of the Sacred College and urged them to choose the next pope without delay. On the following day the emperor's ambassador also delivered a short speech to the assembled cardinals.

Gregory XIII was buried near the door of the Gregorian Chapel for the time being until a suitable tomb could be prepared.[11] On Monday, 15 April, Cardinal Alessandrino,[12] assisted by four other cardinals, conducted the funeral in St Peter's basilica. Two days later, the Jesuit Stefano Tucci delivered the funeral oration in which he mentioned Japan and the Japanese legation.[13]

On Easter Sunday, 21 April, the forty-two cardinals who were in Rome entered the solemn conclave to choose Gregory's successor. As custom dictated, the principal doors of their meeting place were sealed with bricks and cement.[14]

CHAPTER 11

The New Pope

Three days later, on Wednesday, 24 April, Cardinal Montalto was elected by acclamation and chose the name Sixtus V.[1] During his brief five-year reign, Sixtus overhauled and replenished the papal treasury, and, a man of strong character, instituted a relentless campaign against the banditry rampant in the papal states and in Rome itself, ordering the public execution of convicted robbers and sometimes the exposure of their heads on the bridge of Castel Sant'Angelo. A 1704 English version of an Italian account colourfully depicts his strong character:

> He sent for the Govenour of *Rome*, and all the Judges to charge 'em they should administer Justice Exactly: He spoke to them with such earnestness and Vehemence, his Discourse look'd more like Threatnings than Instructions. He perfectly frighted them, when they took leave, with these words, *I come not to bring Peace but a Sword*.[2]

In general, Sixtus was to show himself less favourable to the Jesuits than had been his predecessor, and in fact was considering changing the order's name and constitutions shortly before his death in August 1590. With the disagreement between Jesuits and Franciscans in Japan much in mind, the Jesuits in Rome must have wondered how the new pope would deal with the Japanese legates, but, as the author quoted above tells us, 'He treated the Ambassadors of *Japan* with more respect, receiving them very Handsomly', and they need not have had any anxiety on that score. This author tells us the boys' reception may have aroused jealousy in some circles: 'He receiv'd them and talk'd with them with abundance of Kindness and Freedom ... and shew'd them so much Civility, as made the Cardinals Jealous, and say to one another: *Sixtus treats the Ambassadors of Japan as if he was but Cardinal still, but lives like a Pope amongst us.*'[3]

The Japanese had already visited the new pope at his villa while he was still a cardinal, and two days after his election they went to offer their respects and congratulations. He greeted them kindly and asked how they were faring in Rome. Mancio replied they were overjoyed by his election, and felt blessed to witness the happy event so that on their return to Japan they could recount the new pope's qualities. He further asked the pontiff to help the church in Japan. Sixtus replied he would certainly do so and would take particular care of the boys while they were in Rome.

Before leaving, Mancio presented a memorial, again begging the pope to aid the church in Japan, and Sixtus answered he would deal directly with Acquaviva about the matter. He was as good as his word, for despite the new pope's busy schedule he summoned the Jesuit General on 4 May and told him to consult with Cardinal Carafa,[4] who had a special interest in Japan; anything these two men decided, he said, he would accept. On the following day Acquaviva conferred with the cardinal; they discussed the needs of the church in Japan and formulated proposals, all of which were subsequently approved by the pope. Even though Sixtus was kept busy at this time, he remembered to send a bishop, Master of the Papal Household, to visit the boys and convey his greetings.

The coronation Mass of Sixtus V was celebrated on 1 May in St Peter's basilica.[5] In accordance with the pope's wishes, the boys were not only invited to attend the ceremony but were also asked to take a prominent part in it along with nobles and ambassadors. Julian was still unwell and unable to attend, but the other three Japanese were assigned to bear the poles supporting a canopy over the pope as he entered the basilica. The other pole-bearers were the ambassadors of France and Venice, the duke of Sora, the Marquis of Riano, and Marquis Altemps.[6] But the Venetian ambassador, Lorenzo Priuli, was upset on learning that the Japanese boys would be positioned in front of him in the procession and that he would be separated from the French ambassador, and he accordingly made a complaint. Writing back later to Venice, he explained:

> I then added that orders should be given so that no confusion arise in the chapel, referring to those who had penetrated the ranks of us ambassadors and I said so fully intending to impress on these Japanese gentlemen and ambassadors the simple fact that I wished to avoid a situation in which they might be placed between the French ambassador and myself. Owing to the fact that, even if they have the title of ambassadors of kings, they are nevertheless from such unknown and puny kings. I made it clear that only very unwillingly would I suffer such a thing. And what I said brought about an excellent result, because at the coronation last Wednesday I was given the place beside the French ambassador and the Japanese ambassadors were placed behind me.

The ambassador's protest met with the full approval of the Venetian senate. 'We offer praise that at the coronation of His Holiness, you were able to arrange it so that you were given precedence over the Japanese ambassadors and put beside the French ambassador.'[7]

This small diplomatic flurry is of interest, for it is one of the few contemporaneous reports to disclose that the boys' credentials as legates were not always received with wholehearted acceptance. Yet another diplomatic contretemps in the coronation ceremony involved the Spanish ambassador, who had also been invited to be one of the canopy-bearers, but had pleaded illness to avoid meeting the French envoy at the ceremony. Such were the complications concerning the papal escort, but the boys were probably completely oblivious of these diplomatic niceties as they solemnly escorted the new pope through the basilica. No mention of Priuli's protest is made in Jesuit records; possibly the compilers were also unaware of the incident, or perhaps they viewed the incident as a disagreeable episode reflecting adversely on the Japanese party and therefore to be discreetly omitted.[8]

During the solemn Mass Mancio entered the sanctuary and offered water for the pope to wash his hands; the French and Venetian ambassadors, and also the senior senator, did likewise.

On 5 May, the new pope took possession of the basilica of St John Lateran (San Giovanni in Laterano, 'the mother of all the churches of Rome and of the world'). This was the episcopal seat of the pope as bishop of Rome, and he invited the boys to attend the traditional ceremony. A fine mural painting some four meters in length may still be seen in the Vatican showing in colourful detail the papal procession, depicted in boustrophedonic form, winding its way to the Lateran basilica. Surrounded by clerics and soldiers, Sixtus is prominently seen on horseback in the front row, raising his right hand in blessing. At the beginning of the second row and at the end of the third ride a group of four men on white, identically caparisoned, horses escorted by Swiss Guards in their colourful uniforms; all four are wearing identical tall hats and robes edged with gold.[9] The procession with hundreds of soldiers, standard-bearers, chaplains, keepers of the wardrobes, grooms, banner-carriers, as well as clerics, prelates, nobles, senators and ambassadors, extended for almost a league, and when the beginning of the cavalcade had almost reached St John Lateran, its end was still waiting at St Peter's to begin.

Later in the month the Japanese were invited to visit the new pope in his villa and join him in a meal; again, he treated them with kindness and presented them with gifts. At the end of the month the boys were summoned to the Roman senate, where they were royally treated. The city's senators, magistrates and prominent nobles were present, and it was on this occasion that the Japanese were honoured by being appointed Citizens and Patricians of Rome. After the visitors had been seated in a prominent place, a public orator delivered a speech in which he expressed the Roman people's deep joy at the arrival of these noble youths who professed the Christian religion and had made such a long journey from remote parts to offer homage to the pope. Each boy was then presented with a beautiful vellum scroll on a silver tray, bearing illustrations and the coat of arms of Rome. The appointment entitled them 'to bequeath the title of Roman patrician to their sons, their nephews and all their posterity . . . and to attend the Senate of Rome at any time, to take part in elections, to sit in the judgement seat, to hold both civil and ecclesiastical posts, to hold properties exempt from taxation', and other privileges.[10] At the bottom of the document hung a gold seal from a golden cord; one side of the seal showed an armed woman and the seven hills of Rome.[11] To mark the distinction between the legates and their two companions, the seals of Mancio and Michael were somewhat larger than those of Julian and

Martin. The value of these patents was estimated to be about 800 gold crowns.

To celebrate the auspicious occasion, the authorities had initially planned a banquet for the boys that would cost 1,000 crowns, but then remembering that on a previous and similar occasion Cardinal Marcantonio Colonna[12] had asked for this money to be spent on restoration work in the Franciscan church of Santa Maria in Aracoeli, the senate's official church, it was decided instead that gifts would be prepared for the visitors to take home with them to Japan.

On 29 May, after the Japanese had dined with Sixtus in his palace, they proceeded to his private chapel for, he explained, he wished to appoint them Knights of St Peter. When vespers had been concluded, the master of ceremonies unsheathed four golden swords and offered them one by one for the pope to bless. The French ambassador then girded Mancio with a sword, the Venetian ambassador did the same for Michael, while the Marquis Altemps did likewise with their two companions. The boys were then led to the pope, and each offered him his sword. The pontiff took them one by one in his hand and tapped the shoulder of each boy three times. The swords were then sheathed. Sixtus embraced the Japanese, giving them the kiss of peace, and presented each one with a gold chain to wear around the neck and a pair of golden spurs. With this, the ceremony came to an end and the pope bade the boys goodnight.[13]

But on the following morning the Japanese were back, this time to attend the pope's Mass in his oratory, where each boy received Communion from his hands. As their stay in Rome was drawing to a close, the pope made his final gifts and promises, which turned out to be far more generous than expected. He confirmed his predecessor's annual gift of 4,000 ducats for the seminaries in Japan, and then added another 2,000.[14] They were told that this gift would begin in that same year, and would continue in perpetuity. Other gifts destined for the daimyo who had sent the embassy were handed over, including swords decorated with gold and silver, and a velvet hat. To Bartholomew was presented an apostolic brief promoting him to the ranks of Catholic kings. Then there were sets of liturgical vestments, with a total value of 30,000 crowns, given to the mission. In addition, 3,000 crowns were donated towards the expenses of the legates' return journey. Messages would be sent to all the papal states ordering that the Japanese be treated as honoured guests. Letters would also be despatched to Philip II and the papal delegate in Spain, as well as to Venice, Genoa, and other cities through which they were scheduled to pass, asking that the visitors be made welcome and well received.[15] The party would be escorted from Rome by light cavalry for a considerable distance.

On 2 June, the day before their departure, the Japanese repaired for the last time to the pope's palace to thank him for his kindness and favours. Sixtus replied he would have liked to have done more, and if the boys needed anything else, they should not hesitate to tell him. He would be, he promised, the father of the Japanese mission and would help it in every way possible.

Part 5

Further Travels in Europe

CHAPTER 12

Bologna and Ferrara

The boys left Rome at dawn on 3 June, after spending two months and ten days in the Eternal City.[1] Despite the early hour of their departure, various personages, including the Spanish ambassador, accompanied them for some miles, while a contingent of papal light cavalry escorted them for a whole day. The party, including Mesquita and Nuno Rodrigues, travelled in carriages, together with three wagons to carry their ever-increasing amount of luggage. Wherever they stopped, the Japanese received a cordial welcome, and were accompanied by gentlemen in their coaches with their servants and others on horseback.

The party had received several invitations to visit Naples and intended to travel the 120 miles to that city, a considerable distance from Rome; this of course would take them further from Leghorn, if indeed they planned to sail from there back to Spain. On the other hand it would have been possible to embark from Naples itself. The city, they were told, was one of the noblest of Europe, inferior to no other, boasting of thirteen princes, twenty-eight dukes and the same number of marquesses and counts. Their reception in the city would undoubtedly be spectacular. In his instructions, Valignano had specifically recommended that during their Italian tour, they should visit Naples, in addition to Rome, Venice and Milan.[2]

But the visit to Naples was cancelled on account of the 'adverse nature of its summer weather'.[3] Now the overcrowded city of Naples could certainly become unpleasantly hot in the summer and ridden with fever, but the same was true of other places the party had already passed through. More to the point, the kingdom of Naples, then under Spanish rule, was experiencing a period of political and social unrest, and was perhaps not considered a suitable or safe place for the Japanese to visit. Exactly who made this decision and determined their itinerary is not known, for it is unlikely that Mesquita alone had the authority to do so. Possibly the Jesuit authorities in Rome, in consultation with ambassadors and other officials, worked out the visitors' route.

So the party travelled north[4] and passed through Civita Castellana (where by a mishap nobody was waiting for them), Narni, Spoleto, Montefalco (where they were shown the body of St Clare),[5] Foligno, and on 7 June Assisi, where they were taken to the great church and venerated the relics of St Francis.[6] They did not stop overnight there, but pressed on to Perugia, whose citizens had sent representatives to Rome begging the Japanese to accept their hospitality; the party was received with great enthusiasm: eight miles from the city three orators representing the city, the clergy and the university met the Japanese and delivered speeches of welcome in Latin; four miles further along the road a large crowd was waiting with four richly caparisoned horses for their use. The party continued in the coaches until reaching the outskirts of the city, but then, on request, the boys mounted the horses to allow the citizens to get a better view of the visitors. Greeted by artillery salutes, trumpets, drums and other music, they rode under decorated arches erected in their honour to the cathedral, where the choir sang the appropriate motet, 'Behold, you will call a nation you do not know . . . ',[7] and then on to the Jesuit college, where they spent the night. On the following day the papal legate, Cardinal Spinola, hosted a banquet in their honour and showed them much kindness.[8] In view of all this lavish hospitality, it is hardly surprising that the boys were persuaded to spend three days at Perugia.

Then once more on the road, passing through Camerino, Tolentino, Macerata, Recanati, and finally Loreto, where they spent three days and visited in the basilica the famous Holy House, reputed to be the miraculously transferred dwelling of the Holy Family in Nazareth.[9] Regarding the stay in Loreto, two local Jesuits wrote to Rome reporting on the visit. According to one of the correspondents, the governor of Loreto went out of his way to welcome the visitors. More than a hundred musketeers met the travellers,

1. Portrait of Alessandro Valignano, S.J., 1539–1606, who originated and organized the expedition to Europe.
From J.F. Schütte, S.J., *Valignanos Missionsgrundsätze für Japan*, 1, Rome, 1951

2. Portrait of Philip II, 1527–98. The king received the four Japanese in informal audiences on several occasions.

3. The 1982 re-enactment of the original mission to Europe. 'Mancio' is delivering a speech in Japanese to the Spanish king and queen in Madrid. 'Diogo de Mesquita', in reality Diego Yūki, S.J., stands in the background preparing to read a Spanish translation. Courtesy: Nagasaki Photo Service.

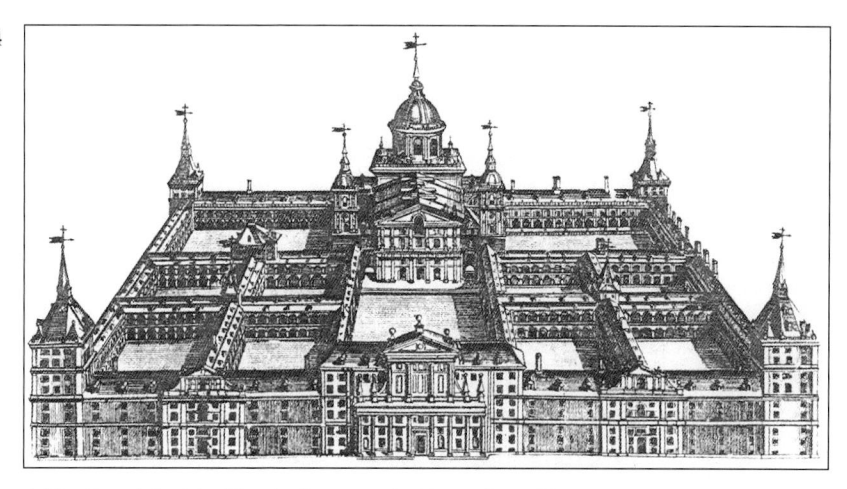

4. The Escorial, visited by the Japanese in November 1584.
From *El Escorial, 1563–1963*, Patrimonio Nacional, Madrid, Vol. 2, 1963.

5. Bianca Capello, the renowned and notorious Archduchess of Tuscany, whom the Japanese met in Pisa in March 1585. It was during a banquet given in honour of the visitors that she danced with Mancio.

6. Pope Sixtus V, whose papal coronation the Japanese attended in Rome on 1 May 1585.

7. Pope Gregory XIII, who received the Japanese in solemn audience on their arrival in Rome in March 1585 and showed them great kindness.

8. The medal ordered by Pope Gregory XIII to commemorate the Japanese visit to Rome. The pope is shown on the obverse, while the reverse (in English translation) reads: 'The first legation and homage from the kings of Japan to the Roman Pontiff, 1585.'
From Hamada Kūsaku, *Tenshō Ken'ō Shisetsu Ki*, Tokyo, 1931.

9. Mural in the Vatican Library depicting the papal procession to St John Lateran on 5 May 1585. Sixtus V is seen in the bottom row, raising his hand in blessing, while three of the Japanese wearing identical costumes are riding on white horses at the beginning of the second row and the fourth at the end of the third row.
From Nagayama Tokihide, *An Album of Collection of Historical Materials Connected with the Roman Catholic Religion in Japan*, Nagasaki, 1924.

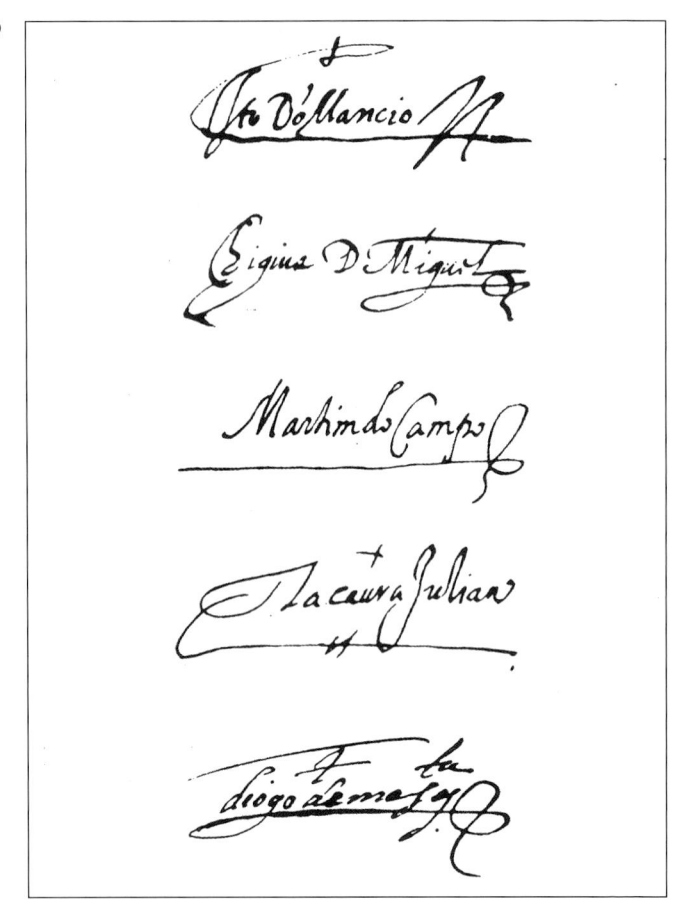

10. Signatures taken from letters and documents of the four Japanese and their mentor Diogo de Mesquita, S.J. From the top: Mancio, Michael, Martin and Julian.
From Yūki Ryōgo, *Roma wo Mita: Tenshō Shōnen Shisetsu*, Nagasaki, 1982.

11. Frontispiece of the text of Martin's speech in Latin at Goa on 4 June 1587 during the return journey to Japan.
From Georg Schurhammer, S.J., *Orientalia*, Rome and Lisbon, 1963.

ORATIO HABITA À FA R A D. MARTINO Iaponio, suo & sociorũ nomine, cũm ab Europa rediret ad Patrẽ Alexãdrũ Valignanũ Visitatorẽ Societatis IESV, Goæ in D. Pauli Collegio, pridie Non. Iunij, Anno Domini 1587

CVM FACVLTATE Inquisitorũ &, Superiorum
GOAE
Excudebat Constãtinus Dourat° Iaponius in ædibus Societatis IESV.
1588

12. Julian Nakaura's certificate of his religious vows, written by him on 21 December 1621 at Katsusa, Kyushu.
From Diego Pacheco, S.J., *Los Cuatro Legados Japoneses de los Daimyos de Kyushu despues de Regresar a Japón*, 1973.

13. Title page of *De Missione Legatorum*, Macao, 1590, originally compiled by Alessandro Valignano in Spanish and here translated into Latin by Duarte de Sande. The book relates the boys' travels in Europe and describes many of the cities they visited.

14. An imaginary depiction of Julian's martyrdom at Nagasaki in October 1633.
From Antonio Cardim, S.J., *Fasciculus e Iapponicis Floribus*, Rome, 1646.

fired a volley in salute, and escorted them to the church with drums and flutes. They were then taken to the governor's mansion and lodged in decorated apartments. As it was a fast day, they were served a simple dinner, but on the following morning they enjoyed a hearty breakfast, and this was followed by lunch at the Jesuit college.

The other Jesuit report strikes a more personal and rather touching note. Although the accounts of Fróis and other Jesuits mention the various attacks of fever suffered by the boys, especially by Julian, the writer of this brief letter expresses concern about the stress incurred by their extended travels through Europe. He states that the boys were not getting enough sleep, and that morning and night they were treated to unaccustomed food, and there was not enough time for them to digest it all, although they generally did not eat much.[10]

The party resumed the journey on 14 June for Ancona, where local nobles and two hundred soldiers met them en route to escort them. As they neared the city, the governor, city officials and a nephew of the pope[11] came out to greet them as artillery in the local fort fired salvos in salute. The travellers lodged in a palace and enjoyed a banquet at which nobles served the guests, and were then on a tour of Ancona to see the sights and be seen by the local population. At night the artillery again fired a salute, and so many fireworks were let off that the city seemed to be on fire. On the following day the Japanese left for Sinigaglia, and then on to Pesaro.

A mile or so from Pesaro they were met by the count of Rovere, a cousin of the duke of Urbino, and were escorted by twenty gentlemen on horseback. Inside the city they were entertained cordially by the duke of Urbino, in whose palace they spent the night.[12] Their host urged his guests to stay longer, but as they wished to attend the celebrated festival of Corpus Christi in Bologna, the travellers politely declined the invitation and continued on their way.

After passing through Rimini, Pesaro, Cesena, Forli and Imola,[13] the party reached Bologna in the evening of 19 June and stayed three days there. They met two cardinals – Archbishop Paleotti of Bologna[14] and the papal legate Cardinal Salviati[15] – who both offered the travellers accommodation in their palaces; not wishing to offend either of the prelates, the boys chose to lodge at the local Jesuit college in keeping with Valignano's directives. The papal legate sent them ample provisions during their stay, while Paleotti treated them, as was his custom, to a somewhat frugal repast, which the boys may well have found a welcome change from the rich food of so many lavish banquets. On the following day, the Japanese went to the cathedral and then took part in the Corpus Christi procession, walking by the side of the papal legate and for a while carrying the poles supporting the canopy over him. The archbishop himself later took the boys to visit various churches and monasteries, in one of which was preserved the body of St Dominic, and in another the seated body of St Catherine of Bologna.[16]

In the same year of the boys' visit, Alessandro Benacci published in Bologna an account of their stay in the city. He included an illustration of their robes, which he describes as follows:

> Portrait and clothes of those Indians [sic] who arrived in Rome on the 23rd of March 1585. They wear two long dresses, the outer one sleeveless, the inner one with sleeves, which go over the shoulders and the breast down to the belt, as the Carthusians or the friars of St Francis of Paula use, but without hood, all in white silk, embroidered in various colours with leaves and lines and drawings of birds and other animals; jewels in the Arabian fashion; a felt hat, a cap with the golden plait and a pleated-collar shirt, both in the Spanish way; a silk belt holding a weapon; a venerable face, of the same colour as an African, short of stature, and roughly eighteen years of age.

Benacci adds a personal description of the Japanese:

> As for the body they are rather short, of swarthy colour, small eyes, thick eyelids, a rather wide nose, a naïve and refined appearance with nothing which resembles a barbarian.[17]

Once more on the road on 22 June, the party headed for Ferrara, for three centuries governed by the powerful Este family. On hearing of their approach, the duke[18] sent the count of Bevilacqua[19] and fifty mounted musketeers to escort the visitors in his own coach to the city. Half a mile further along the road were waiting a hundred mounted guards and six more carriages; and then appeared three companies of light infantry, while just outside the city the duke's uncle was waiting to deliver an official welcome. He entered the carriage with the boys and they rode together through the centre of the city to the massive Castello Estense.

There they were greeted by the duke, reputed to be as wealthy as the archduke of Tuscany, who led the boys from their carriage to an apartment where some years earlier, they were told, the king of France had stayed.[20] There they briefly rested, and then, dressed in Japanese costume, they joined their host in a banquet given in their honour during which musicians performed for their pleasure. After introducing the boys to his wife, the duchess, and also to his sister, the duchess of Urbino,[21] the duke carried the party off to his country estate where the visitors inspected stables housing 150 horses.[22]

On the following day, feast of St John the Baptist, the duke and his guards accompanied the Japanese to the cathedral, where the archbishop celebrated a solemn sung Mass. A sightseeing tour of the city's churches and palaces was also arranged, and the boys admired the mighty city walls on which were mounted many cannons. They had wanted to stay at the local Jesuit college, but the duke would not hear of it, but at least they managed to make a visit and greet the community. They also toured the castle palace, so lavishly decorated with gold and silver, and admired the ornate chapel, the statues made of gold, and the chambers and halls filled with art treasures.[23]

But during their stay Julian once more ran a high fever. The duke ordered renowned physicians to examine him and sent messages every hour asking how the patient was faring. The duchess presented the visitors with silver flowers and other gifts in four boxes for them to take back to give to their mothers in Japan. On the eve of their departure they visited the duchess dressed in their Japanese robes, and presented to the duke one of these robes and a sword belonging to Francis of Bungo. The fact they were giving away their Japanese robes, now considerably worn and faded, indicates their predicament when obliged to make return gifts. Nor were the four boys the only recipients of their host's bounty, for he presented a chain worth fifty crowns to Augustine, their Japanese attendant.

Julian's fever had sufficiently abated for the boys to continue their journey on 25 June, but as a precaution the duke instructed his personal physician and a barber to accompany the party as far as Venice. As they would be travelling along the River Po, he further ordered his own *bucintoro*, or ducal barge, decorated with paintings, gold ornaments and containing three cabins with luxurious beds and furniture, to be prepared to carry the visitors to Venice. Accordingly, the travellers set out and a crew rowed them along the Po. But the vessel did not travel alone, for three other boats accompanied it, one carrying musicians and an escort of armed soldiers, another transporting provisions, and the third serving as a floating kitchen. When the time came for meals, these two last boats drew up alongside and the duke's servants produced a feast as splendid as if it had been prepared back in his palace, all to the accompaniment of pleasant music.

CHAPTER 13

Carnival of Venice

Famous, prosperous and fiercely independent Venice was not to be outdone by other cities in its welcome for the Japanese, especially as reports from its ambassador in Rome indicated that the boys enjoyed the favour and patronage of the new pope, the strong-willed Sixtus V.[1] On 16 June, the authorities of Venice received notice of the party's imminent approach and sent instructions to Chioggia, a city a few miles to the south, to receive the Japanese warmly when they passed through. The order was significantly worded, '. . . as these young men have been greatly favoured and honoured by His Holiness and by all the Roman court, we likewise want to offer them a demonstration of kindness and honour that is appropriate'.[2]

The authorities of Chioggia organized a flotilla of boats to meet the visitors, with the governor going out in a barge beautifully decorated with silken cloths to escort the Japanese ashore. Then came the local bishop, the renowned preacher Gabriel Fiamma, accompanied by all his clergy to greet the visitors and escort them into the city.[3] As the boys disembarked, artillery was fired in salute, fanfares were played, and many ingenious fireworks were let off in welcome. The boys stayed the night in the palace, enjoying a fine banquet in a large chamber, on which occasion the bishop made an eloquent speech in Latin praising the visitors for travelling so far through so many dangers for the sake of religion.

On the following day the party, accompanied by the governor, the bishop, and others, set out for Venice by boat. During their approach to the city, they passed the fortified island of San Giorgio, where the moored ships fired in salute and their crews cheered and waved. At the Santo Espirito monastery, a league from Venice, forty senators, or *Pregadi*, dressed in their velvet and silk robes, came out in boats to greet the Japanese, and after listening to yet another speech, the visitors were invited to board one of the gondolas to make their formal entrance into the city. Escorted by dozens of boats, the boys travelled along the Grand Canal on a roundabout route so that they could take in some of the sights of the city, including the famous St Mark's Square.[4]

When the travellers finally reached the Jesuit residence, they were escorted into the crowded church, which had been lavishly decorated for the occasion, and in front of the high altar, large cushions had been placed on an elevated platform for their use. A solemn Te Deum was sung in thanksgiving for their safe arrival, and then some senators accompanied the boys to their rooms. In addition to the four bedrooms, two other chambers had been put at their disposal, one to serve as a dining-room and the other to entertain visitors. Among these visitors was the papal nuncio,[5] and so many people were milling around that it was not until 8.00 in the evening that the boys could obtain some rest.

Next day, the Japanese paid an extensive round of visits, greeting the patriarch of Venice, as well as various ambassadors and nobles. In all their excursions in the city they were accompanied by the nobleman Constantino Molino, who made sure they lacked for nothing, for during the party's stay in Venice, the senate paid for all their expenses.

The following day was appointed for the visitors to make a formal visit on the Doge and the senate. To add further solemnity to the occasion, many senators arrived in gondolas to escort the travellers to the ducal palace, where so many people were gathered in its halls to see the Japanese that the boys had some difficulty in making their way through.

The venerable Doge, Nicolò da Ponte, aged 88, was seated on a richly decorated throne, surrounded on both sides by senators wearing their purple robes.[6] The boys sat on chairs, two on each side of the Doge, while Mesquita delivered a speech thanking the assembly for the honours accorded to the Japanese. The Doge replied in a friendly manner, and the boys presented him with two robes, the best they had in their depleted wardrobe, and also a sword and a dagger. As the Japanese sword was so novel, they were told it would be placed in public view in memory of their visit, with a notice underneath explaining its origin.[7] Bidding farewell to the Doge and senators, the visitors were then taken to inspect an impressive display of weapons and also the treasury, reputed to be one of the richest in the world. After lunch, they were escorted to the famed Murano workshops to inspect the manufacture of its fine glassware.[8]

The festival of the Apparition of St Mark, the city's patron, was held on 25 June every year,[9] on which occasion one of Europe's most colourful processions was staged. To allow the Japanese visitors to witness this grand spectacle, the celebration had been postponed for a few days until 29 June, the feast of SS Peter and Paul. On that day the boys attended Mass in St Mark's cathedral, from which they were taken to the palace, suitably decorated for the occasion by order of the senate, so that they would enjoy an excellent view of the procession from this vantage point. Venice had indeed a great deal to show, but nothing, they were assured, could compare to the grandeur of this event.

Instead of the dances and similar festivities usually presented on the arrival of princes, the senate judged that in the case of these new Christians, it would be fitting to organize a festival of a more religious nature. The event was more formal than usual and apparently nothing comparable had been seen in the city for many years: Mesquita was told that the event had cost 7,000 crowns to organize. There were shown more than 140 representations of various events in biblical history as well as the martyrdoms of many saints. But these imaginative enactments were not reserved only for ancient history, for the last float featured Gregory XIII sitting on the papal throne and bestowing his blessing on the boys kneeling before him. The senators ordered the more elaborate floats to stop in front of the Japanese to allow them to get a better and longer look at them; the floats took three hours to pass.[10]

On other days the Japanese were shown around the city, admiring the palaces, churches, the Rialto bridge, the fashionable shops selling expensive wares, and the banks which, they were informed, held large reserves of foreign currency. They also visited the castle and the great arsenal, where the Venetian fleet was anchored. For relaxation, they enjoyed a fishing trip and a dinner at sea. On 30 June the boys were received by the Great Council, and on the following day the papal nuncio hosted a banquet for them. On 4 July the visitors returned to the doge's palace to bid him farewell. The senate decided to have the boys' portraits painted in perpetual remembrance of the visit, and Tintoretto, then aged seventy-three but still active, was paid 2,000 ducats to carry out this commission. Below these portraits would be placed inscriptions in Japanese and Italian, explaining who the boys were and the reason for their coming to Europe. The boys would then add their signatures in both Japanese and Roman letters.[11]

This is what a near contemporary had to say, in a modern English translation, about the boys' portraits:

> For the King of Arima, the King of Bungo Cingua [Chijiwa?], and the Prince of Vamusa [Ōmura], he also painted the portrait of Don Mansio, the nephew of the King of Ficenga [Hyūga]; Don Michele, the nephew of Don Protaso, the King of Arima; Don Giuliano Esara [Nakaura] and Don Martio, Japanese Barons of the Kingdom of Fighem [Higen?], ambassadors to the Holy See who also visited Venice in 1565 [=1585]. On a commission from the government [of Venice] he also made another painting of them as a record of their visit. The portrait of Don Mansio was seen in the painter's own home.[12]

Tintoretto had the sobriquet of Furioso for the speed with which he completed his paintings, but it is obvious that the brief and event-filled visit to Venice did not leave sufficient time for adequate sittings. As a result, he apparently completed only Mancio's portrait, and rough sketches of two other boys. Four months later, on 17 October, the senate was still discussing what to do about the unfinished project.[13]

The failure to produce and preserve the works is unfortunate for the paintings by the great Tintoretto, famous for his portraits, would have been of immense interest and enabled us to get some idea of the individual boys' appearances. It is true that sketches made later in Milan still exist in printed form, but they can hardly be considered physiognomic; the amateurish depiction of the boys and Mesquita is crude and purely conventional, revealing little if anything of their individual characters.[14]

Even though the portraits could not be completed before their departure from Venice on 6 July the senate was able to present the party with costly gifts – four marble crucifixes, four large mirrors framed with black wood, four with gilt frames, two large containers full of many glass objects, and rolls of satin, damask and velvet.[15] An earlier plan to present each boy with a silver case containing relics was abandoned, 'because it was not a good thing to deprive the city of Venice of relics for which our ancestors had fought after with such difficulty and labour'.[16] The senate also notified all the authorities in its territories to extend a hearty welcome to the party as it passed through.

Despite the official welcome accorded the Japanese in Venice, some private accounts hint at less enthusiastic attitudes towards the visitors. The cancellation of the original plan to present relics is a case in point. The critical attitude of Lorenzo Priuli, the Venetian ambassador in Rome, who objected to walking behind the boys at the pope's coronation, has already been noted. In addition, a Venetian who saw the party during its stay in his city left the following less than flattering account:

> These Japanese are of short stature, with pale faces, wide noses and thick lips like the Saracens; they look so similar one to the other that it is very difficult to distinguish them; they seem to be people of good breeding.[17]

There can be no doubt that in Venice and elsewhere in Europe the Japanese received a warm and often exuberant official welcome, but this does not mean that critical and unflattering individual views were entirely absent.

■ CHAPTER 14

From Padua to Genoa

So the boys left Venice on 6 July in two boats and resumed their travels. They were accompanied by many senators as far as the church of San Giorgio, where a farewell banquet was provided before they continued on to Padua, some twenty-three miles away. They enjoyed their tranquil progress along the River Bacchiglione, admiring the fine buildings on either side and watching the horses on the river bank pulling their boats forwards. Of special interest was the ingenious system of locks along the river.[1] They reached Padua to find a large crowd of curious onlookers awaiting them as well as magistrates and gentlemen, who conducted them to the Jesuit college, where they were to spend the night.

Padua is renowned for its Franciscan saint, St Anthony, who lived in the city for some years and died nearby, and the Japanese were duly taken to admire the enormous church in which the saint is buried.[2] Also visited was the renowned university, famous throughout Europe and the alma mater of the organizer of their expedition to Europe, Alessandro Valignano.[3] One particular incident during their brief stay in this fair city is of some significance, although not recorded by Fróis. The boys were taken to visit the Orto Botanico, the oldest botanical garden in Europe, which produced a large variety of nutritious herbs used in medicines. There they were introduced to its director, Melchior Wieland, who kindly presented to them a copy of Abraham Ortelius's famous atlas, *Theatrum Orbis Terrarum*, as well as the first three volumes of Georg Braun's illustrated *Civitates Orbis Terrarum*.[4]

On the following day, the party set out for Vicenza, some nineteen miles away, where they were received with the usual acclaim, with twenty carriages meeting the travellers on the road and then escorting them into the city. During their stay, the visitors attended a reception in their honour held in the Teatro Olimpico, a building completed only two years earlier, in which all manner of tragedies, comedies and other forms of drama were periodically staged for the public by erudite men called 'academics'. On this particular occasion the audience was treated to a musical concert as well as an elegant speech by one of the 'academics' in which he expressed joy at the visitors' arrival and praised Japan and its people. This reception hardly differs from scores of other similar gatherings attended by the boys during their travels, except in one respect.

The citizens of Vicenza obviously highly appreciated the visit, and to commemorate the happy occasion, a fresco was painted in the theatre showing the four boys sitting in the front row of the audience listening to an orator holding forth on the stage. But like the fresco showing the pope's procession to the Lateran Basilica earlier that year, the depiction of the four boys unfortunately shows no distinctive features.[5]

On the following day, 10 July, the Japanese resumed their travels, setting out for Verona, where no less than three hundred gentleman on horseback and magistrates in coaches came out of the city to greet them. The boys transferred to one of the carriages for the last stage of their approach, but just outside the city their progress was halted once more when they met a thousand musketeers and other soldiers who fired three salutes in welcome before escorting them into Verona. Here they were carried to the palace with musical accompaniment, then to the Jesuit church, and finally the cathedral. As the Jesuit college was still under construction, the boys passed the night in the bishop's palace. The next day they attended solemn Mass and visited the fine palace of the count of Bevilacqua, where the owner personally showed the visitors his picture gallery, fine library and collection of musical instruments.[6]

The party once more set out, accompanied as usual by coaches and soldiers. The duke of Mantua[7] had expressed his desire to meet the Japanese, and spared no effort to outdo their previous hosts in hospitality. Not content to await the boys within his own domain, he had sent to Verona his secretary, who had accompanied them in a large carriage. The party reached Villafranca at midday, and although the town lay within the territory of Verona, Muzio Gonzaga, one of the duke's sons, met them there and greeted them on behalf of the duke, who because of sickness was unable to come in person.[8]

The Japanese soon entered the duke's domain and found mounted gentlemen and colourfully-dressed musketeers waiting to greet them. A little further along the route a further escort of a hundred light infantry wearing white armour and riding in two lines joined the welcome party. When the travellers reached Marmirolo, seven miles from Mantua, they found the duke's son and heir, 23-year-old Vincenzo,[9] awaiting them. He rode in a richly decorated coach pulled by four fine horses, along with thirty other carriages, and nobles on horseback, and was escorted by 400 light-cavalry soldiers and another hundred mounted gentlemen. The prince received the Japanese in the name of his father, and to show them greater honour he intended to ride on horseback in front of their coach, but the boys insisted he enter their carriage and ride with them.

Crowds lined the road hoping to catch a glimpse of the travellers and greet them, and as they approached the city, the Japanese were met by Scipione Gonzaga,[10] who renewed the welcome of the indisposed duke. Then followed a lengthy salvo from the artillery on the city walls and within the fortress, interspersed with fanfares of trumpets and drums. As the local Jesuits had only recently arrived in the city and could not provide suitable accommodation, the party was taken to the ducal palace, where Vincenzo personally conducted them to their rooms. These chambers had been decorated only recently, and (they were told) the renovation of Mancio's room alone had cost 8,000 crowns.

Happily, the duke had somewhat recovered by the following day and, carried in a chair and accompanied by Vincenzo and courtiers, he went to meet the visitors in their rooms. Showing every sign of affability, he led them to the palace's church of Santa Barbara,[11] where Mass was celebrated with solemnity and music, some of which, they were informed, had been composed by the duke himself.[12] At the conclusion of the service, the duke showed the party around his palace before handing them over to Vincenzo's care. In the afternoon the Japanese returned to the chapel for solemn vespers, at the end of which a rabbi was baptized; the prince was the godfather and asked Mancio to choose Christian names for the convert. After giving the matter some thought, the boy chose Michael Mancio, the names of the two Japanese legates.

Following this liturgy, the prince took the boys in a golden coach to see the city's sights, such as churches, palaces[13] and gardens, and finally to the lake surrounding the city. They boarded a decorated barge lined with crimson velvet and were accompanied by many other boats, while artillery salvos and trumpet fanfares sounded in their honour. The sun had already set, and suddenly bonfires were lit in the palace, on the city walls, and elsewhere, illuminating the scene. On the lake itself there were two boats carrying firewood the height of a lance and on top were fireworks that seemed to set fire to the clouds. Rockets soared into the sky above the palace and other places, while the boats on the lake let off smoke bombs and ingenious fireworks.

This display lasted all of three hours, to the inevitable accompaniment of trumpets and more salutes fired by cannons and muskets. The boys were then driven back to the palace in the golden coach, accompanied as usual by mounted gentlemen, servants bearing torches and musicians playing fanfares.

Next morning, 15 July, the prince escorted the visitors to the church of Santa Maria delle Grazie, some distance outside the city, where they heard Mass. Following lunch at the Carthusian monastery by the side of the lake, the boys enjoyed a fishing trip and, after resting, were taken to see a hunt of mountain pigs in the famous Fontana Woods. On the following day, again accompanied by the prince, they journeyed four leagues out of the city to visit San Benedetto di Polirone, a large Benedictine monastery known as 'the Montecassino of the north', where they were greeted by the abbot, Lattantio Facio, and some hundred and fifty monks. A bell, usually rung only for the reception of a king, was sounded in their honour. The abbot later had a plaque made to commemorate the visit.[14]

But the stay in the city would not have been complete without a visit to the duke's wife[15] and the prince's wife,[16] both of whom greeted the party warmly. As for the gifts showered on the party, Vicenzo presented a suit of armour, two muskets and four clocks, as well as a portrait of himself, to be sent on later. The duke donated four golden boxes containing relics, four broadswords, each worth 200 crowns, with silver scabbards. Following so many formal ceremonies, it must have come as a relief for the visitors to sup privately, at his request, with the prince. After the meal they showed Vincenzo their Japanese robes, presenting him with one of them and a sword – hardly a fitting return gift in view of the spectacular hospitality they had received, but it was, they said, merely a token of their love and gratitude.

The party spent five days in Mantua, 13–18 July, with the duke and prince entertaining the visitors in truly grand style. As Fróis remarks, no more could be imagined as regard honours and favours, and it is difficult to dispute this claim. After bidding farewell to the duke, the boys set out escorted by the prince, his guards, and many coaches until the city gates. From there they were accompanied by gentlemen as far as Gazzuolo, a town belonging to the duke.

Three or four miles from Cremona, the Japanese were welcomed by a representative of the local bishop, Cardinal Niccolò Sfondrati, whom the boys had already met in Rome.[17] Accompanied by eight or nine coaches that would carry the party for the rest of the journey, he informed them that the cardinal sent his best wishes, but was unfortunately unable to come out to meet them in person owing to an indisposition. Escorted by magistrates and a company of light cavalry waiting outside the city walls, the boys made a solemn entry into Cremona and were then taken to the cathedral and the episcopal palace. Although still feeling unwell, Sfondrati greeted the Japanese at the entrance of his palace, and after embracing them, took them inside and accompanied them to their rooms.

During their two-day stay in Cremona, the Japanese attended the cardinal's Mass in his private chapel and then in the cathedral, where they received Communion from his hands. The governor was away, but on hearing of their arrival he hurried back to the city and visited them on behalf of Philip II, for the duchy of Milan was then under Spanish rule. In the king's name, he offered to supply whatever they might need, and accompany them whenever they went sightseeing in the city. An official of the duke of Terranova arrived from Milan and offered to join them and provide whatever might be needed. On their departure, the cardinal presented each boy with a gold cross containing relics, and then the governor and his staff went with the party for two miles out of the city.

On 21 July, the travellers spent the night at Pizzighitone. Before their arrival, a military escort of two companies of soldiers met the party and with much festivity escorted them to the grand palace, where they were royally treated. On the following day they left with the same escort, and were greeted by the local governor with fifteen coaches and light cavalry several miles outside Lodi. The governor received them with honour and took them to his residence, where they stayed for two days. The governor of Milan, the duke of Terranova, was away from the city at the time[18] and had requested the Japanese wait a short while for he wished to return and personally greet them on their arrival on 25 July, the feast of St James. During their stay at Lodi, the boys attended sung Mass, and enjoyed a fine banquet provided by the city, where they were treated to an acrobatic and conjuring display in which the performers jumped and somersaulted with amazing agility and engaged in mock duels with drawn swords.

On 25 July, accompanied by the governor and the principal citizens of Lodi, the party set out for Milan. En route they met a Milanese gentleman with a large escort who had ridden out to greet them on behalf of the city and its citizens. Also to welcome them came the archbishop's vicar general, and then Blasco d'Aragona, a relative of the duke, with a hundred mounted and armed gentlemen, bringing four richly caparisoned horses for the boys to ride as they entered the city.

The duke of Terranova,[19] his two sons and a nephew, together with senators, magistrates and 500 mounted gentlemen, awaited the party outside the walls of Milan, and the duke received the boys kindly and welcomed them to the city. After these formal courtesies had been exchanged, he placed Mancio on his right, while his Majesty's visitor general rode with Michael, the chancellor with Martin, and the president of the senate with Julian. Thus escorted, the Japanese entered Milan and were taken through crowded streets to the Jesuit college where they spent the night.

On the following day, 26 July, the travellers began a round of visits on the bishop of Novara, the bishop of Tortona, the archbishop of Milan, and then the duke's son. The next day the duke of Bavaria's ambassador visited them along with many Ferrara nobles; to be followed by the Venetian ambassador and a nephew of the duke, and other leading people. Finally, the duke himself called and spoke with the Japanese, doubtless with Mesquita, as always, on hand as interpreter.

Archbishop Gaspare Visconte had only recently been appointed to Milan and had arrived in the city on 23 July. He invited the Japanese to attend his first public Mass in the enormous cathedral on Sunday, 28 July, where they received Communion from his hands and afterwards stayed for lunch with the prelate. The duke visited the boys at the Jesuit college and provided a sumptuous banquet for them at his palace, followed by a theatrical performance that greatly pleased the visitors. Every day, in both the morning and afternoon, he sent his son with coaches and guards to accompany the travellers whenever they wished to go sightseeing. They admired the city's palaces, churches and commercial centres, and noted that the finest armour in Europe was manufactured there.

But local skill in casting metal was not reserved for military purposes, and the visitors saw twenty-eight recently cast bronze statues of saints, destined for King Philip's Escorial, each one said to cost six thousand crowns. They were taken to inspect the duke's castle, reputed to be one of the strongest in Italy, and on their arrival more than fifty cannons fired a salute, and as they entered the fortress further salvos of cannons and muskets were sounded. A soldier was to be punished for mistakenly firing too early, but, at Mancio's intercession, was pardoned. Poor Julian was again feeling unwell,[20] and rode a mule during most of the protracted tour. The party was taken to the chapel for Mass and was then treated to yet another banquet, during which Mancio was presented with the keys of the castle.

In his text, Fróis here inserts a verbatim description of the city written by an unidentified member of the party:

> The city of Milan is one of the loveliest places we saw in Italy. It is two-and-half leagues in circumference, and is surrounded by lakes and strong walls, and many high towers around it. The moats are made in this way: any time they want, they can send in water from two plentiful rivers and it enters near the walls and encircles the city. But they do not fill the moats except in time of war. The city has plenty of provisions coming from the estates of the duchy and from other ships. The city is situated on flat ground in the form of a circle. There are many noble houses of 3,000 or 4,000 crowns in value; others are of greater worth.[21]

The rest of this lengthy account may be summarized as follows. Milan is famous for its armour. A plague in the previous year killed 18,000 people in the city. It does not have so many palaces as do Genoa and Venice, but possesses many lovely churches and beautiful monasteries in which live many monks and friars. The cathedral is called the Duomo and is magnificent in size and riches, with many marble statues of Old and New Testament saints. Although begun many years before our arrival, it is still not completed, and it seems they will never finish it or will finish it late, even though work is always in progress there. The top of the cathedral is so high that it can be seen six or seven leagues away. Four or five priests can preach to many people in it at the same time without distracting the others. Finally, it is one of the finest churches in Europe. The fortress is somewhat outside the city in a place slightly elevated, and is well provisioned; reputedly there is none better in Christendom. The local people are polite and well bred, but they spend excessively on clothes for they wear velvet and silk. There is great variety and abundance of food. The duke owns twenty or more cities, all well provided. The body of St Ambrose is buried in the city, while that of St Augustine is in Pavia, four leagues away, but still within the duchy.

During the boys' stay in Milan, Urbano Monte[22] saw the visitors on various occasions and produced the famous portraits, which first appeared in print in 1585, and in the following year were copied in a handbill, published in Augsburg.[23] The half-figure depictions of the Japanese and Mesquita, shown at three-quarter view, are purely conventional and do little to illustrate their individual features.

The identity and age of the portrayed youths are clearly indicated above each figure. The ages of Mancio and Michael are given as twenty, while their two companions are said to be only seventeen years old. Each boy is dressed in identical red European costumes with white ruffs, and in their right hands all carry a tall hat, similar in shape to their hats shown in the Vatican mural of Sixtus V's procession to St John Lateran. As befitting the principal legate, Mancio holds a crown in his left hand, while the other three carry folded fans. Mancio and Michael look to their right, the other two to their left (thus distinguishing the two legates from their two companions?). In contrast to the boys, the lightly bearded Mesquita wears a black cassock and biretta, with a Jesuit crest to the left of his head; his age is not given. An eight-line flowery description in Italian is added below each figure. For example, below Mancio's figure we read in English translation:

This youth, with the crown in his hand,
   Is named Mancio the King.
Come from such a far-distant country
   That he has used up three years on the journey.

But he will never say he has spent his time in vain,
  Having seen, and also conversed in,
The States of Gentle Italy,
  In Rome, in Spain, in Courtly Milan.[24]

Not only does Monte provide these portraits, albeit unskilled and naïve, but he also records that the Japanese arrived in Milan on 25 July and on their entering through the Porta Romana they were welcomed by the governor, magistrates, nobles, and local dignitaries. All the windows of the houses along their route were filled with spectators, especially women. So many people crowded the streets that it was with some difficulty the party managed to reach the Jesuit residence, where they were due to stay. Monte then goes on to provide an eyewitness description of the Japanese visitors that goes a long way to filling out the lackluster illustrations. If his account is not flattering in all respects, his comments are of considerable interest and show the impressions of an educated and sympathetic European. Describing the Japanese, he writes:

> Their stature is rather shorter than average; their complexion is sallow, their eyes small, their eyelids large, their nose somewhat broad; their appearance is ingenuous and refined, and not at all barbarous. Their manner is civil, courteous and modest. Among themselves they show much respect, always observing the same order when walking. As regards eating, they are modest and free, eating everything without waiting to be served. They are moderate and polite, and do not touch food with their hands except bread.[25]

Monte continues his observations by noting that the boys do not drink wine but only tepid water after the Japanese fashion, and usually only once towards the end of the meal. When they eat among themselves, they use some sticks of white wood like ivory as long as a span, and with these they skilfully take any food however distant it may be. They are intelligent, and show mature prudence and much alertness when talking with prelates. Their manners are such that they seem to have been brought up in Italy. They take note of everything they see, but they do not greatly marvel, and in this they show a most noble spirit. They know Portuguese well, Spanish to some extent, Latin in good part, and they understand most of Italian although they do not speak it with confidence. When they talk with princes, they speak in their own native language and use an interpreter. They know how to play European musical instruments and practise in private. They wear fine silk robes of various lovely colours and decorated with Japanese birds and animals. Their socks, made of soft leather, are like mittens with the big toe separate from the others; their shoes are like those of Capuchin friars, that is, without heels, and fastened with just one cord.[26]

All in all, this is perhaps the frankest and most detailed recorded account of the Japanese boys while they were travelling through Europe.

Despite the burst of sightseeing in Milan, the dutiful and responsible Mancio managed to find time to write a letter to the duke of Mantua on 2 August, thanking him for his hospitality during their stay in his city. The text is written in Japanese in seven columns and shows mature calligraphic skill, which may indicate that it was written by Brother George. At the bottom of the document appear Mancio's signature in Roman letters ('Ito D[on] Mancio de fiuga [Hyūga]') and also his *kaō*, or stylized Japanese signature. To the left of the text is written an Italian translation, probably supplied by Mesquita.[27]

Before their departure at the end of the eight-day visit, the duke of Terranova presented each boy with a golden sword, dagger, and belt. News was received from Genoa that some ships were about to sail to Spain, and hoping not to miss this chance of boarding one of them, the travellers bade farewell and left Milan on 3 August. The duke's two sons and a nephew, together with a large escort of German mercenaries, musketeers and light infantry, accompanied the party a considerable distance along their route. At noon on their first day of travel they reached the famed Carthusian monastery near Pavia, some five miles north of Milan. There they were shown the interior of the great church with its abundance of marblework and statues, as well as the celebrated tomb of Gian Galeazzo Visconti, first duke of Milan.

After spending the night there, the travellers continued on to Pavia, and on their approaching the city, they were met by Bishop Ippolito de' Rossi,[28] the governor, and many gentlemen, while a crowd of citizens waited outside the walls to welcome them; as the visitors entered, artillery and muskets were fired in salute.[29] The boys attended Mass in the cathedral and were then entertained in the bishop's palace. They set out again on the following day, accompanied by the bishop and six carriages for one league.

On the same day the Japanese arrived at Voghera, the last town in Milanese territory. There the lord who had accompanied them from the time they entered the duchy, left them, his place being taken by a gentleman, ordered by the duchess of Lorraine and her daughter, the duchess of Brunswick; both ladies ardently desired to meet the Japanese and invited them to visit Tortona, where they were residing.[30] A mile from that city they met Andrea Doria,[31] who escorted them to Tortona and entertained them that evening. On the following day, accompanied by coaches and horses, the party set out for Genoa, capital of Lombardy, and were met by nobles welcoming them. In addition, a mile before the port city four senators and many mounted gentlemen came to meet them, providing them with four horses. On the party's reaching the city gates, four procurators vested in rich togas came out to greet them and lead them to the Jesuit residence, where richly decorated rooms had been prepared for their use.

The authorities had planned to stage a big festival in the visitors' honour, but because of the ships' imminent departure, there was no time for this spectacle; the local people, however, were determined to show the Japanese as much of their city as possible. Together with many senators, the Japanese went to visit the duke, and on reaching his palace, they were greeted by a musket volley fired by the German guards, artillery salvos, and trumpet fanfares. Although indisposed, their host came out of his chamber to greet the boys warmly, and after some conversation, he accompanied them to the front steps to bid them farewell. Only one day could be spent in Genoa, but in that short time the boys, with assigned senators, managed to fit in a great deal of sightseeing, admiring the fine churches and buildings in this 'other Venice'. Among the pious relics seen was a veil of Veronica, on which Christ is said to have left the imprint of his face on his way to Calvary. As a farewell gift, the city presented the party with ample provisions for the voyage to Spain.[32]

The Spanish ambassador called on them, and he was followed by Giannettino Spinola, nephew of Doria, in whose name he served as commander of a fleet of nineteen galiots, and he assigned the party to his well-equipped flagship. Conducted to the ship by four principal senators and other gentlemen, the Japanese boarded the vessel on 8 August at 8.00 in the evening, once more to the sound of trumpet fanfare and artillery salute. On the following day, they set sail for Spain, with numerous memories of the fabulous reception they had received in Italy during their five-month visit.

But, it should be remembered, this extravagant welcome ran quite contrary to the plans of the expedition's organizer, Alessandro Valignano, who in his instructions had explicitly advocated a low-key reception. But once the chain reaction of enthusiastic welcome had started, there was little the party could do to stop it without causing offence to their European hosts.

CHAPTER 15

Spain and Portugal Revisited

The Japanese reached Barcelona without mishap on 16 August and started their journey through Spain and Portugal on their way back to Japan. Their route through the two countries was somewhat different from the road followed on their way to Rome in the previous year. If anything, their reception was even more exuberant than before, doubtless inspired by news of the great favours shown them by Gregory XIII, Sixtus V, Philip II, the Venetian authorities, the duke of Bragança, and dozens of other nobles and bishops. Repetition is, it is true, the mother of learning, but cataloguing in detail all the welcome extended them on their way back through the two countries would be tedious and unnecessary, and a briefer account must suffice. This thought appears to have occurred to Fróis, on whose text the present book is mainly based, for his narrative of the boys' return journey through the Iberian peninsula is appreciably shorter than that of their earlier progress en route to Rome. As Michael remarks in *De Missione*: 'There is no room here to describe everything in the detail that the duty of gratitude demands.'[1] Coimbra, however, is an exception, for as the party had not visited the city and its celebrated university on its way to Rome, Fróis offers a detailed account.

But immediate progress in Spain was halted at Barcelona as Julian fell ill for the fourth time, and for more than three weeks the party stayed at a nearby villa, often making sightseeing expeditions into the city. They visited the cathedral and venerated the tomb of Olegario, bishop of Barcelona, who had died four hundred years earlier.[2] During this enforced delay the Japanese took the opportunity of visiting the great Benedictine monastery of Montserrat, located high among the strangely shaped mountain peaks some thirty miles northwest of the city, and the monks presented the party with a recently published book, which they carried back to Japan, about the sanctuary's history and miracles. During their short visit they were also shown some of the hermitages found in the rugged mountainous terrain.

On Julian's recovery, the Japanese set out to visit Philip II again and thank him for his many acts of kindness both during their previous stay in the capital and in the arrangements made by his officials at later stages of their journey. The king had left Madrid for the summer and was staying at Monzón, where he was dealing with various issues concerning Aragon, Catalonia, and Valencia, and receiving oaths of loyalty from the nobles of these regions in favour of young Prince Philip. The party reached Monzón about 9 September and lodged in the palace of the Patriarch of Venice; there they received visits from the archbishop of Saragossa, the duke of Terranova, and other notables. When these formalities were concluded, it was time to visit the king again.

The boys duly proceeded to the palace and once more met King Philip, the young prince, and the two princesses. Again, they tried to kiss their hands as a sign of respect, but the royal family insisted on embracing them with affection. The king inquired about their impressions of Italy, and, having heard of his illness, asked Julian about his health. The legates then presented Philip with their memorials, which he solemnly accepted. The king told the party that he would cover all their travel expenses from Barcelona, and would provide a coach and horses, and everything else needed, for their future travels. He would further instruct Cardinal Albert in Lisbon and the viceroy in Goa to facilitate their progress in every way possible. He then bade them farewell with every sign of cordiality.

The Japanese then travelled on to the lovely city of Saragossa, capital of Aragon, where they were to stay at the large Jesuit college for three days. The bishop received them at his cathedral, while the choir sang appropriate verses from Psalm 72: 'The kings of Tharsis and the islands shall offer presents; the kings of all the Arabians and of Saba shall bring gifts; and all kings of the earth shall adore Him, all nations shall serve Him.'[3] They visited the famous Nuestra Señora de Pilar, and the celebrated Hieronymite monastery containing the tombs of St Engracia, the fourth-century martyr, and St Lamberto. On the eve of their departure, students staged a play at the Jesuit college in which actors personifying Japan, Spain and Italy declaimed speeches in Latin, Greek and Spanish, repeatedly mentioning the Japanese legation to Europe.

Passing through Daroca, the Japanese travelled on to Alcalá, where they were greeted by Ascanio Colonna[4] and Luis Enríquez de Cabrera y Mendoza.[5] During their four-day stay with the local Jesuit community, Colonna organised a banquet for them together with a theatrical performance; in addition, he presented the boys with a musical instrument, made of cedar wood and called a clavicembalo, decorated with pearls and received from Rome.

In Madrid the boys took leave of the empress, the cardinal of Toledo and the local Jesuit community, and picked up the gifts they had received while staying at Belmonte. On to Oropesa, where the count offered hospitality, but they declined his kind invitation as they wanted to reach Portugal as soon as possible, and they crossed into that country at the end of October.

Duchess Catarina Bragança again entertained the party royally for four days at Vila Viçosa, and on their departure young duke Teodósio and his brothers escorted the travellers, and handed over his coach to carry them as far as Coimbra. A league before reaching Evora, the party was welcomed by city and university officials, with magistrates and two hundred students coming out on horseback to greet them. The ever-indulgent archbishop Theotonio sent them four caparisoned horses, and mounted on these fine steeds the boys rode into the city and were received with acclaim. When they entered the decorated Jesuit church, they met up with the archbishop again and the Jesuit community. They then proceeded to the cathedral, where a solemn Te Deum was sung in thanksgiving for their safe arrival, and a priest offered them a relic of the Holy Cross for them to venerate. Finally, they were able to retire to their chambers, prepared for the visit of Henry III of France a dozen years earlier.[6]

On 7 November the college put on a festival for the visitors, with various lengthy speeches delivered in their honour. The former viceroy of India, Francisco de Mascarenhas, from whom the boys had already received much kindness in Goa, visited them often, and introduced his wife and children. As on their first visit, the archbishop went out of his way to entertain his young guests. On one day he took them, accompanied by gentlemen on horseback, to his pleasant villa in rural Valverde; at other times they visited the Franciscan monastery of Santo António and also Nossa Senhora do Espinheiro, a convent more than a league from the city. The archbishop presented them with gifts worth a thousand crowns, and told them he would cover their travel expenses as far as Lisbon and also provide provisions for the journey. On Sunday he conferred minor orders on some local Jesuits and also on Brother George Loyola in the cathedral, declaring his satisfaction at being the first bishop in Europe to confer orders on a Japanese.

After spending nine days at Evora, the party set out once more, and passing through Setubal they stopped at Val de Rosal, where the Lisbon Jesuits had a pleasant country villa, for a few days' rest. From there they travelled two leagues to the capital along the Tagus in a royal barge supplied by Cardinal Albert. In Lisbon they again stayed at the Jesuit house of São Roque, and several times visited the cardinal, who promised to cover the expenses of their voyage to India and in addition presented them with gifts worth 1,500 crowns.

The travellers were now informed that their ship would not be sailing until March of the following year,1586, and so it was decided to take advantage of this delay by visiting the ancient city of Coimbra. They had received insistent invitations from the Jesuits stationed there, and the city possessed a renowned university in which many Jesuit missionaries had studied.[7]

So in the second half of December the party set out from Lisbon to travel along the Tagus, and passing through Santarém and viewing the Benedictine and Dominican monasteries there, the Japanese approached Coimbra, seat of the premier university in Portugal. News of the boys' reception in Italy and Spain had already been received, and enthusiasm in the university, among both professors and students, had reached fever pitch. Nuno Rodrigues arrived ahead of the party to announce the boys' imminent approach and this news increased the excitement within the city. Four lavishly-decorated chambers had been prepared for their use; in addition, another three would be placed at their disposal, one as a dining-room, another to receive visitors, and the last for Augustine and Constantine. João de Bragança, whom the boys had met at court on their first visit to Madrid, sent his coach ahead for them to use, while he, the city magistrates, and bishop Afonso de Castelo Branco, accompanied by his chapter of clergy and many people on horseback, came out of the city to greet the party. The Japanese were offered four caparisoned horses so that they could leave their coach and ride into Coimbra in full public view.

The students at the university wished to see this procession and began stamping their feet, thus obliging professors to halt their lectures and allow them to gather at windows to view the spectacle. Large crowds lined the streets, with many people sitting on walls and bridges to get a better view. The Japanese crossed the bridge over the Mondego river and entered the city, with Martin and Julian riding in front, followed by Mancio and Michael on either side of the bishop. A member of the senate delivered a speech of welcome, and then shawms played cheerful music from the tower of the count of Portalegre's mansion. While they progressed through the streets, crowds cheered the visitors and ladies sprinkled scented water from decorated windows. The bells of the cathedral and other churches rang out in welcome.

So dense was the crowd when the party arrived at the cathedral that constables had to push and shove so that the visitors could dismount and enter the church, and some students were knocked over and trampled underfoot in the melee. The Rector and senior members of the local Jesuit community had been waiting inside and now emerged to greet the Japanese. After entering the cathedral, the boys knelt in front of the high altar while the bishop, robed in pontifical vestments, presented them with various relics to venerate, including once more the head of one of the eleven thousand virgins of Cologne, while an orchestra of different instruments provided a musical background. Then as the boys sat with the bishop to the left of the altar, a Jesuit delivered an eloquent speech. Finally, in the company of the bishop, the boys were allowed to retire to their rooms to rest.

On Christmas morning the Japanese rode in a carriage to the cathedral to attend Mass celebrated by the bishop and found his chapter of canons awaiting them at the entrance to lead them to four ornate chairs in front of the high altar. At the end of the liturgy the bishop embraced the boys and took them to the main door where they entered the episcopal carriage; such were the crowds that the bishop's and university's bailiffs again had their work cut out to clear the way. In the evening the Japanese went to admire an ornate crib, and were then entertained by João de Bragança and two bishops.

During the last week of the year, the boys received visits from leading citizens and paid visits themselves, often in the company of the bishop. They went to the convent of Santa Clara to admire the ornate tomb of Queen Isabella, and this visit prompted the nuns of the Colas convent to issue an invitation. Accompanied to the convent by the bishop and mounted gentlemen, the boys attended solemn vespers, then spoke through a grille to the abbess and nuns, who treated them to an assortment of sweets and biscuits. Yet another place visited was the famous monastery of Santa Cruz, where they were welcomed by the abbot and senior clergy to the pealing of bells, and then shown the tombs of kings and martyrs within the church. In the evening of 1 January 1586, Bishop Castelo Branco preached in the Jesuit church, praising missionary work in Japan, and later joined the boys for dinner in the community refectory. The meal was graced by speeches given in Hebrew, Greek, Latin, French, Italian, English, Portuguese and even in Japanese, for Brother George Loyola rose to the occasion by delivering an address about his country. This last oration won high praise from the bishop, for whom presumably Mesquita interpreted the gist. The Rector Magnificus, Nuno de Noronha, sent representatives to inquire whether the Japanese would care to visit the university. Mesquita was absent at the time, and so Mancio replied in Portuguese they would be delighted to accept the invitation for they had heard so much about the institution and wished to carry news about it back to their country. Doubtless the Japanese had in fact received reports about the college, for Coimbra was the training college for many of the seminarians destined for the missions in Asia and Latin America. It was a renowned centre of higher learning and was one of the principal works of the Portuguese Jesuits, who had assumed the administration of the College of Arts in 1555.[8]

But not all the events were formal ceremonies, for the bishop appears to have been an understanding man who realized the boys needed some relaxation. So one day he took them off to see some fishing, and on another he escorted them to his villa in the countryside. On their way, they passed by the university, and on learning of their approach the Rector Magnificus interrupted his lecture and came down from his high chair to greet them in the Hall of Public Acts, and took them to see the faculties of Civil Law, Canon Law, Medicine and Theology. In all of these halls the professors stopped their classes and descended from the dais to welcome the visitors, but because so many students were present, the Japanese did not enter but greeted them from the doorway.

A more formal visit to the university was paid on 7 January when the students put on a play about the life and death of St John the Baptist before an appreciative audience. The performance was presented in four acts, showing the saint bidding farewell to his parents, his flight into the desert, his baptism in the Jordan, his warnings to Herod, and finally 'the most cruel beheading of the saint, which was depicted in such a way that the action seemed not to be happening on a stage but in real life'.[9] The play lasted no less than seven hours and was received with much applause.

This marathon event had apparently aroused enormous interest and people had arrived on the previous evening to stake out their places, and such were the crowds that doors were broken down. To get a better view, some students climbed up a flight of stairs, and one of them, a student of Canon Law, fell into a cistern and swam around in the freezing water for some time before being rescued. He was taken off to dry himself in front of a fire and put on new clothes. He later professed himself well satisfied, for in addition to receiving a hearty supper, he was provided a good seat to see the tragedy.

In yet another presentation, direct reference was made to Japan. The four Evangelists drew a triumphal chariot bearing the Christian religion and met Francis of Bungo, Protasius of Arima and Bartholomew of Ōmura, whereupon the three daimyo dedicated themselves to the saints' protection and patronage.[10] Yet another allegorical presentation featured the guardian angels of Europe and Japan, the latter proclaiming the wonderful feats of the missionaries there. His European counterpart declared he had protected the party during their travels in the West and was now handing them back to the care of the angel of Japan to guide them safely home. In yet another play, Asia complained to Ocean about the boys' absence, but the latter referred her to Europe, who assured her they had received excellent treatment. Asia then thanked Europe for her kindness to the Japanese and then entrusted them to Ocean for a safe journey back to Japan.[11]

The presentation of these and other allegorical works finally came to an end, and after spending nearly three weeks in Coimbra, the party left the university city on 9 January and set out once more for Lisbon, on the way visiting the monasteries of Batalha and Alcobaça; in the latter the abbot, wearing miter and episcopal robes, came out to greet the visitors.[12] Cardinal Albert sent the Japanese his carriage to enter the capital, where they again lodged at the Jesuit church of São Roque. During this, their second stay in Lisbon on their return journey, the cardinal again showed them much kindness. He gave them a thousand crowns, which the boys spent on clothes, for doubtless their weeks of travelling over dusty roads made new outfits necessary. A more spectacular gift was promised, for the cardinal told the boys they would be given four Arabian horses on their arrival at Goa and these would be transported to Japan to allow the people there to view such fine examples of horses.[13]

As the time of their departure from Lisbon approached, Cardinal Albert sent a message that the party should decide on one of the five ships sailing to India, and the *São Felipe* was chosen, for it was stronger and bigger than the other vessels. The cardinal further ordered that good cabins, including the captain's, should be assigned to the Japanese, with ample provisions, all at his own expense. He provided such abundant food that people declared it would suffice not only for the ship's voyage to India but also for its return to Portugal. Then in the name of the king, the cardinal donated 4,600 crowns for travel expenses; the archbishop of Evora had given 1,000 crowns as well as many statues, rich fabrics and other costly gifts. In view of the multitude of presents received in the course of their travels in Europe, the *São Felipe* would be carrying exceedingly valuable luggage; and the party took up about half of the limited passenger accommodation.

Finally, the date of embarkation was decided and the boys bade farewell to Cardinal Albert, the nobles of Lisbon, and the Jesuit community, leaving behind, as Fróis tells us, many memories, a fine reputation, and an example of virtue, learning and prudence.[14] On 8 April 1586, the *São Felipe* set sail, carrying on board the four Japanese boys, their attendants, Nuno Rodrigues, Mesquita, and seventeen Jesuits destined for the missions in Asia. The four other ships, on one of which another dozen missionaries sailed, also took advantage of the favourable weather to start out for India on the same day. In addition, a fleet of no less than twenty-eight ships set sail at the same time, destined not only for India but also Brazil and Guinea.

The Japanese boys had spent one year and eight months in Europe.[15]

Part 6

The Return to Japan

■ CHAPTER 16

The Return Journey

The boys' voyage to Europe had taken a total of two-and-a-half years, longer than usual for with God's blessing and good fortune the journey could be completed in two years. Doubtless, the Japanese hoped to reach home more quickly, little realizing as they left Lisbon that their return to Japan would take more than four years. In addition to the delays caused by unfavourable winds, storms, becalming and navigational errors experienced in their voyage to Europe, political developments within Japan were to cause a seemingly interminable delay of nearly two years in Macao on their return journey.[1]

The fleet enjoyed fine weather and sailed together until 6 May, when the ships divided on to different courses to reach their various destinations. A few days later, the *São Felipe* crossed the equator, and sailed further south down the west coast of Africa.

As usual, the favourable weather was not to last, and on 27 June strong winds broke the ship's mainmast yards, and its mainsail and part of the tackle fell into the sea. The crew worked feverishly, cutting away the tackle, gathering up the sail, and clearing the decks of the fallen wreckage. While the captain ordered that new spars be made out of available timber, the ship proceeded using only the smaller sails, until repairs were completed three days later, and the voyage could continue at full speed. On 7 July the ship rounded the Cape of Good Hope in fine weather that allowed fishing, and with line and hook the boys caught more than seventy fish to supply a healthy addition to their diet.

Again, the weather deteriorated and gales so buffeted the *São Felipe* that it lurched from side to side and could hold its course only with the greatest difficulty. But the storm eventually subsided and was then followed by a becalming that lasted for more than two weeks. By 9 August the pilot believed that the ship was nearing Mozambique, but it was then discovered that the vessel was in fact approaching the dangerous Sofala shallows.[2] Land was sighted and the depth of the sea decreased to only fourteen fathoms. The *São Felipe* was dragged into even shallower water, and it was possible to see the trees on the shoreline as well as fires of the local natives hoping to loot the vessel if it broke up on the beach. The ship was now in water only six fathoms deep, and strong winds at dead of night drove it ever closer to shore during a heavy rainstorm. Two ropes had broken, and only one anchor was now holding the *São Felipe* back from land. The crew and the passengers had recourse to prayer, and believing their last hour had come many confessed their sins, while Rodrigues exhorted the boys with words of encouragement and fortitude. The captain dedicated the one anchor and the one remaining rope to the Blessed Virgin, vowing to pay the price of both if the ship escaped from the dangerous sandbanks.

On the following day a light breeze began to blow from land, but did not last long enough to carry the *São Felipe* away from danger, and once more all on board had to depend on the one sole anchor to keep the ship from breaking up on the shallows. More religious devotions were held, and a relic from Christ's crown of thorns was displayed and venerated. More prayers were said, more sermons preached, when on 13 August to the joy and relief of crew and passengers alike a strong wind began to blow offshore, sails were hoisted, and the ship eased its way into deeper water, away from the peril of the shallows. On the following day the passengers' happiness was further increased when they joined up with a small Portuguese ship sailing en route to Mozambique, and little time was lost in meeting up with its crew and exchanging greetings. It was a joyful encounter, but the mood on board the *São Felipe* was clouded by news that the *Santiago*, the ship on which the boys had sailed from India to Lisbon, had sunk in the Mozambique Channel and many of its crew had drowned. Some men managed to get ashore on two makeshift rafts, but on reaching land were captured by local natives and consigned to slavery. This was the fate of six Jesuits, four of whom died from the hardships they suffered. Of the two survivors, one was Pedro Martins, who was to become the first bishop to reach Japan, and so possibly the boys later heard a first-hand account of the maritime disaster.[3]

The *São Felipe* parted from the smaller vessel and reached the Angoche Islands, thirty leagues from Mozambique, on 18 August.[4] It was believed that they would reach the port on the following day, but contrary winds blew them further away until they found themselves eighty leagues from their destination. Soon the ship was in renewed danger as it was sailing in only six fathoms of water. A skiff was lowered to check the situation, and it was found the carrack could proceed, with the utmost caution, through a channel only eight fathoms deep, and in this way it finally reached Mozambique on 31 August. The *São Felipe* fired its two guns as a signal, and a pilot was sent from the fortress to steer the vessel safely into harbour. Thus ended the first stage of the boys' voyage home, a hazardous passage lasting four-and-a-half months, in which their ship experienced storms, becalming, broken sails and danger from sandbanks.

Anxious to reach India as soon as possible and aware that it was already late in the season for favourable winds, the captain decided on a short stay at Mozambique, and within three days set sail to continue the voyage. But the light wind was not sufficient to carry the vessel against the currents, and so in short order the *São Felipe* was forced to return to Mozambique with the doleful prospect of waiting a year before weather would allow it to continue to India. The governor of the fortress, Jorge de Meneses, welcomed the Japanese and treated them kindly throughout their enforced and tedious stay.

The boys remained at Mozambique for nearly six months until March 1587, not only suffering from the intense heat and unhealthy climate, but also worried about the anxiety Valignano must have been experiencing because of their non-arrival in India. To add to their distress, their ship's captain decided to return to Lisbon rather than continue on to India. He reached this decision when another ship, the *São Lourenço*, foundered on its way to Lisbon and arrived at Mozambique in such a shattered condition that it broke up on reaching land. It was agreed that its valuable cargo would be transferred to the *São Felipe*, which would then transport it back to Lisbon. Little did the captain realize that the ship's final landfall would be England, not Portugal.[5] There was now little or no hope that the party could proceed to India that year, especially as access to Mozambique was difficult and many eastbound Portuguese ships bypassed the port altogether and made directly for India.[6]

The party's anxiety was well founded, for Valignano was indeed deeply worried about the boys' non-appearance in Goa.[7] As there was a strong possibility that the party was stranded at Mozambique, Valignano, showing his usual energetic initiative, approached the Viceroy of India and arranged for a swift galiot to be despatched to Mozambique together with a letter to its governor instructing him to send the Japanese, if indeed they were there, to Goa in the same vessel as soon as possible; the viceroy further decided the royal treasury would cover the cost of the boys' lodging in Mozambique and of their voyage to India.

The stranded passengers were overjoyed when the light ship sailed into Mozambique. The ship, in fact, belonged to the governor, but he gladly offered it to the Japanese so that they could proceed to India as quickly as possible. He further donated 2,400 crowns from his own resources to cover expenses.

On 15 March the party finally left Mozambique for the relatively short voyage to India, but no sooner had the ship cleared the port than strong winds suddenly hit the light vessel, and before there was time to lower the sails, the galiot was leaning over at a perilous angle for fifteen minutes, with water pouring into the hold, before the crew managed to cut the tackle and bring down the yards. Fortunately, this manoeuvre was successful and the vessel was able to sail into calmer waters but then adverse winds blew it towards the shores of the kingdom of Melinde.[8] There the passengers and crew stayed for twelve days, taking in fresh supplies and repairing the storm damage. They set out once more and crossed the equator, meeting en route a small Portuguese ship on its way to Goa, and were able to send Valignano a reassuring letter as the other vessel was likely to (and in fact, did) reach Goa before them.

But the travellers' troubles were still not over. Their ship was becalmed for two whole weeks, preventing any further progress, a delay bad enough in itself, but gave rise to increased anxiety. It was now mid-May and winter was fast approaching in India, during which season the ports closed on account of violent storms. It was essential to reach any part of India, even far from Goa, as soon as possible, and once more recourse was had to prayer. On the feast of the Holy Spirit the thorn relic was again exposed on board for public veneration, and happily a week later, on 28 May, the crew spied the Queimados Isles, known to be located only twelve leagues from Goa.[9] On the following day the ship sailed into port amid universal rejoicing and thanksgiving. Valignano had left orders for a twenty-four-hour watch to be maintained, and when the look-out reported sighting the vessel, he and other Jesuits hurried to the harbour to greet the passengers.

On the boys' arrival, everyone in the city, from the Viceroy of India to the humblest citizen, was reported to have rejoiced and given thanks.[10] The viceroy, Duarte de Meneses,[11] received the Japanese kindly and organized equestrian events in their honour and for their entertainment. He paid the debt of 2,000 crowns the party owed to the governor of Mozambique; in accordance with Cardinal Henry's orders, he presented the boys with four horses for them to use during their stay,[12] and also a monthly allowance of 150 crowns while they remained in Goa. During their eleven months in Golden Goa, the Japanese often stayed at the Jesuits' country villa in Santa Anna and other pleasant places away from the heat and sicknesses of the city. Then in addition to their usual programme of studies they were sometimes invited to hunt in the fields of Salsete, a small peninsula nearby that enjoyed an agreeable climate.[13]

On one memorable occasion, 4 June 1587, only a week after the boys' arrival, Martin delivered a speech in Latin at the Jesuit college in the presence of Valignano and others. This public oration, doubtless written or at least polished by Mesquita or someone skilled in Latin, described in eloquent terms the boys' voyages and their travels through Europe, and is notable because its text was published in a fifteen-page pamphlet under the grandiose title, in English translation: 'Speech delivered by Don Martin Hara, Japanese, in his own name and that of his companions on their return from Europe, to Fr Alexander Valignano, Visitor of the Society of Jesus, at the College of St Paul in Goa, 4 June in the year of the Lord 1587.'

It is significant that Martin was again chosen to deliver the speech for he was only the companion of Mancio and Michael, the two official envoys. This pair had always made formal and official addresses during their stay in Europe, but perhaps Martin was chosen for his linguistic talent and, the mission to Europe now completed, there was no longer any need to observe the distinction between the two envoys and their two companions. In any case the speech was delivered at the college as an academic and not diplomatic exercise, possibly to demonstrate how skilful the young Japanese had become in Latin oratory. The boys had, of course, attended many such speeches during their travels in Europe, but this was only the second time one of them, again Martin, had ventured to deliver an address in Latin.

Written in fine classical style, the speech amounts to a paean of praise of Valignano. At the beginning of his oration Martin introduces a reference to Alexander the Great, and mentions the work of the Jesuit missionaries in Japan in driving out false deities. He dwells on the dangers encountered in the boys' long voyages to and from Europe, and their joy at being reunited to Valignano, their dear father. And just as the queen of Sheba journeyed from afar to visit the court of King Solomon to listen to his wisdom, so they, too, have travelled from afar to the Roman court and venerated not one but two popes. Just as the queen of Sheba received kindness and gifts, so, too, had the Japanese been accorded much kindness and generosity by two popes, King Philip, and so many other notables. As the queen of Sheba observed:

> 'How true are the words we heard in our land; but we did not believe the people telling us until we saw with our own eyes and realized that what we had heard was not even half of reality,' so King Philip's achievements are greater than the account we had heard. Blessed are the eyes that have seen such things, and blessed are we who have seen them!

Warming to his subject, Martin exclaims: 'But even more blessed are you, Alexander, great in virtue, who were the principal cause of our experiencing such good!' The speaker relates that Philip II had treated them more as a friend than a king; Cardinal Albert had been kindness itself to them; the archbishop of Evora had been a most generous benefactor. Alexander the Great reached India, but reportedly wept when Anaxorus told him there were other kingdoms he could not conquer.

Turning to Valignano, Martin declaims: 'You, O Alexander, far greater than that great king, have conquered nearly all of India with the weapons of Christ.' He expresses the wish that the same may also happen in Japan 'so that our oppressed country may be freed from the hands of the atrocious enemy'.[14]

This was heady eloquence and must have caused no little satisfaction (and perhaps even some embarrassment) on the part of Valignano, sitting in the audience. Although perhaps appearing strange and artificial to modern readers, the hyperbole, florid style, and references to classical antiquity in the address were customary in speeches delivered in Latin at the time. Who composed the encomium? Certainly not Martin himself. Possibly Mesquita or any of the Jesuit professors teaching at the college in Goa. One charitably presumes that Valignano had no hand in its composition. Nor do we know how fluently and smoothly Martin delivered his speech, although it is surely remarkable that a teenage Japanese was capable of such an accomplishment.

The text of Martin's speech was printed on the press that the party had brought back from Europe, and thus was the first product in the list of books and pamphlets issuing from the famed Jesuit Press. It was no mean feat to have unpacked the press in Goa, get it into working order, and then set up the type to print the document, before dismantling and repacking the machinery prior to setting out on the next leg of the voyage back to Japan. This procedure would later be repeated in Macao, where two substantial books were printed.

As regards the pamphlet containing Martin's text, the title page bears a large Jesuit seal, and then the statement (in Latin): 'Produced by Constantine Dourado, a Japanese, in the Jesuit house.' So not only was the Latin speech delivered by a Japanese, but it was also printed by a Japanese, for both Constantine and Brother George Loyola had taken advantage of their stay in Lisbon to learn the art of printing. Another Jesuit, the Italian Giovanni Battista Pesce, had accompanied the party back from Europe and after studying the art of printing at Goa, made an invaluable contribution when the press was finally established in Japan.[15]

Towards the end of the stay in Goa, Valignano received letters from Japan informing him of Hideyoshi's kind treatment of the missionaries. Just as Nobunaga had personally shown a group of Jesuits around his Azuchi Castle, so, too, had his successor Hideyoshi guided another party through his great Osaka Castle, chatting with them affably and displaying every sign of benevolence. The reports went on to suggest that the Viceroy of India might care to show his gratitude by sending the ruler an official letter of thanks and appreciation together with a suitable gift. Meneses was agreeable, and presents and an ornately decorated letter written on parchment were prepared. Valignano had finished his term of office as Jesuit superior in India and was now free to accompany the party back to Japan in his renewed capacity as Visitor. The viceroy decided, therefore, to appoint him as his ambassador to deliver the letter and gifts, a decision that the Jesuits later regarded as providential.[16]

Writing from Goa on 1 December 1587, to his benefactor Theotonio de Bragança in Evora, Valignano acknowledges the archbishop's long letter written on 20 March of the same year. He reports that the boys arrived in Goa on 29 May after experiencing perils both before Mozambique, where they wintered, and after. The viceroy in Goa has presented them with four fine Arabian horses. He, Valignano, would embark with them for Japan in April, together with Jesuits destined for the mission. The boys would do much good work using their native language, 'for in Europe they were greatly impeded in expressing their ideas for they did not know the language.'[17] The writer laments the loss of the *Santiago*, carrying bolts of rich silk and gold for vestments and decoration of churches that Dom Theotonio had presented to the party.

Good news had arrived from Japan, Valignano continues. In Bungo alone 15,000 people were baptized in 1585–6, and more than 40,000 were preparing to receive the sacrament. As regards the boys, Valignano mentions they have shown him the letters written to each of them by the archbishop in his own hand, and promises they will reply to him soon.[18]

Carrying the gifts received during their stay in Goa as well as those during their travels in Europe, and the invaluable printing press, the party finally left India on 22 April 1588, accompanied by a contingent of seventeen Jesuits destined for the Japanese mission. Also on board were two of the four Arabian horses which Valignano, the viceroy's ambassador, planned to present to Hideyoshi. Doubtless the Japanese would have preferred to take with them all four steeds, one for each boy, but, as it was, transporting even two large horses in a crowded ship and in hot weather raised considerable problems of stabling and feeding, and not a few grumbles were heard on board criticizing the transport of even the two horses. According to one report, a veterinarian, a riding master and a farrier were employed at considerable cost to care for the horses.[19]

But within a few days of the departure from Goa, more serious problems arose than coping with the horses, for the ship strayed off course and was sailing through waters only five or six fathoms deep. No sooner had this danger been avoided than yet another peril was experienced, for the vessel came dangerously close to large rocks and a collision with these would have ended in disaster. But once again this fate was narrowly averted and the voyage continued. The passage to Malacca took seventy days to complete, twice the usual length of time, and the boys stopped there for only twelve days, staying in the Jesuit college. The next stage to Macao lasted twenty-nine days; en route the ship ran into further danger when it approached shallows and rocks, but again managed to avoid these obstacles, finally reaching Macao on 17 August 1588.

With favourable winds the final Macao-Nagasaki stage of the voyage from Europe could be made in less than three weeks and doubtless the Japanese were already looking forward to their imminent arrival home and rejoining their families and friends. Alas for their hopes, they were about to face yet another extended delay of almost two years, caused not only by unfavourable weather conditions this time, but also by recent political developments in Japan.

Both Mancio and Michael sent letters to Rome during their stay in Macao. After recounting the perils they experienced on the voyage from India, they tell of the bad news they received on their arrival in Macao: Francisco of Bungo and Bartholomew of Ōmura, two of the three daimyo they had represented in Europe, had died during their absence. Further, Toyotomi Hideyoshi, virtual ruler of the country, had begun an anti-Christian persecution, ordering missionaries to leave Japan. In his letter to the archbishop of Evora, written in Goa and cited above, Valignano had reported nothing but good news from Japan, for at that time he, like the boys, was unaware of recent developments that had completely changed the fortunes of the church in that country.

As mentioned above, Hideyoshi had followed the example of his predecessor Nobunaga, and had shown himself affable in his dealings with the missionaries, personally conducting a group around his Osaka Castle in 1586. He had also entertained Gaspar Coelho, the mission superior, at Hakata in July 1587 during the ruler's tour of inspection of Kyushu. But within hours of their meting he had abruptly issued a proclamation ordering all missionaries to leave the country for, he asserted, their teaching ran contrary to the traditional religion of Japan. When it was pointed out that it was impossible logistically for all of them to board the Portuguese ship in

Nagasaki harbour, he flew into a rage, threatening to kill any who were left behind and any who tried to enter the country in the future.

The reason for this dramatic volte-face has been widely discussed, but was probably the result of Coelho's interference in domestic politics by rashly offering Portuguese shipping to help the ruler in his military campaigns. Hideyoshi may well have reasoned that if the Europeans were prepared to help him in this way, then it was quite possible for them also to provide aid to his enemies in the future. The ruler's threat to expel or even execute missionaries, however, was probably not intended to be taken too seriously but simply as a warning to the Europeans not to stray into domestic politics.[20]

In the event only three Jesuits left Japan for Macao (and they went there to receive ordination to the priesthood), while the rest continued their work as discreetly and unobtrusively as possible. But the tense and changed situation placed Valignano in a quandary. Ironically, he was carrying a letter from the viceroy of India thanking Hideyoshi for his kindness to the Christian enterprise at a time when the ruler was making wild threats against the missionaries. Also, Hideyoshi was well aware of Valignano's identity as a Jesuit priest and might well forbid his return to Japan. It was at this point that his appointment as the viceroy's ambassador was seen as providential, for Valignano could ask permission to re-enter Japan in that diplomatic capacity. Doubtless, Hideyoshi and his ministers would fully realize the ploy, but might well overlook his clerical status in order to receive the embassy.

The annual Portuguese ship had already left for Nagasaki before Valignano and his party reached Macao, but advance notice of the Visitor's plan had been received and the Captain-Major had promised to look into the possibility of Hideyoshi not only allowing Valignano to return to Japan but also granting him, as ambassador, an audience.

Meanwhile, the party was obliged to remain in Macao with all patience. The piety of the boys impressed the local Jesuits, one of whom reported they lived like religious and might well enter the Jesuit order on their return to Japan, as in fact they did. They had not wasted, he adds, the time during their journey for they had diligently practised playing harp, lute, clavier and rebec,[21] and in the evening of the feast of the Circumcision (6 January) they performed a concert in the church. Mesquita also reported to Rome that his charges were continuing their studies in Macao, singling out Mancio for special praise, and he, too, mentions their diligence in practising instrumental music.[22]

An objective assessment of the boys' musical skill is not possible, but they had practised in their Arima school in Japan and also during their lengthy voyages to and from Europe.[23] It will also be recalled that Mancio and Michael had played on the cathedral organ at Evora, and there is no reason to doubt that they had reached an acceptable standard of musical ability. They also gave at least two musical performances on their return to Japan.

The enforced delay in Macao enabled the printing press to be put to good use, and two substantial volumes were produced, the first appearing in the same year as the party arrived at the port.[24] It also gave the indefatigable Valignano time to compile the first draft of his *Apología* in January 1598, and he later revised the text in Japan.[25]

Friendly officials in Japan were contacted to sound out Hideyoshi's reaction to the proposed visit, and eventually the ruler agreed to meet Valignano in his capacity as ambassador. News of his decision was relayed back to Macao, but as there was no ship leaving for Japan in 1589 as the Captain Major, Jerónimo Pereira, had died, Valignano and the party were obliged to wait until the following year before they could embark.[26]

On 23 June 1590, the party finally sailed from Macao in the ship of Henrique da Costa. In addition to Valignano, the boys, Mesquita and Constantine Dourado, fourteen Jesuits joining the Japanese mission were also on board. Missing, however, was Brother George Loyola, who had died in Macao on 16 August in the previous year. This final stage of the long journey to Europe and back ended on 21 July 1590, when the ship weighed anchor in Nagasaki harbour. Mancio, Michael, Martin and Julian had been away for eight years and five months. Their travels abroad had at last ended.

■ CHAPTER 17

Reception in Japan

The arrival of the boys in Nagasaki caused a considerable stir, for they were the first Japanese to visit Europe and then return to their native land to tell their tale. As noted earlier, two of the three daimyo whom they had represented on their travels had died during their absence: Ōmura Sumitada on 25 May 1587, and Ōtomo Sōrin on 28 June a month later. But within a day of the party's arrival the new daimyo Ōmura Yoshiaki came to the port by ship accompanied by his brothers and other family members.[1] On the following day Arima Harunobu (Protasius) reached Nagasaki with his younger brother Leo. Michael was unwell, so Harunobu, one of the two daimyo he had represented, went to his cabin and talked with him for several hours.[2] Having heard a preliminary account of their travels, the daimyo observed that he now regretted that Leo, who was the same age as Michael, had not accompanied the party to Europe. Some other daimyo and nobles, unable to come in person, sent messages of welcome.

Along with other Christians, the families of the boys arrived to greet the travellers on their return to Japan, and Fróis notes that they and their friends could hardly recognize the travellers. Michael's mother did not recognize her son, nor did Martin's parents recognize him; to add to this catalogue, Julian's sisters did not recognize their brother, while Mancio's mother arrived from Hyūga a little later, and did not recognize him.[3] Fróis's account may perhaps contain a measure of hyperbole, yet possibly does not stray too far from the truth. For at their departure from Japan, the boys were

152

young inexperienced teenagers, but they returned more than eight years later as widely travelled and mature young men in their early twenties. Valignano remarks: 'They have come back so changed from what they were before that they really seem like Europeans', possibly an exaggeration, but in any case hardly an ideal transformation if true.[4]

Although feeling indisposed, Valignano lost no time in contacting two friendly daimyo, Kuroda Yoshitaka and Asano Nagamasa, asking for their help to arrange an audience with Hideyoshi in his capacity as ambassador of the Viceroy of India. The two expressed their willingness to intervene, but as they were on a military campaign and away from court, they suggested he would be well advised to delay his visit to Kyoto so that they could personally be present and facilitate arrangements. This waiting period was utilised by Valignano to pay courtesy visits with the boys to the daimyo of the nearby territories of Ōmura and Arima. At the latter place, Harunobu had recently completed a castle residence and the visitors were much impressed by its splendour. The boys (if we may continue to call them 'boys') also took advantage of the delay by meeting and talking with Japanese, Christian and non-Christian alike, who were obviously curious to learn about their expedition, and doubtless the returned travellers enjoyed recounting their experiences to the attentive listeners.

The boys were also able to show at least some of the gifts they had brought back with them. These included a portrait of the archduchess of Tuscany and a painting of the funeral of Emperor Charles V, father of Philip II; they also exhibited illustrated books concerning Rome and Montserrat. The realism of the paintings and illustrations produced considerable wonder.[5] In addition, they could show the volumes of Braun's *Civitates Orbis Terrarum*, as well as Ortelius's atlas of world geography, which they had received in Padua.[6] The world maps, although not accurate by modern standards, would have come as a revelation to the onlookers, who had little idea of the non-Asian world. Some of the viceroy's fine gifts to be presented to Hideyoshi as well as European coins were also shown to selected visitors. These included the Arabian horse[7] and two fine suits of Milanese armour. These sessions fulfilled to some extent one of Valignano's purposes in organising the legation, for the Japanese were now hearing from their own countrymen firsthand reports of the cultural glories of Renaissance Europe, and would no longer have to rely on foreigners' possibly exaggerated accounts.

In late November, word was received from court that Valignano could proceed to Kyoto and in early December a group of twenty-six men set out. Because of winter conditions and difficulty in finding accommodation en route, the party split into two groups. Mesquita, the boys and some Portuguese merchants travelled by sea, while Valignano, five Jesuits and nine laymen journeyed overland.[8] Strictly speaking, the boys' mission to Europe had ended with their return to Japan, but Valignano included them in his party as doubtless the appearance of the much-travelled foursome would create no little wonder in the capital and add to the embassy's prestige. The visit to Kyoto would also enable the boys to speak about their first-hand experience of Europe while at Hideyoshi's court, again fulfilling one of the objectives of the legation.

The two parties met up at Shimonoseki in the south of Honshu island and then spent five days on a voyage through the Inland Sea. At the port of Muro they remained for no less than two months awaiting further instructions. Again this delay was not wasted as Valignano and the boys received a constant succession of distinguished visitors on their way to or from court to offer New Year congratulations to Hideyoshi. These included Mōri Terumoto (daimyo of Hiroshima and Yamaguchi), Kuroda Nagamasa (Fukuoka), and Sō Yoshitomo (Tsushima), and these lords conversed with the boys and listened appreciatively to their playing European music. As far as meeting influential people was concerned, the delay at Muro at that particular time of the year could not have been more providential.

Among these daimyo was also Ōtomo Yoshimune, 1558–1605, son and heir of Francisco, whom Mancio had represented in the mission to Rome. It will be recalled that on their arrival at Nagasaki, the boys had been met by the daimyo of Arima and Ōmura, but the records do not mention any representative from Bungo. While it is true that Bungo was far further distant from the port than were Arima and Ōmura, there was another reason for this non-appearance. Yoshimune had been baptised as Constantine in 1587 and on the death of his father Francisco in the same year he had inherited the fief of Bungo. But Yoshimune appears to have fallen away from his faith and had even ordered the execution of some Christians, and in Valignano's view it would be completely inappropriate to present to him the papal greetings and honours addressed to his late father.

Possibly to the surprise of the party Yoshimune appeared at Muro, and instead of confronting the imposing Valignano directly he followed the Japanese custom of employing an intermediary, none other than Mancio, his late father's ambassador. Yoshimune had apparently had a change of heart and begged Mancio to intercede on his behalf with Valignano. Mancio listened to his account, questioned him closely, and, satisfied by his sincerity, brought about a reconciliation between Valignano and the repentant daimyo. In his gratitude Yoshimune offered to allow missionaries to work in his territory, and invited Mancio to enter his service. Mancio's assessment of the daimyo's sincerity proved correct, for in his subsequent exile and poverty Yoshimune remained true to his Christian faith.[9]

Finally, news was received from the capital for the embassy to proceed, and the party set out for Kyoto on about 22 February. During their brief stay in Osaka, they were greeted by the outstanding Christian daimyo Takayama Ukon (Justus) and his father Darius. On reaching the capital, Valignano and his companions were housed in one of Hideyoshi's mansions, while Mesquita and the boys stayed as guests of the Christian daimyo Konishi Yukinaga; the rest of the retinue was lodged nearby. Final preparations were made with regard to the viceroy's gifts to be presented to Hideyoshi. In addition to the Milanese armour and the horse, these included a pair of large swords and muskets, a military campaign tent, gilt tapestries and a clock; in accordance with Japanese custom, these gifts, apart from the Arabian stallion, were sent ahead to the court.

On the morning of 3 March 1591, the party set out in solemn and colourful procession for Hideyoshi's Jurakutei palace.[10] As the cavalcade passed slowly through the streets of the capital, large crowds gathered to watch the unusual spectacle of a European procession. In fact, soldiers lining the route had to use force to push back the curious spectators in order to clear the way – a measure that may well have brought back to the boys memories of their European experiences.

The procession was led by two richly-dressed Portuguese on horseback escorting the Arabian stallion, attended by two Indian grooms. The horse attracted much attention, as Valignano had foreseen; Japanese horses were sturdy, it is true, but much smaller in size.[11] Behind rode seven other pages, followed by the four boys, or by this time young men, wearing their black velvet robes edged with gold, personally presented to them by the pope. Then came Valignano, Mesquita and another Jesuit, Antonio Lopes, dressed in black cassocks and carried in litters; they were followed by the interpreters João Rodrigues and Ambrosio Fernandes.[12] The procession was concluded by a dozen Portuguese riding on horseback.[13]

This was to be João Rodrigues's first meeting with Hideyoshi and was an event of some significance, for, remarkably fluent in Japanese, the young Jesuit attracted the ruler's attention and subsequently came to know him well; Rodrigues in fact visited the prostrate Hideyoshi only a week or so before the ruler's death seven years later.[14]

The party finally reached Hideyoshi's palatial Jurakutei (Mansion of Delights), about which contemporaneous Japanese records speak ecstatically of its towers shining like stars in the sky and its roof tiles roaring in the wind like golden dragons. The residence had been completed in 1587, less than four years earlier, and a broad avenue linked it to the imperial palace. One year after its construction, Hideyoshi had been honoured by a four-day visit by Emperor - Go-Yōzei and former Emperor Ōgimachi and their large entourages, and had lavished costly gifts and entertainment on his royal guests. It was rare, indeed entirely unprecedented, for an emperor to pay such a visit on a man who had been born of obscure peasant stock, but then Hideyoshi strove to cultivate relations with the imperial court in order to confirm and strengthen his political supremacy.[15]

On his arrival at the palace, Valignano was greeted by Hidetsugu, Hideyoshi's 22-year-old nephew and heir presumptive, and other ranking officials. Few could have foreseen on that auspicious day that within four years the volatile Hideyoshi would order his nephew to commit ritual suicide and then publicly execute his family and household staff, a tragic instance of the aging ruler's increasing paranoia about safeguarding the succession of his son, Hideyori, born in 1593.[16]

The visitors were ushered into the audience chamber, where Hideyoshi was seated on a raised platform, with daimyo and other nobles assembled in lower positions. Valignano bowed low, advanced, and formally presented the viceroy's letter, enclosed in a handsome casket covered with green velvet and lined with gold silk. The richly-decorated document, dated April 1588 and addressed to

'Quambacudono' (that is, *kampaku-dono*, a title assumed by Hideyoshi in 1586), was personally signed 'Viceroy of India' by Meneses.[17] The text was first read aloud in Portuguese and then in Japanese translation. Valignano, the envoys and the Portuguese then bowed three times.

It was not a little ironic that Meneses's letter thanked the ruler for his great kindness to the missionaries, when only a few years earlier Hideyoshi had issued an expulsion edict that was still, at least in theory, in effect. But if the irony was apparent, and it could hardly have not been obvious, it was diplomatically not mentioned in the audience.

Then followed the ceremony of *sakazuki*, in which toasts were exchanged. Hideyoshi took a sip of *sake* wine, and then sent the cup to Valignano to drink from, a signal honour which the ruler did not always extend to his guests. Attendants then carried in gifts for the visitors. Valignano received two trays, on each of which were piled a hundred bars of silver, as well as a third tray bearing four silk robes. The boys and the Portuguese participants each received five bars and a robe. Hideyoshi had some courtiers express his pleasure at the arrival of the embassy and his thanks to Valignano for the viceroy's gifts. He then retired from the chamber, leaving his nephew to act as host in the banquet that followed.

Eight small tables were placed in front of each guest, and the meal was conducted in complete silence with much solemnity but little festivity. Fróis bleakly relates: 'Everyone ate very little and drank even less.'[18] It must have come as a relief when the meal was concluded and in strolled Hideyoshi dressed quite informally. With Rodrigues as interpreter, he chatted amicably with Valignano, and then talked to the four Japanese who had returned from Europe, plying them with questions about their experiences. He spoke at length with Mancio, noting that he had restored one of his relatives as daimyo of Hyūga and inviting the young man to stay at his court.

This was an awkward invitation, for Mancio and his three companions had already applied to enter religious life and become members of the Society of Jesus. But Mancio was worthy of the occasion, telling Hideyoshi diplomatically that he regarded Valignano as his father and it would be unfilial to leave him, even to enter the ruler's service. Hideyoshi accepted his answer in good part and did not persist in his invitation.[19]

Hideyoshi then asked Michael whether he was related to the house of Arima. This was a delicate matter in view of ruler's relations with the daimyo of Kyushu, and Michael dissembled by saying he was from Chijiwa. Hideyoshi was not satisfied with this reply and further inquired in which fief was Chijiwa located, and Michael was obliged to admit that it was in Arima. The ruler then asked whether Michael was a relative of the daimyo of Arima, to which the boy replied vaguely he believed his father was a relative of Lord Arima. Fortunately, the host did not press the point and passed to other matters.[20]

Next came the boys' recital of Western music,[21] for the ever-imaginative Valignano must have foreseen the possibility of such a musical interlude and had arranged for the instruments to be carried to the palace. The boys also sang Western songs in harmony, but not wishing to take up too much of the ruler's time, they ended their recital, only to have Hideyoshi, apparently greatly pleased by their efforts, demand three encores. He then took each of the instruments in his hands and asked questions about them.

At the conclusion of the musical interlude, the military tent, one of the viceroy's gifts, was erected in a courtyard and a Portuguese showed off the Arabian stallion in the garden for all to admire. Hideyoshi then personally inspected the gifts of European weapons and questioned Mancio and Rodrigues about their use. Finally, two courtiers were told to show the party around the palace, and the visitors were overcome as they admired the decorated apartments, the verandas of highly-polished wood, and the beautiful gardens. At the end of their tour Hideyoshi appeared once more to bid farewell to the visitors. He told Valignano he could stay wherever he wished, but asked that Rodrigues remain behind in Kyoto. The ruler, in fact, invited the young Jesuit that same afternoon to return to the palace and there talked with him until late at night.

On the following day, Rodrigues and Mancio were summoned back to the palace to find a perplexed Hideyoshi trying to regulate the clock he had received from the viceroy. The two visitors spent most of the day there, with the ruler talking about his grandiose plans to invade and conquer China. He again invited Mancio to enter his service, and again the young man managed to decline the offer gracefully.

Valignano's embassy to Hideyoshi had been successfully concluded, but there remained one last duty for the youthful legates to perform. After their return to Nagasaki, the party made its way in May to Arima to present to Harunobu the papal gifts they had brought back from Rome. A sung Mass was celebrated and then Michael handed over the presents: a lignum crucis, a duke's hat, a sword and the papal letter, after which Valignano and the four boys attended a banquet in the castle. Valignano then left Arima, but the youngsters remained for a week of festivities. Harunobu invited Michael to enter his service, but, like Mancio before him, the young man declined the offer.

The boys then travelled to Ōmura to report to Ōmura Yoshiaki, and in the same way presented the papal gifts to him.[22] The daimyo of Arima and Ōmura duly had letters drawn up, and these were sent, together with Portuguese translations provided by the Jesuits, to the pope, Philip II, and Cardinal Henry, thanking them for their kindness shown to the Japanese legates. The boys themselves also wrote letters to the same personages, as well as various cardinals and nobles, announcing their safe return to Japan and expressing their gratitude. Although these letters and copies were sent by three different routes, the ships carrying them were all lost at sea, and so the documents never reached their destinations.[23]

The mission to Europe had now come to an end. The legates had survived the long and hazardous voyages to and from Europe, visited most of the leading cities of Portugal, Spain, and Italy, lived for months in Goa and Macao, met two popes, a future pope, Philip II and his family, and scores of political and religious figures. As members of Valignano's entourage, they had also been received in formal audience by Toyotomi Hideyoshi, the virtual ruler of all Japan.

But it would surely be unfortunate to leave the former envoys and their companions at this juncture without recounting what was to befall them in later years. Their subsequent careers will be recounted in Appendix 1, while the sources on which our knowledge of their expedition is based are discussed in Appendix 2; finally, Appendix 3 will deal with some of the books brought back from Europe. But first one last chapter is needed to enquire why the Japanese legates were received with such enthusiasm in Europe and to evaluate the success (or otherwise) of their mission.

Part 7

Summing Up

■ CHAPTER 18

Assessment of the Enterprise

The enterprise was over: the audiences, receptions and banquets were past history; the church bells had long ceased to peal in the boys' honour; the cannon no longer fired in salute, and it is now time to step back and consider the legation as a whole. To judge, assess and quantify the success or failure of an ambitious project such as the expedition to Europe is no easy task. People's criteria, judgement values and assessment of success are liable to differ. More than four centuries after the event under discussion, how should we evaluate this imaginative enterprise? The modern reader has, of course, the advantage of four centuries of hindsight and so is able to judge the long-term results in light of later events. On the other hand, it is unfair to use twenty-first-century criteria to assess the sixteenth-century project.

Be that as it may, we do know Valignano's purpose for organizing and sending the envoys to Europe, and it is permissible to discuss whether or not his objectives were accomplished, and to what degree, in Europe and later in Japan. Writing to Rome in March 1613, Mesquita speaks enthusiastically about the good work done by Mancio, Martin and Julian, declaring: 'they have fulfilled the purpose of their expedition [to Rome]'.[1] The writer's praise is understandable for doubtless the three acquitted themselves creditably in their later careers, but to obtain a more objective assessment of the legation's success, it is necessary to bear in mind the original objectives of the European journey; here we are on firm ground as Valignano more than once clearly articulated his reasons for organizing the legation. The fact that all four boys survived the lengthy and dangerous journey can perhaps be regarded as one of the enterprise's successes. This observation is not made flippantly, for if one or more of the travellers had died en route (two of them fell ill in Europe, and the dangers involved in ocean voyages have already been recounted), then the legation would certainly not have been regarded as a success.

It will be recalled that the two main purposes of Valignano's ambitious venture were to make Japan better known in Europe and thus gain more recruits and financial support for the Japanese mission, and, secondly, to make Europe, its religion and culture, better known and appreciated in Japan through the eye-witness reports of Japanese who had been there and could report at first hand.

Reception in Europe

As regards the first objective, there can be little doubt that the envoys introduced Japan to Europe in a dramatic, albeit non-permanent, way. As Donald Lach observes: 'That the legates put Japan on the map for most Europeans is beyond doubt.'[2] They attracted enormous attention in the three countries they visited, and appear to have made a favourable impression on heads of state and religious leaders. Fróis's enthusiastic and optimistic account in this regard should perhaps be regarded with a certain caution, but other contemporaneous reports on the whole bear out the validity of his version.

If confirmation is required to support the legation's impact, then we may note that nearly eighty books, treatises and pamphlets were published about the Japanese either during or soon after their European tour. These publications were not limited to the three countries they visited, for accounts appeared in various languages and in other countries and cities, such as Douai, Germany, Paris, Bohemia and Prague, although admittedly most of the publications originated in Spain and Italy; more than half are dated 1585, the very same year of the boys' visit.[3] This impressive list of publications surely indicates that the fame of the legation was not limited to the three countries they visited, nor in fact to Catholic circles. One report lamented that the Japanese had no opportunity of experiencing the work of the reformed church in Germany.[4] Whether or not this generally favourable impression left in Europe was lasting and permanent, there can be no doubt that the fame of the envoys spread far and wide at the time, and drew attention to Japan.

Further, the legation aroused interest and devotion among Jesuits in Europe, for we read that many of them who met the boys volunteered for the Japanese mission. It is likely that not all who offered their services were allowed to embark for Asia as the Society of Jesus had numerous commitments in Europe requiring a constant replenishment of manpower, but nevertheless the boys' presence in Europe undoubtedly aroused added interest in the Japanese mission.

How to account for the boys' enthusiastic reception in Europe? Popular reaction can perhaps be easily explained. Europeans had heard of Marco Polo's mysterious and remote island of Zipangu at the other side of the globe, as well as Xavier's heroic labours in that country, and here for the first time they could view with their own eyes the 'princes' of that land clad in their exotic robes. The Other invariably attracts attention and curiosity, and so in reverse but similar fashion the Japanese were fascinated by the so-called *nambanjin*, or Southern Barbarians. Contemporaneous Japanese screens depict Europeans in their colourful costumes playing musical instruments and languidly conversing in rustic scenes; European knights, battles (even in one screen a colourful rendition of the battle of Lepanto), and weapons are also seen. Just as immense crowds flocked to see the boys passing through European cities, so, too, did Valignano's procession through the streets of Kyoto in 1591 attract many spectators.[5] Just as Philip II and others asked the boys about life in Japan, so Nobunaga and Hideyoshi questioned missionaries about life in Europe. Just as the boys' Japanese robes were copied on at least one occasion in Europe, so in the 1590s there was a craze for European dress in Japan, so much so that Fróis tells us that the tailors at Nagasaki had to work around the clock to satisfy demand.[6]

But there was perhaps an additional factor that served to increase European curiosity. Reference has been made above to the Other, which inevitably attracts attention precisely because it is different. But in the case of the boys their identity was further complicated for it constituted an Other that was remarkably similar to the beholders. Up to that time books had been decorated by imaginary illustrations of monstrous beings inhabiting the distant unexplored regions of Asia, and these quasi-human beings were most emphatically the Other, clearly different from the people who had the good fortune to dwell in civilized Europe.[7] Even when exploration of Africa and Asia failed to discover these grotesque creatures, the peoples of those regions could certainly be identified with the Other as regards their features, complexion, religion, language and customs.

During this period of Iberian exploration and colonial expansion the city of Lisbon, with its port dealing in international commerce, had witnessed the arrival of Asian and African sailors and servants/slaves, but few of these men, if any, would be educated and cultured, and many would not have spoken a European language with any fluency. Now these Japanese boys were from the furthest regions of Asia; their features were certainly not European, and so they were definitely the Other. But in many respects they were the non-Other as well. For the most part they wore European clothes, they spoke passable Portuguese, they studied Latin, they played European musical instruments, they appear to have been educated and well-mannered, and doubtless their many meetings with two popes and Philip II, with counts and cardinals (and even dancing with the archduchess of Tuscany), had given them a certain air of maturity and sophistication. Savages from darkest Asia they were certainly not.

Perhaps the most striking feature of their similarity with Europeans was the boys' display of intense religious piety that was readily observed on many occasions. But they did not worship the alien and pagan deities of the Other, and in fact they were probably more devout in the practice of their Christian faith than were many of the European onlookers. Here, then, was the paradox: they were the Other, but also the non-Other, and thus they brought home to any perceptive mind proof of a somewhat startling, if not disconcerting, discovery – that people inhabiting distant parts of the world, which until recently had experienced little or no contact with Europe, could be just as human, just as civilized, just as cultured, just as Christian, as anyone living in Rome, Madrid or any other part of Europe. It was a salutary lesson, though possibly few were sufficiently perceptive to grasp its underlying significance.

But whatever its cause or causes, such exaggerated curiosity is invariably short-lived, and once the attraction of novelty has dissipated, so, too, enthusiasm rapidly wanes. By their nature fads never survive for long, although some vestiges of interest may continue to linger. But even when enthusiasm faded, as it inevitably did once the boys had returned to their country, European interest in Japan and its people had surely been stimulated and increased, if only for a limited period.

But the popular enthusiasm for the legation would never have reached such heights had not European rulers, both ecclesiastical and secular, gone out of their way to honour the Japanese. In the religious sphere, the Catholic church had suffered grievous setbacks during the Reformation. In the pontificate of Gregory XIII alone Rome had lost England and Sweden, and the church was on the defensive. But the reported rapid growth of Christianity in distant Japan gave reason for hope and optimism; the gains in Japan would offset the losses in Europe. This point is explicitly made in Gonçalves's speech during the boys' solemn papal audience: through Gregory the Great's efforts, England had been converted; now through Gregory XIII's efforts Japan would join the Catholic fold. The piety of these four Asian boys from the other side of the globe – their attending daily Mass, receiving Communion, reciting their prayers, offering homage to the pope, venerating countless relics – was surely proof positive of the bright prospects of the church in Asia. There was, therefore, every reason for the authorities in Rome to welcome the Japanese and shower them with favours and gifts.

The response of the secular authorities was perhaps not so clear-cut and was complicated by a variety of factors, one of which was related to the Church. The three countries through which the boys travelled were Catholic and the pope exerted considerable but varying degrees of influence in each of them. The newly-elected Sixtus V was known for his reforming zeal and strong personality (witness his drastic dealings with brigands), and when word spread that he had shown great favour to the Japanese, there was every reason for the civil authorities throughout the regions to follow his example and extend a similar welcome.

The visit to Venice is a case in point, for that republic staged a particularly elaborate reception for the Japanese, but, as Boscaro points out, the state had no particular interest in developing trade with Japan. But only a dozen years earlier the republic had infuriated Rome by concluding a separate peace treaty with the Turks after the battle of Lepanto,[8] and the boys' visit provided Venice with a convenient opportunity for mending fences. The new pope sent a brief to Venice expressly asking that a welcome be extended to the Japanese;[9] he himself had favoured the visitors, and so Venice, too, would do likewise. This policy is clearly stated in the Venetian authorities' instructions sent to nearby Chioggia. As the Japanese 'have been greatly favoured and honoured by His Holiness and by all the Roman court, we likewise want to offer them an appropriate demonstration of kindness and honour'.[10]

There was also a healthy spirit of competition and rivalry between the cities and states that made up Italy at that time. It must be borne in mind that these regions, although sharing a common language, did not form a unified state as we know Italy today and were often at odds with one and other; indeed, some were under Spanish, not Italian, rule. If at that particular time they were not engaged in armed combat, they could show off their power and wealth in a peaceful, but still competitive, manner by lavishing hospitality on these exotic visitors from the East. And once the chain reaction of enthusiasm had been set in motion, it was difficult to keep in check the ever-increasing abundant receptions.

As regards the situation in Portugal and Spain, the sixty-year union of the Spanish and Portuguese thrones began in 1580 after Philip II of Spain had sent troops into Portugal to bolster his claim to the vacant throne. Philip was half-Portuguese by birth and had a strong claim, but rival candidates, especially Dom Antonio de Crato, were more popular with the general public. To appease Portuguese resentment, Philip had promised to maintain Portuguese laws, administration of justice, civil and military offices, and currency, etc., and to keep separate Portuguese and Spanish colonial and commercial interests abroad. According to the terms of the Treaty of Saragossa, 1529, which demarcated the commercial interests of the two Iberian powers in Asia (a treaty, incidentally, drawn up with no consultation with the peoples living in those regions), the Portuguese believed Japan was located in their sphere of interest. As a result, Jesuits, whatever their nationality, who were destined for the Japanese mission were obliged to set sail from Lisbon; during the course of their long sea voyages, they would stop at Goa, Macao and possibly Mozambique and Malacca, all of which were Portuguese possessions. Further, the Portuguese in Macao enjoyed a highly profitable monopoly exchanging Japanese silver for Chinese raw silk.

There is no reason to believe that King Philip and his young family lacked personal interest in the Japanese visitors as well as curiosity about their country, but in the political context the king had a strong motive for showing favour and kindness to the visitors from Japan, a distant nation that, it was claimed, fell in the Portuguese sphere of interest. In doing so, he would be manifestly fulfilling his promises made to the reluctant Portuguese when he had ascended their throne only a few years earlier. Philip II was now the most powerful monarch in Europe, and once he had made public show of his favour towards the boys, the local authorities in his two kingdoms of Spain and Portugal were bound to follow suit.

There are further considerations that may help explain the enthusiasm in Europe. As the two legates, Mancio and Michael, were still teenagers, it must have been evident that they were not ambassadors in the ordinary sense, prepared to enter into complex and delicate negotiations at national level. The boys occupied centre stage, it is true, but only as visitors, and not negotiators, from Japan. There was no question of their conducting any business that might produce friction and argument; their role in this or that locality was more akin to that of honoured house-guests to be entertained royally for a few days and shown the local sights, without any need to enter into diplomatic or commercial discussions. Most of the places they visited had no contact, whether political or commercial, with Japan, and so no serious negotiations were needed or even possible. The more discerning Europeans, such as the Venetian authorities, may well have suspected that the three Japanese barons whom the boys represented were, in faraway Asia, of insignificant importance and power when compared with the immense wealth and authority of Venice, Florence and Milan.

But to please the pope and Philip II (and Philip I of Portugal), why not lay down the red carpet (to employ a modern idiom)? Such hospitality would certainly do no harm in the short term, and perhaps might do some good in the long. And so the Europeans would treat their youthful visitors with generous hospitality, happily free from the intrigues of international politics and any anxiety of making diplomatic faux pas in their discussions, which in all probability the boys would not have completely understood anyway.

There are also personal considerations to be taken into account. Although, as mentioned earlier, there is little in contemporaneous reports to give us much idea about the individual personalities of the foursome, they appear to have been likeable and well-mannered youths who created a good impression wherever they went. The fact these Asian boys had studied European languages and music served to endear them to their hosts, and especially to court ladies. Their genuine Christian piety was also noted with approval by spectators who observed their devotion in churches, especially their veneration of holy relics. They apparently performed their appointed duties admirably well in their exhausting tour of the three countries, and calmly took in their stride the commotion their presence caused in so many places.[11]

As for the general populace, everybody loves a parade, especially if it features a quartet of affable young men who have travelled from the other side of the globe and were sometimes clad in strange and exotic robes. And if the spectacle included scores of gentlemen dressed in all their finery and riding on caparisoned horses, not to mention escorts of guards in their colourful uniforms blowing trumpets and beating drums, all the better. The people of Rome obviously enjoyed such spectacles and the authorities appeared willing to satisfy them. The cavalcade escorting the boys to their first papal audience was almost half a league long, while the procession in which the pope and the Japanese rode to St John Lateran was nearly twice that length. Parades of such magnitude must have entailed a good deal of organization and expense, but for various reasons the authorities believed that these spectacles were worth the considerable effort and perhaps even politically and socially necessary.

And then there were the church bells ringing and the cannons firing in impressive salute. This was rich entertainment and was free for all to enjoy. In those blissful days before the advent of newspapers, magazines, radio, films and television, such a show came as a welcome break in the monotonous daily routine. And on these occasions, it was not unknown for the wealthy to be generous in distributing alms to the less fortunate.[12]

Finance

So much for the popular and successful reception of the boys in Europe, but it is now necessary to study the long-term results of their expedition. Valignano hoped that as a result of making Japan better known in Europe, the mission's chronic financial problems might be eased, if not solved, by establishing a constant source of economic support. Other Christian missions in Asia and Latin America were located in Spanish or Portuguese colonies, and usually received subsidies from the crown to continue and expand their work. Although falling in the so-called Portuguese sphere of interest, far-off Japan was, of course, an independent nation with no possibility of becoming a European colony. As Valignano explains at some length, it was not possible for the mission to be self-supporting.

Certainly many people, both religious and lay, gave generous gifts of money and materials to the boys during their travels, not only in Europe but also in Goa and Mozambique.[13] These probably covered most of their travel expenses, especially as the Japanese usually received free accommodation as honoured guests in Jesuit residences or in palaces.[14] Some of the items brought back to Japan were of considerable value, especially in view of their novelty. The gifts presented to Hideyoshi in 1591 came from the viceroy of India and did not place a burden on mission funds.

As regards long-term financing of the mission, Gregory XIII promised a regular endowment, and this was confirmed and increased by Sixtus V; archbishop Bragança of Evora offered funds to inaugurate and maintain a new college in Japan. However, it was one thing to promise these endowments, but another to deliver them.[15] This was not necessarily the fault of the donors or of the recipients. Japan was far from Europe, and the dangers of the lengthy voyage have already been recounted. Time and again the members of the Japanese mission were devastated to learn of the wreck of a Portuguese carrack. Not only were the lives of newly-arriving missionaries lost, but also much-needed supplies, money and the proceeds of their investment in the silk trade perished. At other times the non-receipt of financial aid could not be attributed to shipwreck or natural disasters. Japan was far from Europe and colonial officials may well have been tempted to delay or divert monies intended for the Japanese church.

Despite the tumultuous reception of the Japanese in Europe, it is obvious that Valignano's hopes that the legation would produce a permanent solution to the mission's financial problems were not realized. As noted above, on 13 June 1583, Gregory XIII, in his brief *Mirabilia Dei*, had bestowed an annual income of 4,000 ducats for twenty years and 2,000 ducats in perpetuity; in May 1585 Sixtus V increased, in *Divina Bonitas*, this grant to 6,000 ducats.[16] This benevolence was most gratifying for the missionaries in Japan, but from 1585 to 1603 the annual grant of 6,000 ducats was received only once. Clement VIII suspended this income for four years and in 1602 reduced it to 4,000 ducats.[17]

Only a dozen years after the party's return to Japan, Bishop Luis de Cerqueira in Nagasaki repeatedly approached the pope, the king of Spain, the Jesuit General in Rome, and other Jesuit officials in Europe, begging for financial help to support his seminary and the training of an indigenous clergy, but more often than not his pleas went unheeded. Writing to the pope on 1 January 1603, he observed: 'The Catholic King, it seems, does not deem it his duty to support the servants of the Church in this land, as he provided for those in the East and West Indies.' The bishop had heard that the king had assigned him a yearly stipend of 200 gold crowns: 'But these sums of money the King's officials in India give with very bad grace . . . up to the present none of this money has actually been disbursed to me, though I have written to India for it every year and tried every means possible to get it'.[18]

This non-receipt of promised funds for clerical education was also true of the mission as a whole. According to an official report from Japan dated September 1620, an annual grant of a thousand crowns from the royal treasury was due to be paid via Malacca, 'but nothing has been paid for the past fifteen years'. Four years later, rents due from India should have yielded 3,000 crowns, but a storm had destroyed the properties, and 'for six or seven years there has been little yield'.[19] In 1624, money due from Malacca and Goa 'is very poorly paid'.[20] In addition to non-payment owing to distance and storms, there was always the possibility of military intervention, for example, in July 1603 when a richly-laded carrack was seized by the Dutch on the eve of its departure from Macao en route to Japan, and as a result the Japanese mission suffered grievous financial loss.[21]

By 1611 the mission owed 40,000 *pesos* in Portugal, to say nothing of its debts in Goa, Macao and Japan itself. Valignano had written letter after letter to Europe, pleading for financial assistance,[22] and the Jesuits had no other recourse but to request and obtain permission to participate in the Portuguese silk trade, despite canon law prohibiting clerics from engaging in commerce.

While it is true that little could be done to remedy losses owing to destructive storms, shipwrecks and Dutch marauders, it is evident that promised economic aid from Europe was also being withheld on account of bureaucratic mismanagement, whether deliberate or unintended.[23] Whatever benefits the expedition to Europe may have obtained, the mission's permanent financial security was clearly not one of them.

Jesuit Monopoly

As regards retaining the Jesuit monopoly of missionary work in Japan, Valignano was successful, but only in the short-term. Even before the boys reached Rome, Nuno Rodrigues and other Jesuits had lobbied the Roman curia about this matter, with the result that Gregory XIII issued a brief *Ex pastorali officio* on 28 January 1585, expressly reserving Japan for the Jesuits and forbidding other religious orders from entering the country. In light of this document, King Philip II (of Spain, and Philip I of Portugal) ordered the viceroy of India to see that this directive was duly carried out. The viceroy in turn instructed Domingos Monteiro, the Captain-Major of the Portuguese voyage in 1586, to accept no Spanish friars as passengers to Japan. Valignano had every reason to feel satisfied that one of the legation's objectives had been completely achieved, but this satisfaction was not to last long.

The friars considered the 1585 brief had been issued on the basis of false information, and therefore lacked binding force. In any case, at the end of 1586 Gregory's successor, Sixtus V, issued another brief, *Dum ad uberes fructus*, raising the status of the Franciscan mission in the Philippines and granting the friars permission to establish more houses not only in that country but also 'in other lands and places of the above-mentioned India and kingdoms of China'.[24]

Citing this somewhat vague reference in the second brief, friars, not only Franciscan but also Dominican and Augustinian, later entered Japan and began their apostolic work there. An acrimonious controversy ensued between Jesuits and the mendicant orders, a quarrel far more bitter than Valignano had ever foreseen and which caused much harm and scandal within the Church in Japan. It may be argued that this deplorable state of affairs was the result of the friars' taking advantage of a phrase in the second brief. On the other hand, had the Jesuits not opposed their arrival in the first place, the quarrel would not have arisen.

In 1600 Rome issued yet another brief, *Onerosa pastoralis officii cura*, allowing members of other religious orders to sail to Japan, provided they began their voyage from Lisbon and travelled via Portuguese India. Eight years later this restriction was lifted[25] and other religious orders were free to enter Japan as they pleased. But by that time it was too late, for the Tokugawa regime was soon to begin its anti-Christian persecution.

The Bishop

Yet another, perhaps indirect, result of the legation to Europe may be mentioned here. The Japanese mission had not been elevated to the status of a diocese and as a result had no bishop, although obviously the presence of a bishop would increase the mission's prestige and make it better known. There was also a more practical consideration to the introduction of a bishop, for only he had the power to ordain candidates to the priesthood. Many of the young Jesuits landing in Japan, such as Mesquita, were still students yet to complete their theological studies necessary for ordination. As a result, when the time came for them to be raised to the priesthood, they were obliged to sail to Macao and there receive ordination from the hands of the local bishop. Although the voyage from Nagasaki to Macao was relatively short, there would inevitably be a delay at Macao before favourable winds permitted a return passage to Japan.

As a result, for a religious ceremony lasting two hours or so, the ordinands were obliged to spend four or five months away from the undermanned Japanese mission. Further, sea voyages always involved risk, and the relatively short passage from Nagasaki to Macao and back could involve disaster, as has been noted above regarding the return journey of newly-ordained priests in 1582.

So in February 1588 Sixtus V set up a diocese in Japan by his bull *Hodie Sanctissimus*, thus obviating the need to send ordinands all the way to Macao. Valignano himself had opposed the appointment of a bishop, perhaps fearing that such a move might cause an unseemly clash of authority between the prelate and the Jesuit superior of the mission, although in fact this did not subsequently happen.[26] But Rome, mindful of the boys' visit on behalf of the three Christian 'kings' of Kyushu, believed otherwise. A bishop resident in Japan would not only add prestige and importance to the promising mission, but would also obviate the need of ordinands, Japanese and non-Japanese, to undertake the voyage to Macao.

Sixtus V appointed the first bishop of Japan in early 1587 while the legation was still on its return journey.[27] It is ironic that the embassy organized by Valignano indirectly brought about a result which he himself opposed. Had the legation been allowed to remain on a low key, as the Visitor had planned, and had it not become so publicised throughout Europe, the need for appointing a bishop for Japan might not have been considered so important.

The effects of this appointment were not immediately apparent in Japan, for the first prelate, Sebastian de Moraes, died of fever in Mozambique in August 1588 during his voyage to the Indies. His successor, Pedro Martins, was not able to reach Japan until August 1596, and owing to Hideyoshi's edict of expulsion stayed in the country for less than a year, leaving in the following March. He was replaced by Luis de Cerqueira, his automatic successor, who arrived from Macao in the summer of 1598, and for years did sterling work, ordaining fifteen Japanese candidates to the priesthood, including Mancio, Julian and Martin. He died at Nagasaki in February 1614 on the eve of the Tokugawa-ordered expulsion of missionaries. During this time none of Valignano's fears about the appointment of a bishop was realized.

The Jesuit Press

A positive result of the expedition to Europe may be mentioned here, although it cannot be attributed directly to the legation. The shortage of missionaries in Japan was obvious and made it impossible to preach the gospel throughout the whole country. Yet the standard of literacy in Japan was higher than in most other parts of the missionary world, and even before his first arrival in Japan in 1579, Valignano was thinking of importing a press of movable type to spread the Christian message. His experience during his first stay in Japan served to confirm the wisdom and value of this imaginative plan, and when in 1584 he was obliged to remain in India and not accompany the boys to Rome, he instructed Mesquita and Rodrigues to obtain a press in Europe and bring it back to Asia. This was duly accomplished, and, as noted earlier, within a week of the boys' return to Goa in May 1597, Martin delivered his speech in Latin, the text of which was published by the press later in the same year.

During the party's subsequent extended stay in Macao, two bulky volumes were produced. And once the press started operation in

Japan, it turned out an astonishing variety and quantity of books – devotional and liturgical manuals, a Japanese grammar and dictionary, and even adapted versions of *Aesop's Fables* and the Japanese epic *Heike Monogatari*. In all some thirty-five titles are still extant, although extremely rare, and references to twenty more are found in Jesuit records. When the Tokugawa authorities issued the decree of expulsion of missionaries in 1614, the press was packed up once more and shipped back to Macao, where in 1620 it brought out a revised edition of the Japanese grammar.

It is impossible to enter here into detail about the famous press and the variety of its publications during its twenty-four years of operation in Japan,[28] but there remains another factor linking the press to the European visit. It will be recalled that two Japanese, Constantine Dourado and Brother George Loyola, accompanied the boys on their journey to and from Europe, and they apparently took the opportunity of their stay in Lisbon to study the art of matrix-making and printing. As noted above, Brother George died in Macao on the way back to Japan, but Constantine, having entered the Jesuit order in 1595, did valuable work with the press in Japan for many years. So although the press would likely have been eventually shipped to Japan even had there been no legation sent to Europe, the expedition provided an opportunity for a Japanese to receive expert training in matrix-making and printing in both Lisbon and Goa, enabling him to make a major contribution to the work of the Jesuit Press. Thus the introduction of printing with movable type in Japan may surely be associated, at least indirectly, with the legation and can be counted as one of its positive achievements.

Impact in Japan

Owing to the changed political climate, the success of the legation on its return to Japan is less certain. Valignano's plan was for the envoys and their companions to describe to their fellow countrymen the glory and magnificence of Catholic Europe; and so no longer would the Japanese have to rely solely on Europeans who, it was sometimes alleged, might tend to exaggerate the value of their own culture and religion. There would now be Japanese who had seen with their own eyes the splendour of Europe and could provide first-hand accounts.

While awaiting permission to go up to the capital on their return to Japan, the boys met with friendly daimyo and high-ranking officials, who plied them with questions about their experiences in Europe. As noted above, the procession through the streets of the capital undoubtedly caused a stir, and after Hideyoshi had received the legates in solemn audience in his Jurakutei palace, he questioned them about their experiences abroad. Yet the entrance of the four boys into the Jesuit novitiate in July of that year meant that opportunities for their relating their travels to a wider audience were severely curtailed.[29] Throughout the rest of their lives they doubtless talked about their travels in Europe, yet there does not appear to have been made any organized and concerted effort to allow them relate on a wide scale the European expedition to their countrymen.

This is not to say, of course, that they never referred to the subject. In 1613 Mesquita wrote to Rome reporting Mancio's death, adding that he 'was always talking about such things [the visit to Europe], and in this way he did much good. Fathers Martin and Julian also produce much fruit in this way. Encouraged by the news and sights of the things of Europe, they work effectively in the vineyard of the Lord.'[30]

But considering the boys were the first Japanese to visit Europe and return, to meet two popes and Philip II, to be shown around cathedrals, castles and palaces, there appears to have been little or no systematic effort to put their European experience to best advantage and make known to their fellow countrymen the power and wealth of Europe. In this respect much good could have been accomplished had the Jesuit Press published a readable Japanese account of their travels instead of *De Missione*, a text composed in classical Latin that only a handful of Japanese could read, and even then with considerable difficulty. It is strange that such an opportunity, not difficult to accomplish in view of the voluminous and assorted output of the press and the boys' notes written in the course of their travels, was not taken, for to make Europe better known and appreciated in Japan was one of Valignano's major objectives in organizing the expedition.

Considering the eight years spent in travelling to Europe and back, not to mention the many dangers experienced in the course of these travels, it is difficult to understand why the Jesuits did not make greater efforts to publicise the expedition and publish an easily readable Japanese account of the legation. A printed description would surely have attracted much interest and attention, and might have gained best-seller status. Not only would such a work have made the Jesuit mission better known among the Japanese, but it would also have greatly helped to achieve one of Valignano's objectives, that is, to increase Japanese appreciation of Europe, its people, and its culture.

As a result, little revision of Japanese views concerning Europe, as Valignano had hoped to achieve, can be detected. On 1 December 1587, he had written from Goa that when the boys return home, 'without doubt they will make as much (and more) impact in Japan as they did in Europe'.[31] This optimistic forecast was certainly not realized, and their eight years of travel to and from Europe produced few appreciable results in this regard among the Japanese general public.

So we are left with the difficult question, perhaps impossible to answer in a completely satisfactory way, whether or not the legation can be considered a success and fulfilled the aims for which it had been organized. In some respects, such as its reception in Europe, it certainly achieved some remarkable but short-term results; in other aspects, such as the solution of the mission's financial problems and a change of Japanese attitude towards Europeans, its impact was less impressive.

But it cannot be denied that the expedition put Japan on the map in Europe and led to a better understanding and appreciation of the Asian country. Japan was no longer the mysterious, remote island kingdom described so colourfully by Marco Polo, for many thousands of Europeans had seen and admired the young envoys and had read about them in the spate of publications appearing in different countries during and shortly after their visit.

It is not a little ironic that within a few years of their return the boys' island country would again retire into isolation, this time self-imposed, from which it would not emerge until the middle of the nineteenth century.

Envoi

In 1982, to mark the fourth centenary of the legation's departure from Japan, the Japanese post office issued a somewhat unimaginative stamp to commemorate the event. To further celebrate the anniversary, four Kyushu boys were chosen to reenact the expedition. Like the original four, these boys were accompanied by a Jesuit priest and visited Portugal, Spain and Italy. Like the Japanese boys four hundred years earlier, wearing formal Japanese robes they were received in audience by the pope in Rome, by the king of Spain in Madrid and by the president of Portugal in Lisbon, and speeches were read in Japanese. Like the earlier expedition, the boys went sightseeing in all three cities, as well as in Florence and Toledo.

There was, however, one significant difference between the two missions. Mancio, Michael, Martin and Julian took more than eight years to return to their native country in the sixteenth century. The legation in the twentieth century was back in Japan within thirteen days.[32]

APPENDIX 1

The Boys' Later Careers

Before recounting the subsequent careers of the four main participants in the expedition to Europe, let us deal briefly with the men who accompanied them on their travels, and in the first place, the organizer of the mission.

ALESSANDRO VALIGNANO, 1539–1606, was born into a local aristocratic family in Chieti in the kingdom of Naples, and after obtaining a doctorate in civil law at the University of Padua entered the Jesuit novitiate in May 1556. He continued his studies in Rome and was ordained priest there in March 1570. Valignano's administrative talents were soon recognized, and in 1573 at the age of only thirty-four he was appointed Visitor, or inspector, of the Jesuit missions in Asia. This was a position of considerable authority, for in this capacity he was senior to all the Jesuit superiors of those countries and answerable only to the General Superior of the Society of Jesus in Rome.

In this office Valignano made extended stays in India, Malacca and Macao, and finally arrived in Japan in 1579. He remained there for more than two years, studying the situation and formulating his plans to reorganize the mission, insisting that the Jesuits make greater efforts to adapt to Japanese customs and way of life. Valignano was a giant, both in his exceptional height, which impressed Nobunaga and others, and in his ambitious and imaginative plans for the future of the Japanese mission. A man of strong will, he was sometimes inclined to be critical of others who did not measure up to his own high standards.

As regards the qualities and talents of Valignano, Pedro Gómez, superior of the Jesuit mission in Japan, wrote a glowing account in 1593, testifying to his scholarship, learning, charity, prudence, and other virtues; Luis Fróis, who knew him well, also echoes these praises of the Visitor.[1] There is no reason to doubt the sincerity of these appraisals, yet Valignano could be authoritarian at times and also had his critics. These included the Franciscan friars who strongly opposed his championing the Jesuit monopoly of mission work in Japan, as well as members of his own religious order who viewed with alarm the expenses incurred in some of his more ambitious projects.[2]

As we have seen, Valignano travelled to India in the company of the four boys, and there received instructions to remain in that continent as Jesuit superior. But two years later fresh orders from Rome reappointed him as Visitor of the missions in Asia, enabling him to accompany the legates back to Japan and begin his second visitation, which lasted less than two years. After spending time in Macao and India, Valignano returned to Japan in August 1598 for his third and final visitation, this time as Visitor for only Japan and China. This stay was his longest in Japan and lasted until the beginning of 1603.

Valignano returned to Macao, where he died on 20 January 1606 at the age of sixty-seven.[3]

DIOGO DE MESQUITA, 1553–1614. The European most closely associated with the boys during their travels was undoubtedly Diogo de Mesquita, for he was with them nearly every day of their journey (they were separated for only a few weeks in India), accompanying them as their tutor and mentor in the same ship and sharing with them the dangers of sea voyages. On land he spent days and nights riding with them in coaches through Portugal, Spain and Italy. He acted as interpreter in their meetings with two popes, Philip II, and countless other notable figures. The Jesuit Pedro Morejon attributed the boys' virtue to Mesquita, declaring: 'This was due in great part to the good example and formation given them by Father Diogo de Mesquita.'[4] It is hardly surprising that even after the legation had returned to Japan, he kept in touch with the four travellers and showed a lively interest in their subsequent careers.

Diogo de Mesquita hailed from Meiaofrio in the diocese of Lamego, Portugal.[5] Three years after entering the Jesuit novitiate in Goa in April 1574, he was appointed to Japan. Valignano must have been impressed by the young man for he assigned him the responsible post of the boys' mentor when Mesquita was twenty-nine years of age and had lived in Japan for only five years.[6] Moreover, he was still unordained when he set out from Nagasaki in 1582, and was raised to the priesthood in Macao in the same year.

On his return to Japan, Mesquita was present at the historic audience with Hideyoshi in Jurakutei, as recounted above. He was later appointed Rector of the Jesuit college in Nagasaki, an office which he must have occupied with some success as he held the post for fourteen years. During this time he played an active role in renovating the Jesuit property, adding a new building to the college and enlarging the church; he was also involved in the construction of Santiago Hospital in the city, and references to this enterprise are frequent in his letters to Rome. In 1605 a colleague mildly criticized Mesquita, declaring the Rector was over-fond of putting up new buildings, and moreover spent too much time grafting trees in the garden and raising geese and goats, although both of these laudable activities were for the benefit of the patients in the hospital.

Mesquita esteemed the Japanese highly, and freely expressed his admiration. Writing towards the end of his life, he remarked: 'Certainly as regards helping religions and their missions, I have never yet seen in Europe or in India a nation surpassing the Japanese.'[7] He showed this admiration in a practical way by deploring the repeated postponement of ordination of Japanese Jesuits to the priesthood. With Martin Hara much in mind, Mesquita criticizes the injustice of this practice, and observes:

> Our church here in Nagasaki, and the college, is the largest and most crowded of all Japan . . . but the preachers who ascend the pulpit are usually Japanese Brothers, and they do this with just as much fruit and efficacy as our priests could do. These Brothers give just as good account of themselves as do those of Europe; they know enough Latin, and some have preached for ten or fifteen years; they have shown the same or even more religious spirit, to everyone's satisfaction.
>
> I just don't understand why they are denied what is not denied to others from Europe or India . . . . They deserve to receive the priesthood more than I ever did.[8]

Mesquita's views prevailed and in 1608 three of the four boys were finally ordained priests. He maintained a lively interest in his former pupils until the end of his life. 'I may tell you that the Japanese priests have done very well so far; in particular, the three priests Mancio, Martin and Julian are doing very well and are in good health,' he writes in March 1612. He collaborated with Martin in the work of the Jesuit Press, bringing out a Japanese translation of Luis de Granada's *Símbolo de la Fe*. He notes: 'As he [Martin] is the best interpreter we have in Japan he does excellent work translating spiritual books into the language and script of Japan.'[9]

In January 1614 the Tokugawa authorities issued a decree expelling missionaries from Japan, and although sick and elderly Mesquita was chosen to make a personal appeal to Ieyasu to withdraw the edict. He reached Osaka, and from there sent a message to Suruga, where the former shogun was living in nominal retirement, asking permission to present his case at court. His request was rejected and he was ordered to return to Nagasaki.[10]

There Mesquita begged to remain in Japan and not sail into exile in Macao, and his wish was granted. Too ill to travel further, he spent his last days in a straw-roofed hut on the beach at Nagasaki, where he was visited by colleagues and lay people, who found him joyful and composed.[11] He died there on 4 November 1614, three days before the ships sailed from Nagasaki carrying the missionaries into exile. He was sixty-one years old.

CONSTANTINE DOURADO, c. 1567–1620, was born in Isahaya, Kyushu, and became a catechist (or *dōjuku*) residing in a Jesuit house. Only a little older than the envoys, he was chosen to accompany them as an attendant. Along with Brother George Loyola, Dourado learned how to make matrices while in Europe, and later during his stay in Goa studied the art of printing; this training was soon put to good use as his name appears as printer on the title page of Martin Hara's speech printed in Goa in 1588.[12] He entered the Society of Jesus in October 1595, and taught Latin in the Jesuit college in Arima for many years; he is also listed as instructor of instrumental music. Exiled to Macao in 1614, he was ordained priest in Malacca, probably in 1616, and two years later was appointed Rector of the seminary in Macao, where he died soon after.[13]

Why Jesuit records consistently refer to Constantine by the Portuguese name Dourado is not known. In his account of the

European journey Fróis relates that he was fluent in Portuguese, and quotes verbatim his account of Vila Viçosa written in that language,[14] and it is possible that Constantine's father was Portuguese, although Fróis specifically refers to him as 'one of the Japanese boys' accompanying the expedition.[15] According to the historian Matsuda Kiichi, his Japanese name was Kazariya, 'silversmith' or 'goldsmith', which may be the origin of his Portuguese name.[16] This suggestion has some plausibility, for it would have conveniently distinguished him from two other contemporaneous Japanese Jesuits also named Kazariya: Julian, who entered the order in 1589 and died of illness in December 1601, and Justus, who became a Jesuit in 1590 and was exiled, along with Constantine, to Macao in 1614, and died there in 1629.[17]

GEORGE LOYOLA, c. 1562–1589, also born in Isahaya, became a Jesuit in December 1580. Aged only twenty, he accompanied the envoys to Europe two years later, acting as their tutor in Japanese language and literature. He appears to have studied the art of printing while staying in Lisbon. He died of consumption in Macao, aged about twenty-seven, while Valignano and the envoys were waiting to return to Japan.[18]

AUGUSTINE, along with Constantine, accompanied the party as an attendant, but Fróis makes no further mention of him in *Première Ambassade*. The same is true of the Indian boy who briefly appears in the chapter dealing with the first audience with Philip II.

Let us now recount the subsequent careers of the four principal protagonists of the legation.[19]

MANCIO ITŌ, 1569–1612, as representative of the powerful daimyo of Bungo, was regarded on formal occasions as the senior member of the expedition, and it was he who wrote, or at least signed, letters of thanks to European hosts on behalf of the party for their hospitality.[20] Together with his three companions, he was received by Valignano into the novitiate of the Society of Jesus on 25 July 1591, in Kawachi-no-mura in Amakusa, despite the opposition of his mother.

The official catalogue of Jesuits in Japan, 1590–92, records:

> Don Mancio Itō, Don Michael Chijiwa, Don Martin Hara, and Don Julian Nakaura. After they returned to Japan from Rome, they pre-

sented the gifts that His Holiness had sent through them to the Christian lords of Arima and Ōmura. They accompanied Fr Visitor [Valignano] to the court of Kampaku Dono [Hideyoshi]. They then decided to enter the Society [of Jesus], and after they completed for this reason the spiritual exercises [retreat], all four were received [into the Order] with joy and celebration at the Amakusa college on 25 July [1591], the feast of St James. Some months later in the same year, Justus Itō, nineteen years of age and brother of Don Mancio, was also received, after spending many years in the seminary.[21]

The unsettled conditions of the time forced the novices to disperse to different locations, and the four boys took their first religious vows as Jesuits on 25 July 1593. On 6 March of the following year, Mancio wrote in Portuguese to the Jesuit General in Rome, reporting he and his companions had taken vows and entered the Jesuit order; his letter states that it is 'from Japan', but does not name a specific place.[22] Records show that the four studied scholastic philosophy in Amakusa, under the direction of their former mentor and companion, Diogo de Mesquita.

It is difficult to follow their movements from 1597 when the Amakusa college was closed down. The four perhaps continued their studies elsewhere, or perhaps were dispersed to aid missionaries working in different regions. In 1601 Mancio and Julian, together with fifteen other Jesuit students, sailed to Macao, where they studied theology before returning to Japan in 1604.

There were plenty of Japanese students belonging to the order, and it might be expected that in due course the more talented men would receive ordination and become Catholic priests, empowered to celebrate Mass and administer the sacraments. Yet, unhappily, there were missionaries who opposed this promotion, perhaps fearing that European priests in the mission would be eventually outnumbered by Japanese, a development to be welcomed in modern times but still regarded with suspicion four centuries ago in a country so remote from Europe. The Italian Jesuit Celso Confalonieri advocated waiting fifty years before raising Japanese to the priesthood.[23] Even Valignano, the apostle of missionary inculturation and adaptation, had recommended to Rome shortly before his death in 1606 that requirements for Japanese to receive ordination be considerably tightened.[24]

Despite these objections, in September 1608 Bishop Cerqueira finally raised Mancio, Julian and Martin to the priesthood at

Nagasaki.[25] Fittingly enough, their former mentor, guide, interpreter and advocate was present and took part in the ceremony. Mancio worked in Kokura in Buzen province, and also in Yamaguchi and Hyūga. When the local daimyo expelled missionaries from the area in 1611, Mancio was obliged to retire to Nagasaki, where he died, with Mesquita at his side, on 13 November in the following year at the early age of forty-three.

The texts of several of Mancio's letters, written in either Portuguese or Spanish, are extant, although at least one of them, dated 6 March 1594, and sent to the Jesuit General in Rome, was composed in perfect Spanish, and may well have been dictated, or at least corrected, by a European missionary.[26]

MICHAEL CHIJIWA, 1567–1633, represented the daimyo of Arima and Ōmura during the expedition to Rome. On his return to Japan, he entered the Jesuit novitiate and followed the same course of studies as did Mancio, as listed above, but his subsequent career differed sharply.

Although reliable information is scarce, it appears that Michael may well have been affected by the policy of delaying ordination to Japanese candidates.[27] He did not accompany Mancio and Martin to Macao for further studies in 1601, and his name fails to appear in Jesuit records compiled from 1603. In a letter dated 3 November 1607, Mesquita suggests that studying theology might have saved Michael's vocation. According to another Jesuit writing in 1619, ill-health was the reason for Michael's departure from the order; he served under his cousin Ōmura Yoshiaki, but neither abandoned Christianity nor persecuted Christians.

Other reports relate that Michael was living in Tarami in the service of his cousin, the daimyo of Ōmura, had married and had four sons, and was receiving an annual pension of 600 *koku* of rice. According to other accounts, he and his cousin had abandoned Christianity and had joined the Nichiren sect of Buddhism, and Michael was killed by a servant.[28] One of the Europeans living in Japan who chanced to meet Michael was the English merchant Richard Cocks, who, writing to London on 10 December 1614, paints a bleak picture of his state. When commenting on the '3 Japans' who travelled to Europe, Cocks remarks: 'Only it was my chance to be shewed one of these supposed princes, a pore bare fello whoe now hath forsaken his Christian faith and is turned pagon.'[29]

A rumour circulated about 1619 that Michael had died a few years earlier, killed by a servant; according to yet another source, he had been wounded by a servant, but survived the assault. A bizarre story reached Macao in 1638 that Amakusa Shirō, the legendary and possibly imaginary leader of the Shimabara rebellion, 1637–8, was none other than Michael's son, but no other source confirms this startling allegation.[30]

Michael had four sons, the youngest being named Gemba, and a recent discovery, reported in February 2004, has focused attention on this man. A tomb has been identified at a Nichiren temple in Tarami that is almost certainly Michael's. The rear of the stone monument over the tomb bears the name Chijiwa Gemba as its sponsor, while on the front are inscribed the posthumous names of a man and a woman, presumably Michael's wife, who died within two days of each other, the man on Kan'ei 9, 12th month, 12th day, the woman on the 14th; the date of the man's death corresponds to 21 January 1633, in the Western calendar.

But why should Gemba, the youngest son, be mentioned as erecting the monument to his father and mother? The question is easily answered. Of Michael's four sons, the first was banished from the region, the second died young, while the third was adopted into another family, so responsibility for caring for their elderly parents would have rested with Gemba. Although absolute proof is lacking, it appears highly probable that Michael and his wife were buried in this tomb in early 1633 – in which case he died at the age of about sixty-six.[31]

MARTIN HARA, 1568–1639. As regards the subsequent careers of the four boys, Martin Hara's activities emerge the clearest, for not only did he live to an advanced age but his name often appears in Jesuit records. Martin was perhaps the most talented of the four. He was only a companion to the two official envoys of the Kyushu daimyo, it is true, yet he was chosen to deliver in eloquent Latin the public speech in honour of Valignano in Goa in June 1587, although he himself obviously did not compose the ornate text.[32]

Martin also served as interpreter when the Franciscan friars met the Christian daimyo Konishi Yukinaga in 1596.[33] With Mancio and Julian, he completed his studies of formation as a Jesuit, and was active in preaching and catechizing. While still unordained, he was chosen to deliver the homily at the funeral of Pedro Gómez, the

Jesuit superior, in the Nagasaki church in February 1600. Martin's fame as a preacher grew, and in February 1614 he again delivered a panegyric, this time at the funeral of Bishop Luis de Cerqueira.[34]

After the battle of Sekigahara in October 1600, Martin was called on to negotiate the release of five Jesuits who had been imprisoned by the daimyo Katō Kiyomasa. When Martin's efforts were finally successful, Katō summoned the young Jesuit and spoke with him informally. Ironically, one of the Jesuits released through Martin's intercession was none other than Pedro Ramón, who in 1587 had written to Rome denouncing the mission to Europe.

Unlike Mancio and Julian, Martin did not return to Macao for further studies, possibly because his services to the mission in Japan were considered too valuable to allow him to go abroad. Mesquita had kept in close touch with him since their return from Europe and appears to have regarded Martin with special affection. In his indignant letter to Rome, quoted above, he seems to have Martin mostly in mind for he twice mentions him by name as a worthy candidate for ordination. Martin was finally ordained priest in 1608, together with Mancio and Julian.

Martin laboured for six years in Nagasaki, and was appointed the ecclesiastical notary there, in which capacity he witnessed and signed official church documents. The painter Pedro Kano had apparently fallen away from the church, but on 6 March 1603, he signed a document in Kyoto retracting his apostasy, with Martin writing not only his own name but also Pedro's in Roman letters. ('As Pedro Kano cannot write in our letters, he signed his name in Japanese characters, and then asked me to write his name in our letters'.)[35] In January 1605 he gave evidence at a judicial inquiry organized by the Jesuits in Nagasaki to show that the friars had not been welcomed by Ieyasu and that the Jesuits had not hesitated, as was alleged, to preach the Passion of Christ in Japan.[36]

In addition to these labours, Martin found time to render various devotional tracts into Japanese for the Jesuit Press. As noted above, Mesquita regarded Martin as 'the best interpreter we have in Japan'. He translated *Guia de Pecadores*, printed in Nagasaki in 1599, as well as at least a part of *Símbolo de la Fe*, 1611, both written by Luis de Granada, whom he had met in Lisbon in 1584. He also revised the Japanese version of *The Imitation of Christ*, which was published in 1612–13.[37] In 1611, he was appointed socius, or secretary, to Valentim Carvalho, the superior of the Jesuit mission, who had little command of the Japanese language. This appointment did not please some of the Portuguese Jesuits who preferred to keep the administration of the mission in European hands.

As a result of the expulsion edict issued by the Tokugawa authorities in October 1614, Martin was among the sixty-five Jesuits who left for Macao, where he was to spend the rest of his life, ministering to the Japanese Christians living there in exile. One of his duties was to help João Rodrigues in his task of gathering material for a history of the Japanese church, and Martin read and commented on the text. In Rodrigues's manuscript, we read, for example, Martin's marginal comment, written in perfect Portuguese, regarding the author's somewhat loose reference to 'the kingdom of Bungo':

> For many reasons I approve of your calling the *yakata* 'dukes', but to call the state of Bungo a 'kingdom' seems to me an inexact European term. For a man is called a king inasmuch as he is lord of a kingdom, but however large the territories of dukes, they are not called kingdoms but duchies. And so it seems to me better to look for another and more appropriate term.[38]

Martin also comments on the mission to Europe that had taken place nearly forty years earlier. He remarks in Portuguese:

> I'm glad to see what you write about our going to Europe. For you have written the truth and correct the mistakes of other writers in this matter, and you recall the calumnies of the friars, who never stop needling us here.[39]

Martin died in Macao on 23 October 1639, aged about seventy. He was buried there under the floor of the church of São Paolo, along with Valignano, Dourado and João Rodrigues. Most of the great church was destroyed by fire in 1835, but its impressive stone façade exists to this day as a poignant landmark in modern Macao.

JULIAN NAKAURA, c.1568–1633, was the son of the Christian samurai Kozasa Sumiyoshi Jingorō, commander of Nakaura, Yokoseura, in Kyushu, where to this day a monument marks the site of the house in which the boy was born in 1567 or 1568. While he was still young, his father was killed in battle, and Julian, his widowed mother and his two sisters went to live in Ōmura. In 1580 he was one of the first pupils to enter the recently-founded Jesuit college in Arima, reserved for the sons of Christian samurai, and it was here that, together with Martin Hara, he was chosen to accompany the legation to Rome. Understandably, his widowed mother, with no other son, was most reluctant to give permission for him to embark on such a lengthy and hazardous expedition.

On his return from Europe, Julian with his three companions entered the Jesuit novitiate in July 1591 and two years later took his first religious vows with them. He began his apostolic work at Yatsuhiro, but was obliged to return to Nagasaki after the execution of the Christian daimyo Konishi Yukinaga in 1600. After spending three years in Macao studying theology along with Mancio, Julian returned to Japan in 1604. Ordained in 1608, he laboured amid growing tension among the Christians in Arima and then Hakata. The decree expelling religious, both Japanese and European, from Japan was issued in 1614, but unlike Martin, Julian decided, or was ordered, to be one of the twenty-seven Jesuits remaining in the country and continuing to work underground.

A confidential Jesuit report compiled at this time described Julian in these terms:

> Aged 47 years; good health; 23 years in the Society. Has talent, prudence, and ability for preaching, hearing confessions, and dealing with people both high and low. Everything normal. As regards character, more phlegmatic than choleric.[40]

Until 1620 Julian and others worked in the Shimabara region in Kyushu under a daimyo who chose to ignore or turn a blind eye on their presence.

While Julian was visiting and preaching to the persecuted Christians in Amakusa, Higo, and other places in Kyushu, he travelled on foot by night, in lay clothes, staying in the houses of the faithful in remote rural villages, and consoling the Christian refugees.[41] On 21 September 1621, he replied in Portuguese to a letter from Rome. He mentions the increasing violence of the persecution and the growing number of martyrs for the faith. Interestingly, he also refers to the journey he made to Europe more than thirty years previously, declaring that the letter from Europe had

... refreshed my memories of the holy city of Rome, the Supreme Pontiff and the cardinals and Catholic princes, and the acts of kindness and charity I experienced there when I travelled through those parts of Europe. So I thank you for the letter which you sent me from so far, from Rome to Japan . . .[42]

Three months later, Julian took his final religious vows, and the certificate, written in Latin in his own hand, is still preserved in Rome. It concludes: 'In Japan, at the time of persecution, in the village of Kazusa, in the Jesuit chapel in the house of Michael Sukeyemon, 21 December 1621, Nakaura Julian.'[43]

The persecution of Christians intensified. The Great Martyrdom of Nagasaki, in which fifty Christians were executed in one day, took place on 10 September 1622, and Pietro Navarro and companions were burned at the stake in Shimabara on 1 November of the same year. More European missionaries were arrested, imprisoned, and put to death, but probably because of his Japanese nationality, Julian was able to avoid capture in his travels and continue his apostolate. In 1624 he visited the Christians in Hakata, Akizuki and Kokura, but the years of stress and hiding left him exhausted; at times he was unable to walk, and the faithful carried him in a litter from place to place.

In late 1632 Julian, too, was apprehended in Kokura and sent to Nagasaki, where he was imprisoned with other Christians. During his nine months of captivity, he was repeatedly interrogated, and was offered the confiscated lands that had once belonged to his father if only he would deny his faith.

On 18 October 1633, at Nagasaki Julian and seven other religious were submitted to the torture of the *ana-tsurushi*, that is, their bodies were bound tightly and then suspended upside down with their heads submerged in shallow pits that often contained human or animal filth. One hand was left unbound to enable the victim to signal his submission. According to the testimony of those who survived this agonizing torment, no greater torture could be imagined.

The group of martyrs was made up of two Dominican friars, one a Spaniard and the other a Japanese, and six Jesuits, Japanese and European. It is reported that at the site of his execution, Julian declared: 'I am Fr Julian Nakaura, who went to Rome.'[44] After five hours of torment, the Portuguese Jesuit Christovão Ferreira signalled his submission and was released from the torture.[45]

The rest of the group remained firm. One died that night, two others on the following day, and another on the 20th. Julian died on the 21st, another Jesuit on the 22nd, and yet another, Antonio de Sousa, on the 26th. The bodies of the martyrs were burned and the ashes scattered in the sea.[46]

Such was the fate of Julian, aged sixty-three, who as a boy had travelled to Europe and of the four Japanese had always suffered the weakest health.[47]

It is noteworthy that while the four boys appear almost indistinguishable in contemporaneous accounts of their journey to Europe and back, as well as in their crude portraits sketched while in Milan, their subsequent careers in Japan varied widely – one died young in Nagasaki, another spent many years in exile in Macao, another probably apostatized the Christian faith, and in his old age the fourth underwent an agonizing martyrdom in defence of it.

APPENDIX 2

The Sources

The author of the most detailed source of information about the expedition to Europe, *Tratado dos Embaixadores Iapões que Forão de Iapão à Roma no Anno de 1582*, is the Jesuit Luís Fróis, 1532–97, and the present work is based largely on his text. Born in Lisbon, Fróis entered the Society of Jesus in 1548; a month later, he sailed to the Indies as a missionary, and studied in Goa for the priesthood, receiving ordination there in 1561. Soon after, he was appointed to the Japanese mission, founded by Francis Xavier (whom Fróis had known in India), and arrived there in July 1563. Apart from working in Macao 1592–95, he spent the rest of his thirty-four years in that country, dying in Nagasaki on 8 July 1597.[1]

Fróis was, and still is, recognized as the chronicler par excellence of the Japanese mission. Writing seems to have come to him naturally, and he is the author of more than two hundred letters and reports recounting in detail not only the progress and development of the Christian mission but also secular events in Japan. He was well qualified for this work, as he was the provincial superior's secretary for many years, and thus had access to Jesuit reports sent in from different regions of the country. In his later life he also served as amanuensis and interpreter for the Visitor, Alessando Valignano. In addition, during his long career Fróis met Nobunaga, Hideyoshi, and other leading figures on various occasions.

In 1585 Fróis was commissioned to write a history of the Japanese mission and over the next eight years compiled an account that continued down to 1593. Unfortunately, its length and excessive detail did not meet with Valignano's approval, and the complete text was not published until 1976–84 in five volumes.

Fróis did not accompany the expedition to Europe, but obviously had access to its members' copious notes and correspondence on their return to Japan.[2] In several instances in his *Tratado* he provides concrete examples of the diligence with which the visitors recorded what they had seen and experienced during their travels. When describing the tours of Vila Viçosa and Toledo, for example, Fróis interrupts his narrative to remark that he has taken verbatim the following accounts from the notes of one of the Japanese visitors.[3] Then follow detailed and lengthy descriptions, written in Portuguese, supplying more than readers ever need to know about the two places.

Doubtless the boys dutifully took notes in compliance with these instructions, but Fróis's day-by-day account is so systematic, detailed and precise that one suspects that much of his text relies a great deal on printed European sources and a diary-like account compiled by an adult. For example, when describing the oath-taking ceremony in Madrid in 1584, Fróis names the titles of no less than twenty-seven Spanish lords who led members of the nobility in swearing allegiance to the young prince,[4] and it is difficult to conceive how the young Japanese boys, who did not speak Spanish fluently, could have accurately recorded all this information. Other examples of this kind readily come to mind.

It is true that Fróis specifically cites Dourado and quotes his lengthy description of Vila Viçosa verbatim on one occasion, thus indicating that the young man had a remarkable proficiency in Portuguese. He also quotes the account of Toledo, but does not mention the note-taker by name. I believe, however, that it was the boys' mentor and interpreter Diogo de Mesquita, the only adult in daily contact with them throughout their eight-year expedition, who provided the chronicler with much of the necessary information. Mesquita was obviously a man of some stature, for not only had Valignano, a good judge of character, chosen the young Jesuit to accompany the boys to Europe and act as their mentor and interpreter, but also in later life he occupied for fourteen years the responsible post of Superior of the Nagasaki college, the largest Jesuit house containing the largest Jesuit community in Japan. In his text Fróis only twice refers to Mesquita as his source of information, but it would seem he may well have been a major contributor, although this cannot be directly proved.[4]

In addition, by 1585, while the boys were still in Europe, more than forty books, booklets and pamphlets had been published, many of them in Italy and Spain, two of the three countries they passed through, describing different segments of the visit, and it is reasonable to suppose that at least some of these accounts were presented to the party to carry back to Japan.[5]

In the year of their departure from Lisbon, 1586, there appeared in Rome Guido Gualtieri's *Relationi*, 'the most complete description of the envoys' journey' through Europe.[6] In addition to its detailed and accurate account of the boys' travels through Italy, the book contains the texts of the official *Acta* of Gregory XIII's consistory at which the pope first met the Japanese and of his letters to the three daimyo in Kyushu. A study of the texts compiled by Gualtieri (1586) and by Fróis (after 1590) about the boys' experiences in Italy clearly shows so many similarities, even at times identical word-for-word passages, that even if the Japanese did not receive Gualtieri's book before departing from Europe, a copy must have been available to Fróis when he compiled his *Tratado*.[7]

As the party was delayed in Macao for nearly two years and did not get back to Japan until June 1590, it is quite possible that Gualtieri's volume arrived during the extended stay there. It was also during this enforced stop-over in Macao that the imported press printed *De Missione*, and although this work does not provide nearly so much day-to-day detail of the expedition as does Fróis's text, it nevertheless was a valuable source of information. Thus, in addition to the notes taken by members of the party, printed accounts were available to Fróis when he came to compile his account.

Accordingly, on the party's return to Japan, the elderly Fróis was able to compile his *Tratado*, a detailed record of the boys' voyages to Macao, Goa and Lisbon, their travels through Portugal, Spain and Italy, their audiences with the two popes and Philip II, and their return to Lisbon, preparatory to their return to Japan. When exactly he completed this work is not known, but his history of the Japanese mission, running into five volumes, and many extant letters are of formidable length, and it is obvious that writing came easily to him. Fróis accompanied Valignano to Macao in late 1592 and did not return to Japan until July 1595, and there he died in July 1597. In all likelihood he compiled the *Tratado* in the period 1590–1592 while the events of the European expedition were still fresh in memory and interest in the venture still remained high.

Fróis's valuable account remained unpublished until 1942 when the international team of João do Amaral Abranches Pinto, 1893–1965; Okamoto Yoshitomo, 1900–72; and Henri Bernard, S.J., 1889–1975, brought out in Tokyo, after ten years' work, an annotated edition of the first volume of the Portuguese text under the title *La Première Ambassade*. That they were able to complete this superb scholarly feat in Tokyo when the Pacific War was taking a critical turn for Japan is remarkable. The same three editors planned to bring out a second volume recounting the legation's return to Japan, but this sequel never appeared.[8]

As regards the division of labour among the three editors, Abranches Pinto, a specialist in early Japanese-Portuguese relations, presumably was in charge of transcribing the photographic copy of Fróis's Portuguese text. Okamoto Yoshitomo, also an authority in the same subject, contributed much regarding Japanese history and culture.[9] The third editor, the French scholar Henri Bernard, came somewhat later to the project, but the fact that not only the book's title but also its introduction, appendixes, index, and some 920 informative footnotes are written in French surely indicates his major contribution to the publication.[10]

Fróis's *Tratado* remains the chief source of information about the expedition to Europe. My original plan was to publish an annotated translation of this text, but it did not take long to realise that a close English rendition of Fróis's florid style would not greatly appeal to modern readers, who would undoubtedly find its presentation somewhat tedious and excessively pious. In this regard, the author was following the instructions of Francis Xavier, who in a directive dated 1549 exhorted his fellow Jesuits about their letter-writing: 'Let the letters be about the things of edification, and take care not to write matters which are not of edification. Remember that many people will read these letters, so let them be written in such wise that no one may be disedified.'[11] This instruction was all the more applicable to printed accounts that would enjoy a far wider readership.

Following this injunction, Fróis generally adopted a style in which right invariably triumphs over wrong, while anything considered untoward and unbecoming is discreetly omitted. While in my paraphrase of his text I have omitted extreme examples of this approach, some of this tendency inevitably surfaces and should be regarded with a certain caution. It is not that the author is deliberately indulging in pious exaggeration and deception – he was simply following Xavier's dictum to edify as well as inform. Thus, Fróis recounts with obvious relish the kindness, charity and affection invariably shown the boys during their travels; their demeanour and humility aroused universal admiration, wonder and edification, while their piety and devotion often caused onlookers to shed copious tears. Undoubtedly, the young Japanese did create a good impression in Europe, but Fróis's repeated accounts of emotions aroused pall after a few pages.

To provide just one example, when the boys left a monastery in Sintra, Portugal, after a visit of only one day and a half,

> . . . many of those monks were weeping and could not withhold their tears, and this usually happened at all the Jesuit houses and colleges through which they passed, for the Jesuits were so saddened by their departure that they could not help showing their grief by their tears.[12]

The repetitive nature of Fróis's text is also evident. The Japanese party stopped at or at least passed through scores of European cities, and their reception at many of these places was for the most part fairly identical and does not call for repeated descriptions. Instead of a direct translation, therefore, I have paraphrased this invaluable Portuguese text, using it as the principal source of information and making full use of the hundreds of detailed and informative footnotes compiled by the three editors.

De Missione Legatorum

As noted above, *Ambassade* stops short at the party's departure from Lisbon, and thus does not deal with the voyage back to Japan and the party's reception there. Fortunately, this missing information is supplied by a full chapter on the return voyage found in a contemporaneous work published in Latin, *De Missione Legatorum*, Macao, 1590, the first book produced by the Jesuit Press and published even before the legation had returned to Japan; other Jesuit sources also provide additional information about the party after its arrival at Nagasaki. The title page of *De Missione* explains that the text is based on the journals written by the boys and has been translated into Latin by the Portuguese Jesuit Eduardo de Sande.[13] For long it was assumed that Sande was the author of the work, but recent scholarship shows that the text was in fact compiled by Valignano, probably in Spanish, during his and the boys' lengthy enforced stay in Macao from July 1588 to June 1590.[14] Valignano instructed Sande, a scholar with humanistic training and then residing in Macao, to edit and translate his text into Latin.[15]

As an added attraction, the text of *De Missione* is imaginatively presented in the form of 34 Colloquia, or dialogues, between the four boys and Michael's cousins Leo and Linus, who ply the party with questions about their experiences abroad.[16] The dialogues, set in Japan on the boys' return, are obviously fictitious as they were compiled in Macao before the party set sail for Nagasaki. A risk was certainly involved when relating future events as if they had already taken place; for example, we are told that Arima Harunobu was overcome with delight on receiving the papal gifts. It would have caused considerable embarrassment if, on the boys' return to Nagasaki, Valignano had been greeted with the news that the daimyo had been deposed or transferred, or even killed, during the final stage of their travels.[17]

De Missione was conceived as a textbook for students studying Latin at the Jesuit school in Kyushu, and Valignano wrote: 'As the boys in the seminary have such a lack of books, they will greatly enjoy this one.'[18] In another letter, he comments: 'Everyone will be eager to know about it [the legation], and will be impressed if it is immediately imprinted on their souls . . .'[19] This surely shows an overly optimistic assessment of the pupils' language ability, although Valignano was well aware of the low standard of Latin among Japanese students, mentioning elsewhere their 'very crude knowledge of Latin'.[20] Reading and understanding Sande's prose is by no means easy for a European, for in his version compiled in distant Macao, the translator refers to Cicero, Martial, Horace and other classical authors.[21] In addition, the Latin vocabulary employed in the work is at times technical and obscure. For example, Colloquium 28, which describes Venice, contains expressions (given here in English translation) such as 'porphery and ophite', 'adamant, beryl, emeralds', 'alabaster or onyx', 'topazes, chrysolites', and 'Doric and Ionic style', all of which would surely have had little or no meaning for the Jesuit pupils back in Kyushu.

Although Valignano does not mention the possibility, *De Missione* would have made an excellent gift to benefactors in Italy, Portugal and Spain; written in the common language of Latin, the book shows no partiality towards any of these three nations. The work treats things European – monarchy, nobility, papacy, castles, religion, politics, art and culture – in a most laudatory way, and Europeans would find its contents extremely congenial. Colloquia 18 ('Of the Power of King Philip of Spain') and 19 ('Of Various Works Built by King Philip') would have been well received in Spain.[22]

There is evidence that the enterprising Valignano planned to bring out a Japanese version of *De Missione*. The fact that the four boys entered the Jesuit novitiate soon after their return to Japan prevented their authoring such an account; in any case their youth and literary inexperience would not have made them ideal authors. But there were other Japanese who had accompanied them to Europe and could perhaps either translate *De Missione* or else produce an even more interesting account of the legation. The foremost candidate was Brother George Loyola, and Valignano had him in mind for this project, writing from Macao on 25 September 1589, and referring to *De Missione*:

> I also decided that Brother George Loyola should translate it into Japanese and we would take this translation from here to Japan, but it pleased Our Lord that he contracted consumption and his infirmity increased every day, and he was called to the other life on 16 August. This was indeed a great loss for Japan, for in addition to being such a good son, he alone, of all the Japanese Brothers, had seen and well understood the things of Europe.[23]

Thus, no Japanese translation of *De Missione* or some similar account was published, and as a result the mission lost a golden opportunity of promoting its work.[24]

De Missione was intended as a textbook not only for studying Latin but also for acquainting Japanese students with European civilisation, and therefore, despite its title, its treatment of the legation is uneven, unlike Fróis's methodical account. It uses the expedition as a framework on which to hang detailed and idealized descriptions of aspects of European life; its penultimate chapter even deals exclusively with China.[25] Obviously, much of this extraneous information about Europe and China was not supplied by the boys themselves, but was composed by Valignano with possibly Sande's help. Its account of the boys' experiences in Europe is sporadic, but it provides a useful supplement to Fróis's text, especially its chapter (Colloquium 32) on the return journey.

De Missione in places exceeds Fróis's text in length, for example, its detailed chapter on the party's stay in Coimbra, where significantly Sande had studied and taught before setting out for the Indies. In addition, whereas Fróis dismisses the stay in Padua in one short paragraph, *De Missione* goes into considerable detail, describing the visit to Europe's oldest botanical garden there, and mentioning the director's gift of valuable books (see Appendix 3).[26]

So although *De Missione* provides additional information about the expedition, Fróis's text is far more valuable for it depends much more on the notes taken by the Japanese during their travels. In its long description of Lisbon (Colloqium 16), for example, *De Missione* provides considerable detail about the Portuguese capital's palaces, churches, monasteries, chapels, monuments, fortresses, hospitals, leprosarium, port, markets, gardens and fountains (it even identifies Ulysses as the city's founder), but does not specifically state which places the boys actually saw. In contrast, Fróis's text relates exactly where and when the Japanese visited, and in this regard is a more valuable and accurate source of information about the party's day-to-day activities.[27]

Other Sources

Other sources adding to our knowledge of the expedition can be briefly mentioned. Luis de Guzman, S.J.,1544–1605, published his *Historia de las Misiones*, in 1601, in which he devotes some thirty chapters to the boys' travels in Europe. But he adds little information not contained in Fróis's record, and the similarities between the two accounts make it likely that Guzman had access to Fróis's and probably Gualtieri's texts.

An interesting feature of this work is that Guzman, who held the office of Jesuit provincial superior in Spain no less than three times, was Rector of the college in Belmonte when the boys passed through the city in early December 1584 on their way to Rome. They stayed at the college for three days, thus providing the author ample opportunity to meet and converse with them. This personal contact offered a wonderful chance for Guzman to record his impressions of the visitors as individuals, but disappointingly he mentions merely three standard items of pious information that do not add greatly to our knowledge of the travellers.[28]

A somewhat later account is Daniello Bartoli, S.J., *Dell'Historia della Compagnia de Giesu: Il Giappone*, Rome, 1660. Like Guzman, Bartoli, 1608–72, did not have first-hand experience of Japan, nor for that matter did he ever leave his native Italy. Unlike the three previous authors, he never met the boys for he was born some twenty years after their departure from Europe. But in 1646 Bartoli was commissioned to compile an official history of the Society of Jesus, and was given access to letters and documents in the Jesuit archives in Rome, some of which are no longer extant, and he diligently made use of this facility. In his account of the Jesuit mission in Japan, he devotes some seventy pages (pp. 166–242) to the boys' expedition to Europe, but does not offer a great deal of information not contained in the earlier works listed above.

The above four authors (Fróis, Valignano, Guzman and Bartoli) were Jesuits and understandably wrote from the Jesuit point of view, that is, presenting the legation to Europe in the most favourable light possible with little or no indication of any disagreement or discord. We read that in their reception in Europe the boys were admired everywhere they went, they edified spectators by their politeness and piety, and all the arrangements proceeded smoothly.

By and large this state of affairs may well have been the case, but there are instances in secular reports in which a certain note of discord is detected and resentment becomes apparent. An obvious example has already been related above and occurred at the time of the coronation of Sixtus V. The Venetian ambassador, Lorenzo Priuli, vigorously protested against the boys proceeding in front of him in the escort carrying the papal canopy. As he later reported, even if the boys 'have the title of Ambassadors of Kings, they are nevertheless so little known and little esteemed Kings, that very unwillingly would I suffer such a thing'.[29]

Fróis and other Jesuit writers do not mention this incident, and they were possibly unaware of the complication, for it was not likely to have been publicly broadcast. Or perhaps Fróis chose to omit the matter from his account, judging it to be unseemly and not in keeping with the generally optimistic tone of his work.[30]

For this reason contemporaneous accounts of the Japanese mission to Europe written by lay people are valuable inasmuch as they provide an additional dimension to our understanding of the party's reception, although many of the brief comments refer to the travellers' visit to one particular place and not to their stay in Europe as a whole. Mention has already been made of the Venetian ambassador's indignation, but there are other examples of some discord. In *Antiche Ambasciate Giapponesi*, Berchet records some less than flattering remarks made by onlookers in Italy; in *Asia in the Making of Europe*, Lach offers valuable references, some of them obscure, to many texts and articles, and briefly touches on Protestant reaction to the legation and disappointment that the visit to Europe had been limited to only three Catholic countries.[31]

Doubtless there are further sources of information buried in the archives of the cities, towns and monasteries the boys visited, but it would take a lifetime to track them down and evaluate their contents. Professor Adriana Boscaro has uncovered valuable documents regarding the visits to Venice and elsewhere, while Judith Brown, 'Courtiers', presents interesting excerpts from letters written about the boys' stay in Florence

Yūki Ryōgo, S.J. (formerly known as Diego Pacheco), has spent many years studying the mission to Europe, and his books, in Spanish, English, and Japanese, contain much new material. His research into the subsequent careers of the boys after their return to Japan has proved invaluable for the present account.

APPENDIX 3

Azuchi Screens and Braun's Cities

Owing to the hurried preparation for the legation to Europe, there was not sufficient time to collect and prepare adequate gifts in return for all the largesse the Japanese were to receive during the course of their travels. Even had there been the opportunity to do so, Valignano did not foresee or desire the boys' public and enthusiastic reception in Europe and the resulting need for a plentiful supply of return gifts. Time and again during their travels they must have felt embarrassed by their inability to make fitting return for the expensive presents lavished on them, especially in view of the Japanese tradition of scrupulously making suitable return gifts.

We have seen that the boys received costly gifts in Rome, Venice, Florence and elsewhere, and were unable to make adequate reparation. On several occasions they donated some of their used, and possibly worn, Japanese robes, which, although having novelty value, hardly qualified as suitable gifts to present to nobles. When they were shown around the Escorial, they managed no more than write a few words in Japanese as a remembrance of their visit. Even at the beginning of their stay in Europe, they offered Cardinal Albert, Philip II's representative in Portugal, no more than an inkstand made from rhinoceros horn, which could hardly be considered a suitable gift to present to such a distinguished figure.

There was, however, one particular item that Valignano had given to the party as a present for the pope in Rome, for the primary objective of the legation was to pay homage to the pontiff. The gift was a pair of screens, or *byōbu*, depicting Azuchi castle and city which they gave to Gregory XIII in the afternoon of 3 April 1585, and this present deserves some explanation. As a good deal of unpublished information is available about these screens, we may perhaps pause here to describe this outstanding gift, one of the few that the legation carried that in any way corresponded to the wealth of presents showered upon the boys by European princes and prelates.

Byōbu, hence the Portuguese and Spanish *biombo*, folding screen, are large, free-standing screens, generally produced in pairs of four or six hinged panels, anything from 3.0 to 6.0 feet tall. At the time of the boys' departure from Japan, such screens were much in vogue, depicting on a gold-leaf background scenes of nature, views of Kyoto or other cities, or even famous battles in Japanese history. The Italian merchant Francesco Carletti, who arrived in Japan in 1597, noted that these screens open and shut like a fan, in such fashion that when the panels are unfolded, they are 'kept in an upright position on the floor by the folds or angles thus formed'. The hinged panels 'are made of several thicknesses of paper stuck together like pasteboard, which are then pasted on both sides of a wooden framework'. They feature 'all sorts of pictures of different kinds of birds and flowers and beautifully painted designs of all kinds'. The Jesuit Gaspar Vilela remarked on the realism of the paintings: 'They were painted so realistically that the spectator seemed to be looking at the actual thing which was thus portrayed; indeed, on one of these *byōbu* there was depicted so naturally some snow lying on bamboos that without any doubt at all it appeared no less real than the snow which falls in its proper season.'[1]

Although these pairs of screens could be folded up, they nevertheless remained bulky objects to transport in ships to Europe and in coaches through Portugal, Spain and Italy, and it is remarkable, but a cause for satisfaction, that the screens presented to the pope in 1585 survived undamaged the long and perilous journey from Nagasaki to Rome.[2]

This was no ordinary pair of screens, for they had been presented to Valignano by the ruler Oda Nobunaga himself, then at the height of his power. Nobunaga had established his headquarters at Azuchi, a strategic site on the east bank of Lake Biwa and some twenty miles from Kyoto. There he constructed his castle, and also city, where he obliged daimyos to build their mansions in lavish style. The first of Japan's three unifiers, he had inherited a minor fief in Gifu, but by a combination of good fortune, military genius and ruthlessness had eventually succeeded in controlling about half of the country. He showed particular favour to the Jesuit missionaries, partly out of his curiosity about the visitors from the West and partly, perhaps mainly, in an attempt to offset the political and military power of the Buddhist establishment.

Jesuit writers have left glowing accounts of the magnificence of Azuchi, and Fróis's eyewitness description is justly famous:

> On top of the hill, in the middle of the city, Nobunaga built his palace and castle, which as regards architecture, strength, wealth and grandeur may well be compared with the greatest buildings of Europe. Its strong and well-constructed surrounding walls of stone are over 60 spans in height and even higher in many places; inside the walls there are many beautiful and exquisite houses, all of them decorated with gold and so neat and well fashioned that they seem to reach the acme of human elegance. . . . In a word, the whole edifice is beautiful, excellent and brilliant. As the castle is situated on high ground and is itself very lofty, it looks as if it reaches to the clouds and it can be seen from afar for many leagues.[3]

The Jesuit chronicler did not base his account on merely exterior observation, for Nobunaga enjoyed showing off his castle to the Europeans, and gave Valignano and a party of missionaries and faithful an extended tour in April 1581, insisting they inspect not only the building's exterior but also its interior, even the kitchens and stables.[4] Thanks to the ruler's largesse, the Jesuits were also allotted an excellent site in the city and inaugurated a school there for the Christian sons of gentry.

Of additional interest, the castle appears to have incorporated features of European architecture, such as the empty central space extending from the first to the top floor of the central tower, and the pulpit-like platform jutting out of the second floor into this space. Fróis's account is of particular interest, for Azuchi castle and city were destroyed following Nobunaga's assassination only a few months after the boys left for Europe in 1582, and as a result few written and no pictorial records have survived.

Valignano visited Nobunaga at Azuchi twice in April and August 1581, and the warlord, impressed by the Italian's towering height, presented him with a pair of screens depicting the newly-constructed castle and city with its dozens of fine mansions of his principal retainers. According to Jesuit letters, the screens were the work of 'the foremost painter of Japan', and Nobunaga himself had overseen the work and ordered alterations in places where he considered the depiction was inaccurate. The following extract from the annual Jesuit letter for 1581 recounts with suitable embellishment the background of this largesse and may be quoted at some length. It also provides an example of the somewhat effusive and optimistic style of Jesuit letters of those days:

> As the Father [Valignano] left to visit Christians, Nobunaga bestowed on him favours even greater than those he had shown in the past, and the fame of these spread throughout all of Japan resulting in much credit with everyone. One particular favour was the following.
>
> Nobunaga had ordered to be made some decorated panels such as the Japanese lords have and are much esteemed among them; they are called *byōbu*. One year earlier he had commissioned the most famous painter in Japan to produce them, and said that this new city with its fortress should be accurately depicted thereon as he did not want anything to differ from reality; the artist should paint the lake, the houses, and everything else as accurately as he could. He spent a great deal of time on this work, for anything he [Nobunaga] thought differed from reality he made him erase and paint again. Finally, it was completed to his satisfaction.
>
> The panels became famous throughout the court because they were so accomplished and perfect, they were the work of a famous painter, and they satisfied Nobunaga, who held them in high esteem. . . . Their fame reached the emperor, who sent word to Nobunaga to show them to him; he was so pleased by them that he made known to Nobunaga that he desired them for himself.
>
> But Nobunaga made excuses, for he did not want to give them to him. Knowing that the Father [Valignano] wished to leave, he sent him a very friendly and courteous message, declaring that as he was going such a long distance by ship . . . he wished to give him something as a souvenir and a sign of the love he bore for the Fathers so that he could take it with him when he returned to his country. . . . And so he ordered his *byōbu* to be sent for him to view: if he liked them, he could keep them; if he did not, then he could return them. And while we were still opening this message to read it, there suddenly arrived a gentleman with another message from Nobunaga, saying he would soon send the *byōbu*. . . .

The Father [Valignano] sent word how pleased he was with the *byōbu*, and this greatly satisfied Nobunaga, who declared that this would make the Father understand the great love he had, for this work so much pleased him, and that although the emperor had asked for it, he had refused for he wished to give it to the Father. In this way it would make known throughout Japan the high esteem in which he held him and be proof of his favour. He could give him a thousand crowns, but this would not be so much, for he did not lack gold or silver, but to deprive himself of something he so liked and give it to the Father – this was really something to show his esteem.

This matter soon became known throughout the city and then the neighbouring kingdoms, with both Christians and non-Christians astounded by something so novel as Nobunaga granting such a great favour to the Father, and they called him indeed fortunate. Lords and gentlemen began to come to our house to inspect the *byōbu*, and among them came Sanchichi Dono [Nobunaga's third son], who showed much happiness and joy, and talked about the favour his father had shown the Father.[5]

Now the principal interior decorator of the castle was the outstanding master painter Kano Eitoku, 1543–90, and it may be presumed that he either painted the screens or at least supervised their production. Although the fortress was destroyed within six years, a contemporaneous account of its interior decoration provides a detailed record of Eitoku's work there.[6] To satisfy popular demand, Valignano had the screens put on public view in churches in Kyoto, Sakai and Bungo.

This, then, was the pair of screens presented to Gregory XIII in Rome, and their artistic and historical value was immense. Artistic because of the illustrious Eitoku's participation in their production, and historical for within five months of the boys' departure, Nobunaga was attacked by enemies, and died a violent death; in short time his Azuchi castle was plundered and destroyed by marauding peasants. The fortress had been completed in 1579 and thus lasted a mere five or six years before its ignominious destruction, and as a result of its brief existence there is little contemporaneous Japanese description of the building.

The pope, therefore, received a priceless gift of great value, at least in Japan, but sad to relate the Azuchi screens disappeared from view shortly after their presentation and perhaps were allowed to disintegrate and rot in storerooms or cellars. The fact that their recipient, Gregory XIII, died within a week of receiving them, and there then followed a transition period before his successor was crowned, may have something to do with their disappearance.

There is only one further reference to the missing screens. Philips van Winghe, 1560–92, a young artist, humanist and antiquary from Louvain, lived in Rome 1589–92 (with a five-month stay in Naples in the summer of 1591). In his correspondence with the great Ortelius, compiler of *Theatrum Orbis Terrarum*, he mentions his contacts with many artists and men of letters in Rome. He knew, for example, Fulvio Orsini, 1529–1600, the librarian of the influential Cardinal Farnese, brother of Paul III, and the list of his acquaintances comprises an artist's who's-who of Rome in his day. He also obtained an illustration depicting the coronation of Sixtus V, a ceremony which the boys had attended four years before the artist's arrival in Rome.[7]

During his stay in Rome, Winghe must have viewed the Japanese screens as two of his simple sketches showing an Azuchi tower and gateway were engraved and published in the 1647 edition of Vicenzo Cartari's celebrated *Imagini delli dei de gl'antichi*. The illustration of the tower has no caption, but below the gateway print we read that the picture is the work of Philips Winghe and shows 'a temple of a Japanese deity', copied from a gift donated by 'the Japanese Ambassadors to Pope Gregory XIII'.[8] Precisely where and when Winghe saw the screens is not known.[9] No further reference to the Azuchi screens can be found.

Today, the ruins of Azuchi castle may still be visited on a tranquil hillside near the banks of Lake Biwa, and the overgrown and crumbling stone walls and steps of the mighty fortress inevitably bring to mind Bashō's moving haiku:

The summer grasses –
All that is left
Of a warrior's dreams.[10]

The above account deals with the principal gift presented by the boys to the pope; whatever their European hosts may have thought about it, the value of the screens back in Japan was immense.[11] In contrast the most significant presents received by the legates during their European travels were not fine swords or silver ornaments, but illustrated books that, although expensive, were not of immense financial value. The visitors, it is true, were presented with a great variety of valuable gifts in the course of their travels, but like the Azuchi screens, probably none of these presents has survived to the present day. But the donation of these books was to exert considerable influence back in Japan.

While staying in Padua the boys went to visit Europe's oldest botanical garden and there met the director, Melchior Wieland, aka Guilandinus, who presented them with two works, one in one volume, the other in three.[12] The first is specifically mentioned in *De Missione* by title and author: *Theatrum Orbis* by Abraham Ortelius, while the three-volume set is described as 'the most famous cities of the world depicted and published most ingeniously'.[13] Although no editor or title is mentioned in this second case, there can be no doubt that the text refers to Georg Braun and Franz Hogenberg, *Civitates Orbis Terrarum*, the first volume of which was published in Cologne in 1572. This work eventually appeared in a total of six volumes, the second and third published in 1575 and 1581; the remaining three were published after the boys' departure from Europe, the sixth and final one appearing as late as 1617.[14]

Much can be said about Abraham Ortels or Wortels (Ortelius is the Latin form of his name), 1527–98, the Antwerp cartographer, and his major work containing seventy maps of different regions in the world, all engraved in uniform size and style. Ortelius himself did not compile these maps, but reproduced the works of some eighty cartographers, presenting the latest cartographical information available. The maps of European regions are, of course, depicted with considerable accuracy, those of Asian regions less so, but nevertheless they are a considerable improvement on earlier versions. Interestingly, the title page of this large volume is illustrated by an engraving showing Atlas bearing the world on his mighty shoulders, and Ortelius's work may be considered the first atlas, in the modern sense of the word, to be published in Europe, although that honour is often attributed to the work of the Flemish cartographer Gerardus Mercator, 1512–94. Ortelius's atlas became justly famous and was reissued in no less than fifteen editions in four languages within ten years.

Living on remote islands off the Asian mainland, the Japanese had scant knowledge of world geography. They knew, of course, about their neighbours Korea and China, and they had heard of India, which they called Tenjiku, where the Lord Buddha had been born. In addition, Japanese merchants and adventurers had settled in the Manilla area of the Philippines, and doubtless by accident or design had visited Formosa and regions of southwest Asia; they would be active in Siam early in the following century. But their geographical knowledge of the rest of the world, including Africa and Europe, was extremely hazy. European world maps admittedly labelled vast areas in the northern and southern regions of the globe as *Terra incognita*, it is true, but they were far superior to anything Japanese cartographers could produce.

Doubtless some world maps had been imported in the first forty years of Japanese-European relations, but the arrival of this bulky volume of so many finely printed maps must have come as a startling revelation to those who had the good fortune to study the atlas on the boys' return. There still exist to this day Japanese screens, produced towards the end of the sixteenth century or the beginning of the seventeenth, depicting world maps with fair accuracy, and it is more than likely that Ortelius's volume served as a basis for these reproductions.[15]

Georg Braun's first three volumes of *Civitates Orbis Terrarum* contain views of cities around the world, mostly presented from an elevated angle. Here again, this work would add greatly to Japanese understanding of foreign countries, although the various cities tend to be represented in ideal fashion. There are still three Japanese screens which show four, twelve and twenty-eight cities of the world respectively.[16]

The depiction of Paris and Venice in these screens is undoubtedly based on the illustrations in the first volume of *Civitates Orbis Terrarum*, although London, Cologne and Amsterdam, also appearing in the same volume brought back to Japan, are completely different. The Kobe screen shows elevated views of Rome and Lisbon in great detail, but the latter view is contained in a later volume of Braun and so presumably could not be the exemplar brought back by the boys and copied by a Japanese artist. Braun includes a view of Rome in his first volume, but the depiction of the city on the screens differs considerably. Yet the great detail clearly shown in the screen depiction of Rome – St Peter's, Castel Sant'Angelo, the Colosseum, the bridges spanning the Tiber – is remarkable, for here was a Japanese artist, who had never left his native country, producing with amazing accuracy a picture, admittedly a copy, of a city he had never seen, or visited.

One further point may be mentioned here concerning the influence of *Civitates Orbis Terrarum*. In the foreground of the pictures of the various cities are often shown local men and women clad in their regional costumes, with the former sometimes carrying swords and lances. Similar portrayals of the inhabitants of the depicted localities are found in the screens showing cities of the world and in other Japanese screens painted in Western style.

The similarities and differences in the depiction of Braun's cities and of those featured on the Japanese screens need to be studied in greater detail, but the boys' volumes of *Civitates Orbis Terrarum* and *Theatrum Orbis Terrarum* undoubtedly helped to introduce the outside world to the Japanese who viewed these works and thus expanded their limited world view. Little could Melchior Wieland have realized in July 1585 that his generous gift of books to the boys would eventually produce such far-reaching results and impact in far-away Japan.

There may perhaps be additional influences more difficult to pinpoint, for details included in European engravings and reproduced, usually in simpler form, in Japanese screens have been detected. For example, an elephant and its howdah appearing in the colourful *The Battle of Lepanto* screen has obviously been copied, in a less skilful manner, from the engraving *The Battle of Zama* (202 BC), while the chariot horses are similar to those in another engraving. Mounted figures in other screens are definitely based on engravings of the Emperors Vespasian and Otto, and the castle in two other screens has obviously been copied from an engraving of *Pyramus and Thisbe*.[17] It is unlikely that either missionaries or Portuguese merchants would have been able or willing to transport these engravings featuring themes of antiquity halfway around the world to distant Japan. The Dutch imported illustrated books, it is true, but these illustrations probably reached Japan too late to be incorporated into the *namban byōbu*.

It is impossible to know definitely how these illustrations came into the hands of Japanese painters, but the likelihood that the prints, perhaps contained in books, were among the many gifts the legates brought back from Europe cannot be lightly dismissed.[18]

Notes

Preface
1 Kaempfer, *History*, 1, p. lxvii; Lach, *Asia*, 1:2, p. 705.

Acknowledgments
1 Further information about these two basic works is provided in Appendix 2.
2 For a pictorial record of the places visited by the boys, Yūki, *Roma wo Mita*, provides dozens of photographs taken as the author followed the party's route through Europe. Fr. Yūki has made a profound study of the expedition to Europe, and I owe a great deal to his extensive research.

Chapter 1: Christianity in Japan
1 Polo, *Book*, 2, pp. 253–54. Some authors believe Polo never reached China, but whether he did or not does not diminish the influence of his book of travels.
2 Columbus, *Voyage*, p. 106.
3 Schütte, *Introductio*, p. 429.
4 Valignano, *Sumario*, p. 240, n. 18.
5 Quoted in Cooper, *Southern Barbarians*, p. 137.
6 As was his custom, Valignano put in writing detailed instructions concerning the purpose, administration, curriculum and daily timetable of these institutions. Schütte, *Valignano's*, 1, pp. 346–54.
7 Valignano, *Sumario*, pp. 312–30.
8 As Fróis dolefully notes, 'If you visit a noble thirty times a year, you must take a gift on each occasion.' Quoted in Cooper, *Rodrigues the Interpreter*, p. 240. To economize, Valignano reached an agreement with the Christian daimyo that missionaries would not be required to present gifts on each visit, but this concession did not last long. Valignano laid down in detail the types of gifts that Jesuits should present to people of different social ranks. Schütte, *Valignano's*, 2, pp. 184–87; Valignano, *Cerimoniale*, pp. 250–69.
9 For example, Duarte de Meneses, fourteenth viceroy of India 1584–88, drew up a lengthy report in 1584 concerning 'the Laws, Customes, Revenues, Expenses and other matters of the Portugall Indies', which includes a list of the annual grants paid to each of the forty parishes and various mon-

asteries in the Goa region. Purchas, *Hakluytus Posthumus*, 9, pp. 178–84.
10 *Cartas*, 2, ff. 88v-89. Rodrigues, 1539–1604, had been the rector of the Goa college.
11 Ibid, 2, ff. 168v-69; Valignano, *Sumario*, pp. 340–44.
12 Valignano, *Sumario*, p. 334, n. 4; *Documenta Indica*, 14, pp. 38*–39*; Cooper, *Rodrigues the Interpreter*, pp. 239–47.
13 Valignano, *Adiciones*, p. 393, n. 3. These words were repeated by the Jesuit João Rodrigues as late as 1620 in the Introduction of his history of the Japanese mission. Rodrigues, *Rodrigues's Account*, p. 6.
14 Valignano, *Sumario*, p. 337.
15 Cooper, *Rodrigues the Interpreter*, p. 242. This moving document is titled, 'Memorial made by the Father Visitor of China and Japan while suffering great life-threatening pains and weakness.'
16 Following Chinese usage in this regard, the Japanese often referred to the Iberian visitors as *Nanbanjin*, or 'Southern Barbarians' ('southern' because their ships arrived in Japan from the south). Although too much should not be read into this expression, it was obviously not intended as complimentary.
17 Cooper, *They Came*, p. 41.
18 Ibid, p. 42.
19 Abranches Pinto & Bernard, '*Instructions*', p. 396.
20 Burnett, 'Humanism', p. 457.
21 Details of this controversy between Jesuits and friars, Portuguese and Spaniards, are given in Boxer, *Christian Century*, pp. 154–60; Cooper, *Rodrigues the Interpreter*, pp. 123–26; and Moran, *Japanese*, Chapter 7. A recent valuable account, Correia, 'Alessandro Valignano Attitude', discusses the political and commercial aspects of the matter, but concentrates on the different world-views of the Jesuit and Franciscan orders, with the former willing to adapt to different cultures and circumstances.
22 A general account is provided in Moran, *Japanese*, Chapter 7; Valignano's views on the matter are given in his *Sumario*, Chapter 9. The issue was extensively discussed at a conference of senior Jesuits in Bungo in December 1581. Schütte, *Valignano's*, 2, pp. 216–20.
23 An account of the origin of this antagonism is given in Satow, 'Origin'.
24 The Franciscan viewpoint is expressed in Ascensión & Ribadeneira, *Relaciones*.
25 Quoted in Abranches, Pinto & Bernard, '*Instructions*', pp. 395–96 and also at greater length in Moran, *Japanese*, pp. 8–9. Note that Valignano mentions here the first two issues listed above – lack of finance and lack of Japanese understanding of Europeans – but says nothing about preserving the Jesuit monopoly of missionary work in Japan. In his *Apología*, p. 64, Valignano denies the purpose of the legation was to obtain a papal brief maintaining the Jesuit monopoly, but in his lengthy list of instructions to Nuno Rodrigues, who accompanied the party from India to Europe, he orders him to inform the king and the pope that 'neither bishop nor friars should come to Japan'. *Apología*, p. 64, n. 45. In view of their subsequent criticism of the mission to Europe, the friars evidently believed that one of the legation's aims was to lobby in Rome for a retention of this monopoly. Ibid, p. 52.

Chapter 2: Preparing the Legation

1 A Japanese named Bernard had in fact reached Europe as early as 1553. Baptized by Xavier in Japan, he entered the Society of Jesus in Lisbon, studied

pp 12-19 THE JAPANESE MISSION TO EUROPE, 1582-1590

    in Coimbra, and travelled through Spain and Italy. He died in Coimbra in February 1557. Schurhammer, *Xavier*, 4, p. 65, n. 2. But Valignano's legation was the first Japanese party to reach Europe.
2 An excellent general account of the legation in given in Moran, *Japanese*, pp. 6–19.
3 Jesuit archives, Rome, JapSin 10 (IIb), f. 335.
4 Much detail regarding the families of Mancio and Michael is provided in Fróis, *Ambassade*, pp. 9–16, with their family trees on pp. 14–15; also, Valignano, *Apología*, pp. 56–57; Okamoto, *Kyūshū Sankō*, pp. 22–25. Martin was also called Martin Campo, the Portuguese translation of his surname, and he sometimes signed his name in this way.
5 Abranches Pinto & Bernard, *'Instructions'*.
6 *Cartas* 2, f. 17v. Other Jesuit accounts use the same or similar references.
7 Among the more bizarre references to the boys may be mentioned 'two kings of India' and 'Indian princes'. Fróis, *Ambassade*, p. 126, n. 475, & p. 139.
8 Even in a modern publication, a Portuguese scholar refers to the boys as 'daimyo', which they were certainly not. Sande, *Diálogo*, p. 55, n. 28.
9 Valignano, *Apología*, p. 64; Jesuit Archives, Rome, JapSin 10 (11b), f. 337v.
10 Valignano, *Apología*, p. 59. Valignano probably mentions 'the most Serene Princes' because Fray Martín had ironically referred to the legates as 'these most serene princes'. Ibid, p. 52; Asensión & Ribadeneira, *Relaciones*, p. 124.
11 Valignano, *Apologia*, p. 52; Ascensión & Ribadeneira, *Relaciones*, p. 60.
12 Valignano, *Apología*, p. 52; also Ascensión & Ribadeneira, *Relaciones*, pp. 124–5.
13 Jesuit Archives, Rome, JapSin 10 (IIb), f. 337v.
14 Farrington, *English Factory*, p. 257. Cocks mentions three Japanese instead of four, but was not alone in this error. Richard Hakluyt, c.1552–1616, refers to 'the 3. Princes of Japan, that were in Europe'. Hakluyt, *Principal Navigations*, 6, p. 442. In his *Essai sur les mœurs*, 2, pp. 316 & 794, Voltaire also mentions the *'trois princes japonais chrétiens'* who went to Rome. The mistake may have originated in Julian's absence from the papal audience and the coronation Mass in 1585.
15 Fróis, *Ambassade*, pp. 158–59.
16 Ibid, p. 175.
17 Schütte deals with Ramón's statements in detail in his *Valignano's*, I, pp. 258–63; see also Pacheco, *'Cuatro Legados'*, p. 19, n. 1.
18 Valignano, *Apología*, pp. 59–61.
19 Fróis, *Ambassade*, p. 7.
20 Ibid, p. 28, n. 109.
21 Fróis, *Ambassade*, p. 6, n. 43.
22 Valignano, *Sumario*, pp. 86–87. Writing from Cochin in October 1583, Valignano mentions 'the four boys aged fifteen'. *Documenta Indica*, 12, p. 828.
23 Coelho, Nagasaki, 15 February 1582, in *Cartas*, 2, f. 17v.
24 Abranches Pinto & Bernard, *'Instructions'*, p. 402. Regarding study abroad, Valignano later changed his mind and sent seventeen Japanese seminarians to Macao in 1601. He even wanted some Japanese Jesuits to study in Europe, but this plan aroused so much opposition among missionaries that even the strong-willed Visitor was obliged to drop the idea. Schütte, *Textus*, p. 405, n. 95; *Documenta Indica*, 14, pp. 654–55; Pacheco, *'Cuatro Legados'*, pp. 31–32.
25 Valignano, *De Missione*, p. 11.

26 Schütte, *Valignano's*, 2, p. 266. The fathers of Julian, Mancio and Michael had all been killed in battle: Mancio's and Michael's fathers in 1577, and Julian's in 1569. Yūki, *Roma wo Mita*, p. 16, and *'Julian Nakaura'*, p. 3.
27 To justify his return to Europe, Valignano reported to Rome about the party: '. . . it is not suitable they go to Rome except in my company, for their relatives in Japan felt deeply about this, and I could get their consent only on condition that I would bring them back to Japan.' He says it was essential they be treated hospitably in Europe, 'and in no way does it seem this can be done except in my company'. Valignano, *Apología*, p. 58, n. 25.
28 *Cartas*, 2, f. 17v.
29 Having travelled from Europe to Japan, Valignano was well aware of the perils and hardships of the voyage. He provides a graphic account of this subject in his *Historia*, pp. 11–16, and also *De Missione*, p. 336, mentioning storms, fire, becalming, rocks, shipwreck, sickness and death. More on the wretched conditions and numerous deaths on board is given in Cooper, *Rodrigues the Interpreter*, pp. 28–32. Details of the many shipwrecks on the Lisbon-Goa route are given in Mathew, *History*, pp. 259–72.
30 As related below, one of the party, Brother George Loyola, died of consumption in Macao, aged about twenty-seven years, on the return journey. His death took place exactly a year after the Japanese reached Macao, and may perhaps not be attributed to the hardships experienced during the long voyage.
31 Diogo de Mesquita, 1553–1614, was a Portuguese Jesuit who entered the Jesuit order in April 1574. Details of his life are given below in Appendix 1.
32 Another was the Spaniard Gil de la Mata, who reached Japan in 1586. He was chosen to represent the Japanese mission at a meeting of senior Jesuits in Rome, leaving from Nagasaki in 1592 and returning six years later. He was again chosen for the same duty in 1599, but was drowned when his junk sank before reaching Macao.
33 Despite his surname, Constantine was Japanese (or perhaps his father was Portuguese?). A possible reason for the use of his Portuguese surname is suggested in Appendix 1.
34 The diocese of Macao had been established by papal bull in January 1575; the bishop had under his jurisdiction both Japan and all of China, although it was understood he would always remain in Macao. Magnino, *Pontificia Nipponica*, pp. 16–20.
35 Valignano, *De Missione*, Introduction; translation by J. F. Moran. Luis de Guzman met the boys in Spain and reported: 'They noted down with much care everything they saw and wrote it all up in detail so that they could refer to it later with more certitude and accuracy.' Guzman, *Historia*, 2, p. 294.
36 This expedition should not be confused with the much larger legation led by Hasekura Tsunenaga, 1571–1622, on behalf of Date Masamune, the powerful daimyo of Sendai. This embassy left Japan in October 1613 and travelled via Mexico, and while in Europe Hasekura met Pope Paul V and King Philip III. The party returned in September 1620, but the anti-Christian persecution had begun in its absence, and so the legation made little or no impact in Japan. Materials concerning this mission are found in *Dai-Nihon Shiryō*, part 12, volume 12.

The first national embassy from Japan to the West was led by Iwakura Tomomi, 1825–83, and visited the US and European countries from December 1871 to September 1873.

Chapter 3: Passage to India

1 One passenger on a voyage to India in 1597 wrote: 'God pardon the man who built her and erected so many and such high upper works upon so small a keel.' Quoted in Boxer, *Tragic History*, p. 25, n. 8. For a graphic description of the harsh and unhealthy conditions on board such ships, see Ibid, pp. 10–24. Further information about carracks is given in Mathew, *History*, pp. 288–92.
2 Details of these rutters are given in Mathew, *History*, pp. 29–34.
3 Pyrard, *Voyage*, 2, p. 196.
4 The carracks usually had upper, middle and lower decks, with the cabins of the Captain-Major, pilot and other officials on the middle deck. For the layout of these three decks, see the illustrations in Boxer, *Tragic History*, p. 277.
5 Fróis, *Ambassade*, p. 8, gives the date of departure as 28 February, but most other sources state the 20th. Fróis's text says nothing about the voyage from Nagasaki to Goa, but his editors include, pp. 16–20, a most useful account compiled from other sources, such as Guzman and Gualtieri.
6 Probably *shōgi*, the Japanese board game most similar to Western chess.
7 The daily routine followed by Jesuit missionaries on board ships sailing to India at this time is described in Brockey, 'Jesuit Missionaries'.
8 Linschoten, *Voyage*, 1, p. 147. Despite Linschoten's observation, the silk trade was in fact extremely complicated. Cooper, 'Mechanics'.
9 Valignano, *Sumario*, p. 176*. A lengthy account of the negotiations, with Valignano's prominent participation, is given in Colín, *Labor evangélica*, pp. 265–308.
10 Fróis, *Historia*, 3, p. 287, but *Cartas*, 2, f. 82v, gives the date as 6 July.
11 Vivid accounts of this shipwreck are plentiful: Fróis, *Historia*, 3, pp. 286–291; Pedro Gómez, Macao, 13 December, 1582, in *Cartas*, 2, ff. 82v-85v; Pérez, *Puntos do que me alembrar*, in Schütte, *Textus*, pp. 387–91; Boxer, *Great Ship*, pp. 44–45.
12 Boxer, *Great Ship*, p. 44.
13 Linschoten, *Voyage*, 1, p. 5. A detailed account of the food available on board these ships is given in Mathew, *History*, pp. 248–51.
14 *Documenta Indica*, 12, p. 827.
15 Valignano, *Sumario*, p. 346. Not only does the text of this work provide much information, but the learned commentary and notes of its editor, the late José Luis Alvarez-Taladriz, supply invaluable material based on first-hand sources.
16 While the Portuguese began using this system in India in 1583, politico-religious reasons delayed its introduction in Britain until as late as 1752.

Chapter 4: From India to Europe

1 Pyrard, *Voyage*, pp. 76–88.
2 In his Instructions, the meticulous Valignano had laid down on which formal occasions the boys should wear their Japanese robes. Abranches Pinto & Bernard, '*Instructions*', p. 394.
3 'A most sumptuous construction.' Pyrard, *Voyage*, p. 49.

NOTES   pp. 36-39

4 *Documenta Indica*, 12, p. 899. Fonseca's career had been eventful, for as royal chaplain he accompanied the youthful King Sebastian, 1558–78, on his ill-fated crusade to Morocco and was present at the king's death in the battle of Alcazarquivir; the friar was taken prisoner, but later ransomed. Linschoten entered his service and sailed with him to India. During the voyage the archbishop quelled a riot on board with his strong personality. Linschoten, *Voyage*, 1, p. 6; Cooper, *They Came*, p. 31. The boys would meet another cleric captured at the battle and then ransomed, for the Jesuit Pedro Martins was in Goa at the time of their visit and later became the first bishop to reach Japan. Valignano, *Sumario*, p. 117, n. 30; Cooper, *Rodrigues the Interpreter*, p. 109.
5 Mundy, *Travels*, 1, p. 64.
6 Pyrard, *Voyage*, 2, pp. 3–17, 49, 53, 59, 63, & 199.
7 Linschoten, *Voyage*, 1, p. 181.
8 Valignano, *Sumario*, p. 179; Schütte, *Valignano's*, 1, p. 37.
9 He strongly expresses his disappointment at length in a letter to the Jesuit General in Rome, written in Cochin on 28 October 1583. He writes that Mesquita is a very good man and can look after the boys well, but lacks experience and authority in high-level negotiations. Valignano, *Apología*, p. 60; *Documenta Indica*, 12, pp. 829–33. It is likely that Valignano, with his forceful personality and experience as Visitor, would have made a greater impact in Rome and elsewhere than did the much younger Mesquita. Valignano consoled himself that perhaps he would be able to accompany the boys on their return journey back to Japan, as actually happened. *Documenta Indica*, 12, p. 890.
10 Rodrigues was travelling to Europe in any case, to attend a Procurators Congregation, or a meeting of Jesuit representatives from around the world. This was due to begin in Rome on 15 November 1584. Abranches Pinto & Bernard, 'Instructions', p. 392, n. 18.
11 Conveniently listed in ibid, pp. 391–403.
12 Valignano would have preferred Rodrigues to accompany the party until Rome, but realized his need to go ahead for the Jesuit meeting scheduled to be held there. *Documenta Indica*, 13, p. 452.
13 *Documenta Indica* p. 453, n. 28; Valignano, *Apología*, p. 60. The Jesuit Luis Perpinhão joined the party at Lisbon for this purpose, while others escorted the boys through Spain and Italy. *Documenta Indica*, 13, p. 453, n. 28; Fróis, *Ambassade*, p. 40, n. 151.
14 Valignano was insistent on this point and mentioned it several times, going so far as to say: 'As they live among the [Jesuit] Brothers, they know nothing of what is happening outside except what we wish them to know.' *Apología*, p. 60; *Documenta Indica*, 12, p. 842. He certainly advocated a tight rein be kept on the boys.
15 *Cartas*, 2, f. 89. Archbishop Bragança, 1530–1602, son of the fourth duke of Bragança, tried his vocation as a Jesuit as a young man, but left the order after six years, remaining a firm friend and subsidizing the publication of the two-volume Jesuit letter-book, *Cartas*, Evora, 1598, often quoted or cited in these pages. He corresponded not only with Valignano but also with St Teresa of Avila. Fróis, *Ambassade*, p. 37, n. 142; Valignano, *Sumario*, p. 176.
16 It is significant that Martin was chosen for this duty as he was not one of the two official legates. At Goa on the return journey to Japan, it was also Martin

who delivered a public speech in Latin, perhaps indicating that, of the four boys, he was the most skilled in that language.
17 Linschoten stayed two weeks in Mozambique and reported that 'divers of our men fel sicke and died, by reason of the unaccustomed ayre of the place, which of it selfe is an unwholesome land, and an evill aire by meanes of the great and unmeasurable heat'. Linschoten, *Voyage*, 1, p. 35.
18 Montanus, *Atlas*, p. 32.
19 Imported goats, cattle and crops have, alas, since devastated the island's original rich vegetation.
20 Mundy, *Travels*, 3:2, pp. 415–16. Linschoten stopped at the island in May 1583, and left a detailed description. *Voyage*, 2, p. 258.
21 Whether or not the boys showed their wonderment either here or elsewhere in Europe is not known. In the Introduction of *De Missione*, we read that although they regarded many things as wonderful, 'in conformity with Japanese manners, they gave no outward sign of surprise', thus displaying the difference between the exuberant character of the Europeans and that of the more reserved Japanese. On their return journey, Valignano was told that in all the dangers experienced in their long journey, the colour of the boys' face never changed nor did they ever lose their composure, much to the amazement of onlookers. Valignano, Goa, 1 December 1587, in *Cartas*, 2, ff. 231v-34. In his account of the boys in Milan, Urbano Monte mentions that they 'do not greatly marvel'. Gutiérrez, *Prima Ambascieria*, pp. 67–68.
22 Lisbon was an international centre of trade and distribution, with hundreds of Portuguese ships bringing a large variety of goods from Africa, India, Ceylon, Malacca, Sumatra, China and Japan. Russell-Wood, *World*, pp. 123–32.
23 'Japanese party' is written advisedly for, as noted above, a Japanese named Bernard had reached Europe some thirty years earlier.

Chapter 5: Portugal

1 They later gave the pope a similar cup. The gift is not entirely improbable. In 1532 Pope Clement VII presented to Francis I of France, among other gifts, a 'unicorn's horn'. It was probably a narwhal's tusk. Knecht, *Catherine*, p. 17.
2 Valignano, *Cerimoniale*, Chapter 4. This demonstration was not perhaps a complete success, for there is no record of its being repeated during their stay in Europe. Perhaps the boys were considered too young to be putting on a public display of drinking alcohol.
3 The Hieronymite religious order, named after St Jerome, 340–420, flourished in Spain and Portugal during the sixteenth and seventeenth centuries. Philip II much favoured the monks and, as will be seen later, entrusted to them the administration of the Escorial.
4 Exactly which screens these were is not clear. The boys later presented the pope with screens depicting Azuchi castle and city, but they also carried a screen, received in Macao, showing a map of China. Abranches Pinto & Bernard, 'Instructions', p. 398; Fróis, *Ambassade*, p. 35, n. 133.
5 The ingenious and playful use of water power was much in vogue in nobles' gardens at the time. The boys later witnessed another example at the Villa Pratolino near Florence.
6 These translations must have been handwritten, for the Jesuits began printing books only after the boys had returned to Macao and Japan.

7 It was in Lisbon that Mesquita obtained the famed movable-type printing press for use in Japan, but it is not clear whether this purchase was made during this stay in the capital or on the return journey eighteen months later. In any case, the party would certainly not have transported the bulky press through Spain and Italy, and then back again to Lisbon. Pacheco, 'Diogo de Mesquita', pp. 439–40; Laures, *Kirishitan Bunko*, p. 9.
8 Valignano, *De Missione*, pp. 183–84. Unfortunately, many of these gifts were lost when the *Santiago* was wrecked on its return voyage to India. Valignano, in *Cartas*, 2, f. 232v.
9 The organ had been built by an Italian master as recently as 1562. Grove, *New Grove*, 13, p. 739.
10 The tapestries were laded on to the *Santiago* sailing from Lisbon in March 1585, and were lost when the ship was wrecked off Mozambique on 19 August later that year.
11 Caterina,1540–1614, was the widow of Duke João Bragança, who had died only two years earlier. Caterina had given birth to ten children, four of whom had died before the boys' arrival. Despite his youth, Teodósio, 1568–1630, had already experienced no little hardship. Taking the place of his ailing father, he had joined King Sebastian's ill-fated crusade and had been captured in Morocco, but later ransomed. The boy was descended from the royal family, and when Portugal regained its independence from Spain in December 1640, it was a Bragança, the son of Teodósio, who was summoned to Lisbon from Vila Viçosa to become King João IV of Portugal.
12 Fróis, *Ambassade*, pp. 50–53. Much of Constantine's account – the lavish silverware, tapestries, stables, and hunting reserve – can still be seen and admired today. An illustration showing a tournament of *cañas* is given in ibid, facing p. 30.
13 The duke had three younger brothers, the youngest of whom , Felipe, was only three, and two sisters.

Chapter 6: Spain and 'the Most Potent Monarch'

1 Fróis, *Ambassade*, pp. 58–60. According to legend, the statue was buried for safekeeping after the Saracen victory in 711, but was found by a shepherd in 1326. The basilica, now in the custody of the Franciscans, is still a centre of pilgrimage.
2 Fróis, *Ambassade*, pp. 64–68.
3 Gianello Turriano, 1500?–85, was born in Cremona, but moved to Spain in 1529, and worked for Charles V for many years; on the emperor's death in 1558, he transferred to the service of Philip II. His famous clock, with its 1,800 wheels, was probably based on an earlier model constructed by another horologist. Turriano invented the system for raising water from the Tagus to supply Toledo with drinking water, as well as devising ingenious moving figurines and contributing to calendar reform. He died in June 1585, nine months after the boys' visit. In 1987 the Juanelo Turriano Foundation was founded in Madrid to study and publish his works. García-Diego, *Juanelo Turriano*.
4 Iñigo López de Mendoza, 1536–1601, the fifth duke of Infantado. The Mendoza family was extremely powerful, and the splendour of its palace in Guadalajara was renowned.
5 The boys would meet Dom João again during their visit to Coimbra.

6 The three chapters are part of Valignano's *Historia del Principio*, which he completed in Cochin in June 1583, while still in the company of the boys. They deal with China's administration, imperial rule, mandarins, punishments, language, religions, army, climate, topography, and other topics. Abranches Pinto & Bernard, '*Instructions*', p. 398, and Valignano, *Historia*, chapters 26–28.
7 Cristóbal de Moura, c.1538–1613, a 'Castilinized Portuguese', was the king's confidential minister. He had played a prominent role in negotiating Philip's succession to the Portuguese throne, and served as Spanish ambassador and then twice as viceroy in Portugal. He was present at Philip's death on 13 September 1598. Five days later another powerful ruler, Toyotomi Hideyoshi, died in Japan.
8 Maria of Spain, 1528–1606, married Emperor Maximilian II of Austria, 1527–76, in 1548, and after her husband's death became the Dowager Empress. She resided in the Descalzas Reales convent, formerly a palace, in Madrid, which she and her sister Juana, 1535–73, widow of Prince John of Portugal, furnished with fine works of art.
9 Antoine Perrenot de Granvelle, 1517–86, was made cardinal in 1561, and served as viceroy of Naples for four years. He played a large role in the election of Gregory XIII in 1572, and in the negotiations leading to Philip II ascending the Portuguese throne in 1580.
10 'I don't know who it was', according to Fróis, *Ambassade*, p. 79, thus indicating that this incident was noted down by a member of the Japanese party.
11 Luis Enríquez de Cabrera y Mendoza, d. 1596, the seventh Admiral of Castile. At this point the meticulous Fróis lists by title no less than twenty-seven nobles who took the oath. *Ambassade*, p. 81.
12 Much of this account is based on Valignano, *De Missione*, pp. 195–97, in which Leo is made to remark that the same sort of allegiance ceremony was also held in Japan. In 1598, in the last weeks of his life, Toyotomi Hideyoshi assembled leading daimyo more than once to swear loyalty to his eight-year-old son Hideyori, but with far less success than in the Spanish case. Berry, *Hideyoshi*, pp. 234–35. *De Missione*, p. 197, also explains the traditional rivalry between Toledo and Burgos.
13 In the words of a contemporaneous Englishman. Parker, *Philip II*, p. 159.
14 The concession must also have pleased Mesquita, who on 15 November wrote from Madrid to the Jesuit general superior in Rome complaining about the difficulty he was experiencing in fulfilling Valingnano's directives. Yūki, *Shinshiryō*, p. 74.
15 A reference to the *kataginu*, a stiff, sleeveless shoulder garment worn by nobles on formal occasions.
16 As reported in Guzman, *Historia*, 2, p. 236.
17 Philip's personal life was tragic, for he was widowed four times. His teenage daughters Isabella, b. 1566, and Catarina, b. 1567, were children of his third wife, Elizabeth of Valois, while his son Philip, 1578–1621, was born of his fourth wife, Anne of Austria, who had died four years before the Japanese arrived. The king's wives had suffered five miscarriages or stillborn children, while three young sons and a daughter had died before the age of eight, two of them since the boys' departure from Japan. Philip's mentally unstable son Don Carlos, born of his first wife, Maria of Portugal, had died in 1568 at the age of twenty-three in virtual confinement. In Japan also, the death rate

among children, even of aristocratic families, was brutally high. Bolitho, *Bereavement and Consolation*, pp. 3–5.

18 The Japanese language aroused considerable interest in Europe, and a curious reference to it is found in John Eliot's textbook of French conversation published in London, 1593, when referring to the *'foure yong princes or kings, or sonnes of the kings of Iapan'*. Eliot declares: *'I heard them speake in passing along thorow the streetes: their words are almost all of one sillable, their speech princely, thundering, proud, glorious and marvellous loftie.'* Eliot, *Ortho-epia Gallica*, p. 37.

19 The Portuguese texts of the three letters are given in Fróis, *Ambassade*, pp. 90–92. Their style and content make it evident that they were not personally composed by the daimyo.

20 Count of Mayalde and Ficallo, 1533–1606, one-time viceroy of Portugal and man of letters. He was the fifth, and the favourite, of the eight children of the fourth Duke of Gandia, 1510–73, who after losing his beloved wife in 1546 entered the Society of Jesus, was elected its third superior general in 1565, and is now known as St Francis Borja.

21 Gaspar de Quiroga, 1512–95, whom Philip II much admired, was made cardinal in 1578. Appointed Inquisitor General in 1575, he supervised publication of a two-volume index of forbidden books, 1583–84. The boys had already seen him shortly before leading the bishops in the oath-taking ceremony.

22 Fróis, *Ambassade*, p. 98.
23 Ibid, p. 99.
24 San Gerónimo, 'Memorias', pp. 395–96.
25 Fróis, *Ambassade*, pp. 103–04. *Torinoko* is a type of thick, smooth Japanese paper. The renowned Jesuit José de Acosta, 1540–1600, mentions seeing examples of the boys' writing after his return to Spain from Latin America in 1587. Acosta, *Natural and Moral History*, 1, pp. 400–01.
26 An elephant and a rhinoceros, presumably the same beasts, had lumbered through the cloisters of the Escorial in October of the previous year. San Gerónimo, 'Memorias', pp. 368–69.

Chapter 7: From Alcalá to Alicante

1 Such credentials were extremely useful for travellers. Montaigne, 1532–96, passed through Italy four years before the boys' arrival and relates: 'At Ferrara they kept us waiting a long time at the gate on account of the passports and certificates of health, and the same at all the places.' *Diary*, p. 100.

2 On various occasions, Enrique de Guzman, 1540–1607, second count of Olivares, went out of his way to help the Japanese party in Rome. His son, born in Rome three years after their visit, became the famous count of Olivares who dominated the Spanish government during the reign of Philip IV.

3 Guzman, *Historia*, 2, p. 295.
4 The text of the king's letter, dated 24 November 1584, to Arteaga is given in Fróis, *Ambassade*, p. 109.

Chapter 8: The Road to Rome

1 Francesco de' Medici, 1541–87, who had been granted the title of archduke by Emperor Maximilian II in 1576, was greatly interested in natural science, chemistry and alchemy, and spent much time working in his laboratory.

A contemporary report mentions his 'melancholy disposition'. Hibbert, *Florence*, p. 188.
2 Pietro de' Medici, the duke's second younger brother.
3 Nor is there any mention of the two leaning towers in Bologna. Thanks to feats of modern engineering, the tower in Pisa now tilts a safe 5°, and in December 2001 the general public was once more allowed to enter and climb to the top.
4 Mesquita hesitated because the archduchess was none other than the celebrated Bianca Capello, 1548–87, Francesco's long-time mistress whom he had secretly married in 1578 within a month of the death of his first wife, Joanna of Austria. The duke and duchess died of fever within a few hours of each other only two years after the boys' visit, thus inevitably giving rise to rumours of mutual poisoning. The Florentines lost no love for the Venetian Bianca and 'imputed to her more crimes than she had time to commit'. Steegmann, *Bianca Capello*, p. 228.
During his visit to Italy, Montaigne dined with the archduke's family in November 1580, and describes the archduchess as 'handsome, according to Italian ideas, a pleasant and dignified face, big bust and breasts as they like them'. *Diary*, p. 109.
5 This was merely a matter of public politeness as Pietro and his brother Cardinal Ferdinando, 1549–1609, loathed Francesco's wife Bianca, and on her death two years later the cardinal, Francesco's successor, ordered her to be buried in an unmarked grave. Incidentally, Pietro, who treated the Japanese visitors with so much affection and loving kindness, had murdered his wife Eleanora de Toledo in July 1576. He has been described as 'passionate, jealous, dissolute and without a redeeming quality of any kind'. Young, *Medici*, p. 604.
6 Fróis, *Ambassade*, pp. 128–29, and Valignano, *De Missione*, pp. 215–16.
7 Brown, 'Courtiers', p. 894, points out the political aspect of this visit, for the Order of Santo Stefano was the institution 'by which the duke sought to establish his naval supremacy in the Mediterranean'.
8 His mother, Isabella de' Medici, the archduke's favourite sister, had been strangled by her husband, Paolo Giordano Orsini, on 16 July 1576, some eight years before the boys' visit. Thus Francesco's sister and sister-in-law, Eleanora (see n. 16), were murdered within one week.
9 The pious Alessandro de' Medici, 1535–1605, was elected pope in 1605 and took the name Leo XI, but died within less than a month of his coronation.
10 Fróis, *Ambassade*, pp. 130–31.
11 Francesco had built the palace ('a fairy palace of beauty and delight') for Bianca and its construction took fifteen years. It was demolished in 1822. Steegmann, *Bianco Capello*, pp. 172–73; Hibbert, *Florence*, p. 357. Montaigne also visited the Villa Pratolino in 1580 and left a description of these fountains and the aviary. *Diary*, pp. 105–07.
12 The Palazzo Vecchio, with its slender tower reaching a height of more than 300 feet, is still a prominent landmark in Florence today. Borsook, *Florence*, pp. 38–41.
13 The fountain was planned by Ammannati and completed in 1575; the giant statue of Neptune is not highly regarded. Ibid, pp. 47–49.
14 Valignano, *De Missione*, p. 219: 'two giants made of polished stone, each on a column, with their clubs raised on high and threatening to kill two men,

about the same size, under their feet'. Perhaps a reference to Michelangelo's *David*, 1503, and Baccio Bandinelli's *Hercules and Cacus*, 1533. The giant *David* does not carry a club nor is he trampling anyone under foot, but these two statues are often considered as a pair. The visitors must have viewed *David* and one can only guess how they reacted, for standing statues of human beings (as opposed to deities) were uncommon in Japan. To add to their wonderment, the statue towers some three-times life-size and is completely naked, other features not encountered in Japanese culture.

15 According to Valignano, *De Missione*, p. 219, the boys viewed statues of a man and woman, looking at each other and holding a chain that could be extended across the palace's main entrance. The armless male was the work of Vincenzo de' Rossi, about 1535, and may represent Philemon, while the other, by Bandinelli of the same date, may be of Philemon's wife Baucis, the couple who showed hospitality to Jupiter and Mercury. These figures are technically called herms, that is, statues on columns used as signposts, boundary markers, or (as in this case) chain-posts. Borsook, *Florence*, p. 33.

16 According to Valignano, *De Missione*, p. 230, the boys saw this ingenious clavicembalo several days later in Viterbo, and not in Florence. Other discrepancies in time sequence between the two texts are noted in Fróis, *Ambassade*, p. 139. A description of this instrument a given in Valignano, *De Missione*, p. 230; English translation in Harich-Schneider, *History*, pp. 470–71.

17 Full descriptions are given in Borsook, *Florence*, pp. 55–58, 219–20 & 279–80.

18 A brief contemporary account about the visit to Florence mentions the boys were not more than eighteen years old and were still beardless. It lists some of the decidedly modest gifts they presented to the archduke, including a pot made of black perfumed wood and a piece of the same wood, and two sheets of paper made from the bark of a tree on which were written in their language the names of God and the Virgin Mary. The report confirms that the boys wrote down 'all the notable things of our city'. Berchet, *Ambasciate*, pp. 53–54.

19 Such was their devotion, the boys wished to make one more visit to the Virgin, but this was not allowed, for 'Neither the highest kings nor emperors had been shown [the Virgin] more than once'. Brown, 'Courtiers', pp. 897–98, quoting from a letter written by Raffaello de' Medici on 13 March. This rebuff is not reported by Fróis.

20 It may seem strange that a pious teenager should ask for a portrait of a married lady, but the Latin text in *De Missione*, p. 228, implies that he did request a portrait of her and not of her husband, the archduke. This is confirmed in a letter dated 1 March 1585 (quoted in Brown, 'Courtiers', p. 895), in which Antonio Inglese mentions this choice of gift. 'And this he wants to take to Japan so that the women may see how much these [women here] exceed them in beauty and style.'

21 Further discussion on this point is made in Brown, 'Courtiers', pp. 892–93. Raffaello de' Medici accompanied the boys on these expeditions and lost no time in sending reports to the archduke. Ibid, pp. 895–97.

22 Fróis, *Ambassade*, p. 141, n. 520. This remark is contained in a private letter, written a few days later and still preserved in Siena. The observation appears exaggerated, but the boys' obedient attitude towards Mesquita has already been mentioned.

23 Characteristically Fróis does not mention this untoward incident, but it is reported in other sources. Fróis, *Ambassade*, p. 142, n. 522.
24 A distinguished jurist, Ugo Buoncompagni, 1502–85, had taught law at Bologna and was not ordained to the priesthood until he was about forty. He had been elected pope in May 1572 thanks to the intervention of Philip II, who had used his power of veto to prevent the conclave's first choice from ascending the papal throne. Spanish intervention also brought about his successor's election. Pastor, *History*, volume 20, deals with Gregory XIII in detail. Today, Gregory is best remembered by two institutions bearing his name, the Gregorian University in Rome and the Gregorian calendar, devised and introduced under his auspices.
25 Nuno Rodrigues mentions the need for guards in a letter written in Civita Castellana on 3 June 1585. Yūki, '*Atarashiku*', p. 13.
26 Giacomo Buoncompagni, 1548–1612.
27 The incorrupt body of St Rose, 1235–52, is preserved in Viterbo, and is carried in procession around the city every year on 4 September.
28 During his career, Alessandro Farnese, 1520–89, son of the first Duke of Parma and nephew of Pope Paul III, was often employed as papal ambassador to conduct negotiations in European courts. The Farnese palace at Caprarola was designed by the celebrated Giacomo Barozzi da Vignola, 1507–73, student of Michelangelo.
29 Claudio Acquaviva, 1543–1615, had been elected the fifth Superior General of the order in 1581. He and Valignano had been fellow students in Rome. In fact, the two men had much in common – both came from noble families, both were appointed to the highest offices in the Jesuit order while still in their thirties and both were outstanding administrators. Schütte, *Valignano's*, 1, pp. 9 & 30–36.
30 Crasset, *History*, 1, p. 377.
31 As quoted in Boscaro, 'The First Japanese', p. 9. The text of Acquaviva's letter to Valignano explaining the change in plan is given in Fróis, *Ambassade*, p. 143, n. 526, and Valignano, *Apología*, p. 62.

Chapter 9: The Papal Audience

1 Montaigne was received in private audience by Gregory XIII on 28 December 1580, and left the following memorable description: 'He is a very handsome old man, of the middle height and upright, his face full of majesty, a long white beard; at this time more than eighty years old, as healthy and vigorous at that age as one can possibly wish, without gout, without colic, without stomach trouble, and without any subjection; of a gentle nature, exciting himself little over the affairs of the world; a great builder, and in this respect he will leave in Rome and elsewhere a particularly honoured memory.' *Diary*, p. 125.
2 The procession's exact route through the city is given in Fróis, *Ambassade*, p. 153, n. 568.
3 Giacomo Savelli, d. 1587, had been promoted cardinal in 1539; he belonged to one of the four most influential Roman families.
4 Further details are given in Fróis, *Ambassade*, p. 154, n. 571.
5 Purchas, *Hakluyt Posthumous*, volume 12, p. 254.
6 Ibid, p. 32. Portuguese text in Fróis, *Ambassade*, pp. 173–76. The sequence of events in Fróis's narrative is somewhat suspect, and a more logical version is

presented in ibid, p. 156, n. 575. From the style of the letters it is obvious that they had not been composed by the daimyo themselves.
7 Fróis, *Ambassade*, pp. 163–72. English summary in Pastor, *History*, volume 20, pp. 462–64. The speech was later published and the party took back a copy to Japan. Valignano, *De Missione*, p. 235.
8 Purchas, *Purchas his Pilgrimes*, p. 32.
9 Filippo Boncompagni, a nephew of the pope. Also present at the banquet was Cardinal Philippo Guastavillani, another nephew.

Chapter 10: The Stay in Rome

1 Valignano, *De Missione*, p. 257 bis, explains that by custom ambassadors stood on these occasions as if guarding the pope, while other people remained seated.
2 Further details of this ceremony are supplied in Valignano, *De Missione*, pp. 241–46. On Maundy Thursday 1581 Montaigne attended the same ceremony at the same church. Having ridden to Santa Maria sopra Minerva in a procession of 25 richly caparisoned horses, Gregory XIII bestowed promissory notes of 35 crowns to 107 young women, who could cash the notes and receive a white dress 'when they have found a husband'. Montaigne, *Diary*, p. 162.
3 The boys also appear to have met Bernard Maciejowski, the representative of the Polish King. Ermakova, *'Tenshō Ken'ō Shisetsu to Pōrando'*.
4 'The first legation and homage from the kings of Japan to the Roman pontiff, 1585'. See Fig. 8.
5 Much detailed information about these doctors and Julian's diet is given in Fróis, *Ambassade*, p. 183, n. 654.
6 These screens, which Nobunaga had presented to Valignano, depicted Azuchi castle and city. Their origin is a matter of some interest and is related in Appendix 3. Writing from Rome on 5 April, one correspondent mentions the gifts presented by the Japanese – 'they only gave a desk and a table on which a town erected by that king of Bongo is engraved', and a few other items, including 'a cup made from a bone of a rhinoceros' ('all things of low value'). Boscaro, 'First Japanese Embassy', p. 15. In fact, the screens were of immense artistic and historical value back in Japan.
7 Regarding the traditional seven churches of Rome, see Montaigne, *Diary*, pp. 152 & 153–54; Valignano, *De Missione*, p. 257. The boys also visited the eight Jesuit establishments in Rome, including the German and English colleges. Valignano, *De Missione*, pp. 248–51.
8 Fróis refers to the duke, mentioned several times earlier, as the pope's nephew, although in fact he was Gregory's natural son, born before the pope was ordained priest. 'Nephew... Euphemistically applied to the illegitimate son of an ecclesiastic'. *Oxford English Dictionary*, 10, p. 324. Although Fróis diplomatically refers to him as 'nephew', Gregory himself never made any secret of his paternity, and on his becoming pope he appointed his son governor of Castel Sant'Angelo and later granted him other titles and offices.
9 Pastor, *History*, volume 20, pp. 634–36, deals with the pope's final days.
10 Bishop of Ripatransone since 1572, Sasso was appointed cardinal in 1593.
11 Gregory's tomb, surmounted by an imposing seated statue of the pope with his right hand extended in blessing, is located within the basilica.

pp 97–101   THE JAPANESE MISSION TO EUROPE, 1582–1590

12 Cardinal Michele Bonelli, 1541–1604, performed this duty in his capacity as Vicar General of Rome. He was known as Cardinal Alessandrino from his birthplace near Alessandria in northwest Italy. As papal legate, he had visited Spain and Portugal in 1571 to form a league against the Turks.
13 The relevant part of his speech is given in Fróis, *Ambassade*, p. 191, n. 681.
14 A detailed and somewhat idealized account of the procedure followed in electing a pope is given in Valignano, *De Missione*, Colloqium 25, but, as in many other passages in this book, it is improbable this text is based on the boys' notes.

Chapter 11: The New Pope

1 Born as Felice Peretti in 1521 near Montalto and the son of a peasant, the new pope entered the Franciscan novitiate at the age of twelve and eventually became vicar general of the order. His election came as a surprise, for he had been out of favour with his predecessor and was living in semi-retirement. When the conclave was split between the Medici and Farnesi factions, Montalto emerged as a compromise candidate and was elected. Pastor, *History*, volume 21, pp. 8–23; this volume deals with the reign of Sixtus V in great detail.
2 Leti, *Life*, p. 173. Concerning brigandage in Italy at the time, see Pastor, *History*, volume 20, pp. 539–41.
3 Ibid, p. 178.
4 Antonio Carafa, 1538–91, nephew of Paul IV, was a classical scholar pf some renown. Created cardinal in 1568, he was appointed director of the Vatican library, and was an active member of the council created to correct the texts of the missal and breviary.
5 One of Sixtus's many accomplishments in Rome during his short reign was to complete the construction of the basilica's dome. A mural in the Vatican Library, shown in *Spazio*, 13:1, p. 11, depicts the crowds in front of the cathedral at Sixtus's coronation and the dome is clearly shown to be incomplete.
6 Marco Sittico Altemps, 1533–95. The un-Italian family name derived from the castle of Hohenems, in present-day Austria, where the duke was born; the name was first italinized as Alta Emps and then Altemps. Pius IV was his uncle on his mother's side. After following a military career, Altemps was made cardinal in 1561 and appointed bishop of Constanza. He reconstructed a medieval villa in Rome, now known as the Altemps Palace.
7 Quoted in Boscaro, 'First Japanese Ambassadors', p. 17, and 'Popular Reaction', p. 4.
8 Perhaps on account of this protocol contretemps, Priuli did not send back to Venice a flattering description of the boys, reporting: 'They are short of stature . . . of swarthy complexion . . . of bad mien and bad colour of flesh'. Quoted in Boscaro, 'First Japanese Ambassadors', p. 10.
9 This mural has often been reproduced, notably in *Spazio*, 13:1, 1982. See Fig. 9. Valigano, *De Missione*, pp. 276–78, provides a detailed description of this procession.
10 Tucchi, 'Japanese Ambassadors', p. 68.
11 This was a common decorative theme and was also to be found on the letter from the Viceroy of India that Valignano presented to the ruler Toyotomi Hideyoshi in Kyoto six years later. The Latin text of Julian's and Michael's certificates is given in Berchet, *Ambasciate*, pp. 68–71; Yūki, *Shinshiryō*,

pp. 80–81. In 1615, Hasekura Tsunenaga, leader of the second Japanese mission to Europe, received the same honour in Rome, and his tattered illuminated scroll, with similar wording, is reproduced in *Dai-Nihon Shiryō*, part 12, volume 12, p. 240.

12 Marcantonio Colonna, 1523–97, was a zealous cleric, becoming archbishop of Taranto in 1560, and then of Salerno; appointed cardinal in 1565, he attended the Council of Trent. Not to be confused with his kinsman of the same name, hero of the battle of Lepanto.

13 In a despatch to the Doge dated 1 June 1585, the Venetian ambassador, Lorenzo Priuli, mentions this ceremony in some detail. Berchet, *Ambasciate*, p. 72.

14 Gregory XIII's brief *Mirabilia Dei*, dated 13 June 1583, donated an annual 4,000 crowns for twenty years, and this was increased to 6,000 crowns by Sixtus V in *Divina Bonitas*, 22 June 1585. Schütte, *Textus*, p. 189, nn. 12 & 13; Magnino, *Pontificia Nipponica*, pp. 24 & 35.

15 The Latin texts of three of these letters – to Philip II, Cardinal Albert in Lisbon, and the authorities in Genoa – all dated 26 May are given in Magnino, *Pontificia Nipponica*, pp. 33–34.

Chapter 12: Bologna and Ferrara

1 It was during their meetings with Acquaviva that the foursome asked to enter the Jesuit novitiate. While still with the boys in Cochin in 1583, Valignano had foreseen the possibility of their becoming novices, but did not want them to do so in Rome, 'because they may see and learn matters which may turn out to be bad to know in Japan'. Acquaviva wisely counselled his visitors to wait until they returned to Japan before entering the order, as in fact they later did. *Documenta Indica*, 12, p. 843; Abranchas Pinto & Bernard, 'Instructions', p. 402; Fróis, *Ambassade*, p. 207.

2 Abranches Pinto & Bernard, 'Instructions', p. 402. Valignano had been born in the kingdom of Naples.

3 Valignano, *De Missione*, p. 283. Even though the Japanese did not visit Naples, *De Missione*, pp. 283–84, contains a detailed account of the city and obviously this account could not have been based on the boys' notes. It may be noted that Valignano came from the Naples region.

4 On the journey from Rome to Genoa the party was accompanied by the Italian Jesuit Ippolito Voglia, who sent back numerous reports to Rome. Japanese translations of a score of these letters is given in Yūki, *Shinshiryō*, pp. 101–226. Many of the cities the Japanese passed through are engagingly described in Montaigne, *Diary*, pp. 171–86.

5 That is, St Clare of Montefalco, c.1268–1308, not the better-known St Clare of Assisi, 1194–1253, who was born and is buried in nearby Assisi.

6 Their reception in most of these places (except Civita Castellana) was more or less identical – a welcome by the governor and officials with guards outside the city, reception at the local cathedral and veneration of relics, and a banquet accompanied by music.

7 Isaiah, 55.5.

8 Belonging to an illustrious Genovese family, Filippo Spinola was made cardinal in 1583. The boys would later meet his nephew, Carlo Spinola, a Jesuit who reached Japan in 1602 and died as a martyr at Nagasaki in September 1622.

pp 108–111 THE JAPANESE MISSION TO EUROPE, 1582–1590

9 While in Loreto, Mancio wrote a letter, dated 13 June, to the Jesuit General, thanking him for his kindness to them in Rome and reporting on the reception enjoyed since leaving the city. A Japanese translation of the letter, written in Spanish in Mesquita's handwriting, is given in Yūki, '*Atarashiku Hakken*', pp. 11–12. Montaigne, in *Diary*, pp. 178–81, offers a lengthy account of the holy house of Loreto, where he piously left a tablet on which the names of himself, his wife, and daughter were inscribed.
10 Japanese translation in Yūki, '*Atarashiku Hakken*', pp. 13–16.
11 Sixtus V was born in the village of Grottamare near Ancona.
12 Francesco Maria II, 1548–1631, the last duke of Urbino. As a young man he had distinguished himself in the battle of Lepanto. Dennistoun, *Memoirs*, 3, pp. 129–249. According to Valignano, De *Missione*, p. 289, the duke had just returned from hunting (to account for his not receiving the party earlier?), but according to Guzman, *Historia*, 2, p. 272, he had in fact been speaking to Paolo Giordano Orsini (see p. 222, n. 8), whom the boys had met in Rome. Orsini had fled to Venetian territory on the election of Sixtus V, for he had murdered not only his own wife but also on 27 June 1583, his lover's husband Francesco Peretti, who happened to be the new pope's nephew. Orsini died in November of that year, while his lover, Vittoria Accoramboni, was assassinated on 23 December in Padua to avenge the honour of the Orsini family. Fróis, *Ambassade*, p. 215, n. 754.
13 They were duly entertained at all these places, even at Rimini, where the governor, uninformed of their impending arrival, hurriedly organized a fitting reception within fifteen minutes.
14 Gabriel Paleotti, 1524–97, was made cardinal in 1565 and appointed bishop, and then archbishop, of Bologna in 1576. In the consistory following the death of Sixtus V in 1590, he received a substantial number of votes.
15 Antonio Maria Salviati, 1507–1602, was sent twice to France as papal legate by Pius IV; Gregory XIII raised him to the cardinalate and appointed him papal legate in Bologna.
16 St Dominic, 1170–1221, was the Spanish founder of the Order of Preachers, better known as the Dominican Order. St Catherine, 1413–63, was a mystical writer and abbess who was born and died in Bologna.
17 Alessandro Benacci, *Avisi Venuti Novamente da Roma* . . ., Bologna, 1585. Quoted in Boscaro, 'First Japanese', p. 12, 'Popular Reaction', p. 5, and *Sixteenth Century*, p. 44. Alessandro Benacci, d. 1590, belonged to a well-known Bologna publishing family and produced half-a-dozen booklets about the boys. Regarding another of his works titled, in English translation, 'Account of the Voyage and Arrival of the Most Serene Japanese Princes in Europe, Rome, and Bologna', Boscaro notes its text shows that, such was popular demand for information, the booklet was published *before* the Japanese reached Bologna. Boscaro, *Sixteenth Century*, p. 84.
18 Alfonso II, 1533–97, was the fifth and last duke of Ferrara. Although married three times, he produced no heir, and after his death Ferrara reverted to administration by a papal legate.
19 Mario Bevilacqua, 1536–93, patron of the arts.
20 This is an interesting remark as it pinpoints the boys' apartment. On hearing of the death of his brother Charles IX in May 1574, the future Henry III returned from Poland to France via Italy, and was feted in Venice and Ferrara.

While in the latter city in July, he stayed in the castle's lavishly decorated Mirror Suite, with its famous frescos still unfinished.
21 Writing about his travels in Italy four years before the Japanese arrived, Montaigne notes that the duchess of Urbino, ten years older than her husband, and the duke were not on good terms and lived apart. *Diary*, p. 190. The duchess, Lucrezia d'Este, 1535–98, may have been more than thirteen years older than her husband. They were married in 1570, but it was not a happy union and within a few years they parted and lived separately; her close friendship with the poet Tasso is well known. Dennistoun, *Memoirs*, 3, pp. 135–36, 152–54 & 317–21.
22 Guzman, *Historia*, 2, p. 275.
23 Whether or not they were shown the grim subterranean dungeons, in which so many people had met a miserable end, is not recorded.

Chapter 13: Carnival of Venice

1 Concerning Venice, Colloquia 27 & 28 in *De Missione* deal in part with the visit, while Colloquium 29 is devoted to a detailed account of the city, most of which does not treat directly with the visit and probably is mainly Valignano's composition.
2 Quoted in Boscaro, 'Popular Reaction', p. 3. In other words, Venice did not wish to be bested by Rome in its display of hospitality; in addition, the new pope approved of the Japanese legation. Interestingly, this was not the first time a young ambassador had passed through Chioggia en route to Venice, for in 1579 Archduke Francesco of Tuscany (see p. 221, n. 1) sent his half-brother Giovanni, then aged only twelve, to thank the Venetian senate for its good wishes on the occasion of his second marriage. Like the Japanese, young Giovanni performed his duties admirably and enjoyed twelve days of banquets and sightseeing. Steegmann, *Bianca Capello*, pp. 199–200.
3 Gabriel Fiamma, 1533–85, was a minor poet and man of letters, who had been appointed bishop of Vicenzia by Gregory XIII.
4 At this point, Valignano, *De Missione*, Colloquia 27 & 28, provides a long description of the basilica and the ducal palace, and with its wealth of detail the account appears to depend on sources other than the boys' notes. Like a Baedeker guidebook, the text tells us that Venice had 70 parishes, 31 monasteries, 28 convents, 14 hospitals, 53 plazas, 160 marble and 23 bronze statues, 450 bridges and reputedly 10,000 gondolas.
5 Lorenzo Campeggi, 1547–85, nuncio in Venice since 1581.
6 Da Ponte had been member of the senate since 1522 and was the 87th doge since March 1578, dying shortly after the boys' visit. He had attended the later sessions of the Council of Trent, 1545–63, not as a theologian but as an observer to protect Venice's political interests. Tintoretto's painting of him kneeling before the Virgin and Child, with a suitable accompaniment of saints and cherubs, may still be seen in the Sala del Collegio in the ducal palace, not far from where the Japanese boys met him. Tietze, *Tintoretto*, plate 235.
7 The sword was still on display until at least 1773.
8 A description of the shipyards and Murano glassworks is given in Valignano, *De Missione*, pp. 318–21.
9 The universal feast day of St Mark falls on 25 April, but Venice also celebrated the Apparition of St Mark on 25 June to commemorate the discovery of his

remains, stolen from Alexandria in 828, hidden in a stone pillar in Venice, and said to have been found on 25 June 1094.

10 A lengthy eyewitness description of the 1585 procession, compiled by a notary, Nicolò Doglioni, is given in Berchet, *Ambasciate*, pp. 123–38. He confirms that the senate had postponed the event, in which thousands of people took part, so that the Japanese could view the spectacle. He lists the floats depicting Biblical figures (starting with Adam and Eve) and saints, but makes no mention of any representation of the pope blessing the Japanese boys. But both Frois, *Ambassade*, p. 228, and Valignano, *De Missione*, p. 315, refer explicitly to this final float.

11 In a letter to Rome written shortly after leaving Venice, Mesquita provides exactly the same information concerning the inscriptions and names written in Japanese and Italian. He remarks that the portraits were to be hung in a chamber together with the those of doges and senators. Japanese translation of his letter in Yūki, '*Atarashiku*', pp. 16–17. A letter written in Italian and Japanese, praising Venice but with the signatures written by the same hand, is preserved in the Vatican Museum, and is probably a preliminary draft of the presentation document. Reproduced and translated in Satow, 'Origin', pp. 136–39.

12 Ridolfi, *Life*, pp. 77–78. Carlo Ridolfi, 1594–1658, published his detailed and standard account of Tintoretto's life and work in 1642.

13 Boscaro, 'Popular Reaction', p. 6; Berchet, *Ambasciate*, pp. 79–80.

14 In contrast, no less than two portraits of Hasekura Tsunenaga, leader of the second Japanese mission to Europe, 1613–20, are still preserved in Sendai and in the Galleria Borghese, Rome. In the former he is wearing European clothes, in the latter, still in perfect condition, he is dressed in exotic Japanese robes, decorated with a colourful pattern of deer and plant shoots. Okamoto, *Namban Art*, fig. 49; Sakamoto, *Namban Bijutsu*, figs. 66 & 67.

15 Rodrigues mentions two large crates of valuable glassware and another containing velvet and other items. *Documenta Indica*, 14, p. 56.

16 Quoted in Boscaro, 'First Japanese Ambassadors', pp. 18 & 19. In his letter, Mesquita notes that Venice had plenty of holy relics and there had been a desire to present some to the party, 'but for some reason they did not give any'. Japanese translation in Yūki, '*Atarashiku*', p. 17. According to Boscaro, it was common for Venice to give relics to distinguished visitors, and she suggests the change in plan indicates the republic was not interested in the legates as such, but rather in improving its strained relations with Rome. While other Italian cities sometimes referred to the Japanese as 'the Indian kings', in their letters the shrewd Venetians usually, but not always, called them 'the Japanese gentlemen' or 'the young Japanese'. Berchet, *Ambasciate*, pp. 54, 62 , 71, 73, 76, 79 & 85.

17 Both quotations in Boscaro, 'First Japanese Ambassadors', p. 10. The remark about the difficulty in distinguishing the boys is a classic case of viewing the unfamiliar Other. This feature is especially noticeable in the depiction of the boys in the Milan sketches.

Chapter 14: From Padua to Genoa

1 Montaigne, *Diary*, p. 93, passed along the same route in November 1580 and also remarks on the horse-pulled boats and the locks.

2 St Anthony of Padua, 1195–1231, an outstanding preacher, was born in Lisbon, but spent his short adult life in France and Italy. His body was transferred to Padua in 1263. In popular belief, he is the saint to approach to recover lost articles.
3 The alma mater of Dante, Petrarch and Galileo as well.
4 Melchior Wieland, c.1529–89, was born in Königsberg, but in his writings often used the Italian or Latin forms of his name, Villandino or Guilandinus (the latter appears in Valignano, *De Missione*, p. 323). During his extensive travels he was shipwrecked, captured by pirates and ransomed for 200 *scudi*. He was appointed director of the botanical garden in 1561. To avoid interrupting the narrative, the significance of his gifts is later discussed in detail in Appendix 3.
5 Vicenza is famous for its fine buildings designed by the outstanding and influential classical architect Andrea Palladio, 1508–80, and the Teatro Olimpico, completed in 1583, is his last work.
6 Bevilaqua palace/castle dates from 1336 and in recent years has been restored to some of its original splendor after suffering damage from fires and occupation by Austrian troops in the nineteenth century and German military in the twentieth.
7 Guglielmo Gonzaga, 1538–87, a competent, at times autocratic, ruler and fervent patron of music.
8 The duke suffered constantly from gout and arthritis. Simon, *Renaissance Tapestry*, p. 227.
9 Vicenzo Gonzaga, 1562–1612. Despite Fróis's rosy account, Vicenzo was on bad terms with his father. Rubens's portrait of father and son is reproduced in Fenlon, *Music*, p. 120. Vicenzo had reputedly killed the Scottish scholar, and his father's favourite, James ('The Admirable') Crichton, b. 1560, in a nocturnal street brawl in Mantua. The date of this incident is uncertain, but as Crichton published a eulogy on the death of St Charles Borromeo, who died on 3 November 1584, the brawl may well have taken place as late as 1585. The decline of the Gonzaga family is generally associated with Vicenzo's reign. He led three fruitless expeditions against the Turks in 1595, 1597 and 1602. In popular belief, the infamous Duke of Mantua in Verdi's opera *Rigoletto* may be identified with Vincenzo.
10 Sixtus V appointed the bishop and scholar Scipione Gonzaga, 1542–93, Patriarch of Jerusalem in 1585 and two years later promoted him to cardinal. The pope often made use of his skilful diplomatic and religious services to carry out his policies.
11 Guglielmo had the basilica of Santa Barbara built 1563–72. Fenlon, *Music*, pp. 95–101; illustration and plan are given in ibid, pp. 87 & 97.
12 This may well have been true as Guglielmo was passionately interested in music, was in correspondence with the great Palestrina, and published anonymously several works of sacred and profane music. Fenlon, *Music*, pp. 87 & 94. The scores of four of his polyphonic Masses are given in *Gonzaga Masses*. Vincenzo was also enamoured with music and invited Monteverdi to his court.
13 The boys visited the famous Palazzo de Te, but one wonders whether they were shown some of the more explicit frescos, such as the depiction of the drunken naked Bacchus, surrounded by unclad fauns and ladies. Illustration in Simon, *Renaissance*, between pp. 182–83.

14 The Latin text of this plaque is given in Berchet, *Ambasciate*, p. 86. The noted poet, composer, and Benedictine monk Angelo Grillo, 1557–1629, was present, and at the abbot's request wrote a poem to mark the event.

15 Eleanora of Austria, daughter of Emperor Ferdinand I, whom Guglielmo had married in 1561. They had two daughters and one son, Vincenzo.

16 Eleanora de' Medici, eldest daughter of the archduke of Tuscany, was Vincenzo's second wife. He had married Margherita Farnese in April 1581, but the marriage was annulled on grounds of non-consummation, and the 16-year-old Margherita was packed off to a comfortable convent. Before Vicenzo could marry his second wife, the Tuscan authorities demanded a witnessed test of his virility. Then followed a farcical series of events in true comic-opera style until the famous *La Prova*, or 'The Test', accounts of which entertained the European courts, took place (successfully, after some mishaps) in Venice. Vicenzo happily married Eleanora in the same month, April 1584, just one year before the boys' visit. Simon, *Renaissance*, pp. 240–45. The affair is written up in satirical fashion in Peyrefitte, *Prince's Person*.

17 Niccolò Sfondrati, 1535–91, had been bishop of Cremona since 1560 and was made a cardinal in 1583. He would later succeed Urban VII as Pope Gregory XIV in December 1590, but reigned for less than a year.

18 Because of a disagreement over protocol, the duke did not wish to be present to greet the new archbishop, Gaspare Visconti, on his solemn entry into Milan, and had temporarily left the city. Gutiérrez, *Prima Ambascieria*, p. 40.

19 The Sicilian Carlo d'Aragon, d. 1599. He was also Marquis of Avola, Prince of Castelvetrano, Count of Burgeto, Grand Constable of Sicily and Captain General of His Catholic Majesty in Italy. Gutiérrez, *Prima Ambascieria*, p. 39; *Enciclopedia Universal*, vol. 60, p. 1475.

20 According to Rodrigues, Julian had a fever lasting little more than twenty-four hours. *Documenta Indica*, 14, p. 47. Further details of the stay in Milan are given in ibid, pp. 44–45.

21 Fróis, *Ambassade*, pp. 245–46.

22 An account of Urbano Monte, 1544–1613, cartographer and man of letters, is given in Gutiérrez, *Prima Ambascieria*, pp. 37–38.

23 Although the figures depicted in the Augsburg print are obviously based on the Milan portraits, they are not completely identical and, if anything, are more delicately reproduced. Mesquita's figure has been reversed and he now turns towards his left; in addition, his hands are resting on what appears to be a desk; Michael's left hand now touches a table.

24 All five Italian poems with English translations are given in Boscaro, *Sixteenth Century*, pp. 174–82

25 Gutiérrez, *Prima Ambascieria*, p. 67.

26 Gutiérrez, *Prima Ambascieria*, pp. 67–68. Despite this account of their Japanese robes, the boys are portrayed wearing European dress in the portraits provided by Monte.

27 The letter, still preserved in the State Archives of Mantua, is reproduced in Lach, *Asia*, 1:2, between pp. 656–57.

28 Bishop of Pavia, 1564–91. As noted in Valignano, *De Missione*, p. 338, he was promoted to cardinal shortly after the boys' visit.

29 Readers weary of so many references to artillery salutes will be consoled to learn that numerous references to this subject in Fróis's account have been

prudently omitted here to avoid tiresome repetition. Perhaps even the boys understandably became a little tired of this thunderous welcome, however well-meaning it was intended. In *De Missione*, p. 338, Michael is made to note at this point: 'Our entering the city was celebrated by the usual noise of muskets and cannons'.

30 Christina, 1522–90, duchess of Lorraine, was the daughter of King Christian II of Denmark and at the age of eleven married Francesco Maria Sforza, duke of Milan, who died in 1535. Six years later she married Franz, duke of Lorraine, with whom she had three children. Her youngest child was Dorothea, who married Duke Erich II of Brunswick in 1576; he died in Pavia only a year before the boys' visit. Christina lived in Italy for health reasons from 1579 until her death in Tortona eleven years later. Her portrait in mourning dress by Hans Holbein the Younger is justly famous and made Henrry VIII wish to marry her. Fróis assures readers that both mother and daughter were mirrors of sanctity and virtue, but there is no record of the Japanese actually visiting them, although presumably they did so.

31 Not the famous admiral Andrea Doria, who had died in 1560, but his grand-nephew and successor, Giovanni Andrea Doria, 1539–1606, commander of the Mediterranean fleet. He had not distinguished himself in the battle of Lepanto.

32 Official senate documents detailing hospitality arrangements and expenses incurred are given in Berchet, *Ambasciate*, pp. 88–90.

Chapter 15: Spain and Portugal Revisited

1 Valignano, *De Missione*, p. 324, J. F. Moran's translation.
2 The incorrupt body of Olegario, 1060–1137, is still venerated in Barcelona cathedral.
3 Quoted also in Moran, *Japanese*, p. 11.
4 Ascanio Collona, 1560–1608, son of Marcantonio Collona, hero of the battle of Lepanto, was made cardinal in 1586; his intervention in the stormy conclave of 1592 resulted in the election of Clement VIII against the wishes of Philip II.
5 The boys had seen Cabrera y Mendoza in the previous November when, as Admiral of Castile, he had led the nobles taking the oath of loyalty to Prince Philip.
6 See p. 228, n. 20, above.
7 Presumably to simplify his narrative, Fróis in *Ambassade* has the boys visiting Coimbra during their journey between Evora and Lisbon, as a result stopping at the capital only once, not twice, before setting sail to India. Valignano in *De Missione*, and Guzman, *Historia*, 2, p. 291, provide the more likely account of their itinerary, presented here.
8 Burnett, 'Humanism', p. 463; Valignano, *De Missione*, pp. 360–61. Colloquium 31 in this latter work is devoted to a detailed description of Coimbra and its university.
9 Valignano, *De Missione*, p. 360. The new bishop of Coimbra, Afonso Castelo Branco, had just arrived in the city, and the play was doubtless performed also in his honour.
10 Burnett, 'Humanism', p. 467; Valignano, *De Missione*, pp. 360–61.
11 Burnett, 'Humanism', p. 465; Valignano, *De Missione*, pp. 358–59. Staging such plays was a feature of Jesuit education at the time, and in Swiss colleges

alone at least thirty-nine plays dealing with the Japanese mission and the Christian daimyo were produced. Immoos, 'Japanese Themes', pp. 86–87. On his arrival in Goa in 1583 Valignano was greeted by similar theatrical performances at the Jesuit college. *Documenta Indica*, 12, pp. 898–99. This practice extended even to Japan, where allegorical plays with Christian themes were staged by students at the Kyushu college in honour of Bishop Martins in 1596. Cooper, '*Teatro Jesuítico*'; also Fróis, *Historia*, 5, p. 435.

12 The former monastery commemorates the victory of John I over Spanish forces at Aljubarrota in 1385, while the latter was founded in 1153 and was in the care of Cistercian monks.

13 The first part of the promise was fulfilled, but as will be seen later, only one horse reached Japan and was featured prominently in a procession through Kyoto.

14 Fróis, *Ambassade*, p. 264.

15 According to Bartoli, *Historia*, p. 292, the ship had made an earlier attempt to sail at the end of March, but within a day head winds had obliged it to return to port. In *Ambassade*, p. 264, Fróis relates that the party embarked on 8 April, but Valignano, *De Missione*, p. 365, gives the date as 12 April. The former perhaps refers to the passengers boarding the ship, the latter to the ship's departure.

Chapter 16: The Return Journey

1 An account of the return voyage is not included in *Ambassade*, and the content of the present chapter is largely based on Valignano, *De Missione*, Colloquium 32, and Guzman, *Historia*, 2. There is some doubt about the accuracy of various dates mentioned here in the text.

2 Sofala was a region in Mozambique, where the Portuguese established a fortress in 1508; for some time gold was mined in the area, thus giving rise to speculation that the place might be identified with Ophir, whence Solomon obtained his legendary wealth. But Sofala was notorious for its unhealthy climate and its treacherous coastal shallows, and was a place to be avoided at all costs. Sofala is often mentioned in accounts of shipwrecked sailors. Boxer, *Tragic History*, passim. Friar João dos Sanctos, O.P., laboured there for some six years and left a description of the place: Purchas, *Hakluytus Posthumus*, 9, pp. 198–202.

3 Cooper, *Rodrigues the Interpreter*, pp. 109–10; Valignano, *De Missione*, pp. 370–71. A lengthy account of the wreck of the richly laden *Santiago* on 19–20 August 1585, is given in Brito, *História Trágico-Marítima*, 2, pp. 49–93. The ship sank in the Baixos de Judia, also called Baixos da India (now known as Bassas da India), which Friar João dos Sanctos correctly located at 22° South. Purchas, *Hakluytus Posthumus*, 9, p. 198.

4 Angoche, situated at 16° S, is a port in the north of present-day Mozambique, and has many off-shore islands and shallows in its vicinity.

5 On its return voyage, the *São Felipe* had the misfortune of encountering the fleet of Sir Francis Drake, who captured the carrack near the Azores on 9 June 1587, and seized its rich cargo of tons of spices, porcelain, silk, velvet, jewels and bullion, worth millions of pounds. Passengers and crew were provided with shipping to return home, and some hundreds of black slaves imprisoned on board were liberated. The *São Felipe* was then sailed to Plymouth, England, where it arrived on 26 June. All apart from

the enormous value of the seized cargo, confiscated documents found on the ship revealed the huge profits to be obtained from Asian trade and this information indirectly led to the foundation of the East India Company in 1600.

6 Linschoten stayed in Mozambique for two weeks in 1583 while food supplies and water were loaded on board. He reports on the prevalence of fever and disease in the extreme heat, and Portuguese shipping tended to avoid landing there whenever possible. According to Linschoten, 'divers of our men fel sicke and died, by reason of the unaccustomed ayre of the place, which of it selfe is an unwholesome land, and an evill aire by meanes of the great and unmeasurable heat'. *Voyage*, 1, pp. 34–35.

7 Writing from Cochin on 20 December 1586, Valignano expressed his 'affliction and worry' about the boys' non-arrival, but detailed news received from four other ships that had arrived together at Goa on 27 September led him to believe the party had been delayed at Mozambique. *Documenta Indica*, 14, pp. 423–25.

8 According to Linschoten, Melinde was 'a kingdome of it selfe, holding the lawe of Mahomet'. 1, p. 36. Situated at 3° N, it was reportedly the first port of call after Vasco da Gama rounded the Cape of Good Hope in November 1497. The place is located on the south-east coast in present-day Kenya.

9 The small Queimados Isles served as a useful marker for ships approaching the port.

10 Valignano later wrote to Philip II announcing the arrival of the boys and thanking the king for his kindness towards them. *Documenta Indica*, 14, pp. 669–70. Although the passengers reached Goa safely, two Jesuits had died on board since leaving Lisbon. Ibid, p. 698; Guzman, *Historia*, 2, p. 292.

11 Duarte de Meneses, 1537–88, count of Tarouca, had been taken prisoner at the battle of Alcazaquivir in 1578, but was later ransomed. A talented administrator, he was much admired by King Philip, who extended his three-year term of office by an additional two years. Valignano, *Sumario*, p. 117, n. 30. Meneses, however, did not live to complete this extension in office.

12 Details about these animals are given in Yūki, 'Horses'. Speaking from first-hand experience, Pyrard, *Voyage*, p. 79, praises the fine horses he had seen in Goa; most, he asserts, had been imported from Persia, but the best had come from Arabia.

13 For Salsete, see *Documenta Indica*, 14, p. 33*.

14 Other quotations from the speech are found in Moran, *Japanese*, p. 6. The full Latin text is given in Schurhammer, 'Obra raríssima', pp. 749–53.

15 Laures, *Kirishitan Bunko*, pp. 19–20.

16 One of the Franciscan friars in Japan alleged that Valignano was not the viceroy's genuine ambassador. Ascensión & Ribadeneira, *Relaciones*, p. 197, n. 114. This seems highly unlikely as Meneses's letter to Hideyoshi, carried by Valignano, still exists in Kyoto. See p. 237, n. 17, below.

17 This is one of the few references frankly admitting in a private letter the boys' lack of fluency in European languages.

18 *Cartas*, 2, ff. 231v-34.

19 Yūki, 'Horses', p. 2.

20 Further details in Boxer, *Christian Century*, pp. 140–52. The annual Jesuit letter of 1588 points out that Hideyoshi's volte-face occurred exactly two

months after the death of Bartholomew of Ōmura and forty-two days after the death of Francis of Bungo, two of the most staunch Christian daimyo in Kyushu. *Cartas*, 2, f. 203.

21 The clavier here was probably a spinet, that is, a small harpsichord with plucked strings, while a rebec was a bowed lute or fiddle. There is no way of knowing which boy played which instrument. For European musical instruments with reference to Japan at that time, see Waterhouse, 'Southern Barbarian Music', pp. 363–4, and Harich-Schneider, *History*, pp. 463–70 & 474–5.

22 Lourenço Mexia, Macao, 8 January 1589, in Jesuit Archives, Rome, JapSin 11 (Ia), ff.16–16v; Mesquita, Macao, 14 November 1589, in ibid, 11 (II), ff. 192–92v.

23 During their travels the four boys may have been coached by the talented Constantine Dourado, for he was later recorded as teaching not only Latin but also instrumental music in the Kyushu school. Schütte, *Textus*, p. 555. All four boys also taught instrumental music at this school during their Jesuit training. Fróis, *Historia*, 5, p. 434.

24 The two books published in Macao were João Bonifacio, S.J., *Christiani Pueri Institutio*, 1588, and Alessandro Valignano, *De Missione Legatorum*, 1590 (more about the latter work is given in Appendix 2). When the anti-Christian persecution broke out in Japan, the press was shipped back to Macao in 1614, where it produced João Rodrigues, S.J., *Arte Breve da Lingoa Iapoa*, 1620.

25 This was a treatise in which he attempted to refute Franciscan criticism of aspects of Jesuit work in Japan, including the despatch of the legation to Europe.

26 In September 1589 Valignano reports that the party's baggage had been stored on board ship, but, to their disappointment, had to be unloaded because it was too late for the favourable monsoon winds. *Documenta Indica*, 15, p. 323.

Chapter 17: Reception in Japan

1 Ōmura Yoshiaki, 1568–1615, baptized as Sancho, had succeeded his father in 1587.

2 The fact that the daimyo, on hearing of the ship's arrival, left his fief, hurried to visit Michael, and spoke with him for several hours appears to confirm the boy's appointment as his representative.

3 Fróis, *Historia*, 5, p. 188. Valignano also confirms that their mothers did not recognize the boys. *Documenta Indica*, 15, p. 518.

4 Quoted in Moran, *Japanese*, p. 173; also pp. 174 & 176.

5 Valignano, *De Missione*, pp. 143 & 247. When twenty years later the Spaniard Sebastian Vizcaino showed a portrait of Philip III and family to Tokugawa Hidetada, the shogun greatly admired the work, marvelling at the realism and colouring, and borrowed the painting to show to his family. Cooper, *They Came*, pp. 120–21.

6 For further details about these two works and their impact in Japan, see Appendix 3.

7 The two horses had certainly reached Macao safely and were destined for 'the Lord of Japan'. Lourenço Mexia, Macao, 8 January 1589, in Jesuit Archives, Rome, JapSin 11 (Ia), f. 16. One of them must have died either in Macao or en route to Nagasaki.

8 The decision for one party to travel overland may have been influenced by the fact that the Arabian horse was being taken as a gift to Hideyoshi, and transporting the large animal in a small coastal vessel would have caused problems.
9 Two years later Yoshimune earned Hideyoshi's wrath by withdrawing his troops during the Korean campaign; he was stripped of his fief and, in the words of Valignano, was left with scarcely enough rice to maintain eight or ten servants. Valignano, *Apología*, pp. 67 & 104–05. Fróis, *Historia*, 5, pp. 279–89, deals with the events in Muro in great detail.
10 A more detailed account of the embassy and the audience with Hideyoshi is given in Cooper, *Rodrigues the Interpreter*, pp. 75–81.
11 The English merchant John Saris commented that the horses he had seen in Japan were 'the size of our middling Nags', although they were admittedly 'very full of mettle'. Bernardino de Avila Girón was even more critical, declaring: 'The very best [horse] in Japan is only fit to carry firewood'. Cooper, *They Came*, pp. 142–43.
12 Fernandes was a Portuguese Jesuit who had entered the order in 1579; imprisoned in the anti-Christian persecution, he died in 1620.
13 Among the Portuguese was the cartographer Ignacio Moreira, who diligently took measurements wherever he travelled in Japan. Schütte, 'Ignacio Moreira'.
14 For Rodrigues's subsequent dealings with Hideyoshi, see Cooper, *Rodrigues the Interpreter*, pp. 83–104 & 185–87.
15 Details of this extravagant gathering are given in Berry, *Hideyoshi*, pp. 183–87.
16 Hideyoshi's ruthless extermination of Hidetsugu's household (in addition to his wife and three young children, some thirty members of his staff were publicly executed in Kyoto) is described in ibid, p. 219.
17 The document still exists in Kyoto in perfect condition for all to admire, and has been designated a National Treasure. Its Portuguese text is given in Fróis, *Historia*, 5, pp. 302–03. For further details and photos, see Cooper, *Rodrigues the Interpreter*, pp. 77–79 & fig. 4, and *Southern Barbarians*, fig. 8.
18 Cooper, *Rodrigues the Interpreter*, p. 80.
19 Writing to Rome on 14 March 1592, Mancio related: 'This unexpected question startled me, but the Lord inspired my reply'. Valignano reported that he had worried for several days in case Hideyoshi decided to keep Mancio in his service. Valignano, *Apología*, pp. 68–69.
20 In fact his father was brother of Arima Yoshinao and Ōmura Sumitada, thus making Michael a cousin of the current daimyo of Arima. Pacheco, '*Cuatro Legados*', p. 25, n. 9.
21 See Harich-Schneider, *History*, p. 471. Chapter 14 ('The First Introduction of Western Music') of this work contains much valuable material on the subject. But when dealing with the boys' travels in Europe, the author tends to assume without evidence they met all the famous musicians then residing in the cities the Japanese visited.
22 As two of the three daimyo represented by the legation had died during the boys' absence, the papal gifts and honours were presented to their successors.
23 Valignano, *Apología*, p. 67, n. 51. It was customary to send from Japan copies of important letters by three different routes, or *vias*, via Goa, the Philippines and Mexico, in the hope that at least one would reach its destination.

pp 163–171 THE JAPANESE MISSION TO EUROPE, 1582–1590

Chapter 18: Assessment of the Enterprise

1 Pacheco, 'Diogo de Mesquita', p. 438.
2 Lach, *Asia*, 1:2, p. 705.
3 Boscaro, *Sixteenth Century*, lists these publications, providing much information and reproducing their title pages. At least one more pamphlet, dated 1585 and published in Olomouc, Bohemia, has since been found. Vasiljevova, 'Unknown'. All these publications deal specifically with the legation, but many other works, including those of Acosta, Cocks, Kaempfer, Scheuchzer and Voltaire, mention the boys in passing. The French historian Jacques-Auguste de Thou, 1553–1617, also refers to the legation in his renowned *Historia*, Book 81. Kaempfer, *Kaempfer's Japan*, p. 479, n. 4.
4 Lach, *Asia*, 1:2, p. 702.
5 As another instance of the Japanese fascination with foreigners, the periodic processions of Korean ambassadors to the shogun's court drew immense crowds in Edo (present-day Tokyo). See Toby's aptly titled article, 'Carnival of the Aliens'.
6 Cooper, *Rodrigues the Interpreter*, p. 104.
7 Consider, for example, the imaginative woodcuts showing quasi-humans ('men that have no head or eyes, and their mouth is in their shoulders') and strange beasts appearing in Sir John Mandeville's *Travels*, a fourteenth-century text that circulated in at least ten European languages and was still being reprinted during the Japanese visit. Whether or not readers of *Travels* still believed these quasi-humans existed in Asia is another matter. But as late as about 1620, the Jesuit João Rodrigues was happily writing in Macao about a 300-year-old Indian, a 700-hundred-year-old Japanese, and shellfish changing into birds. Rodrigues, *João Rodrigues's Account*, pp. 102–03 & 111. European attitudes concerning Asia are ably discussed in Higgins, *Writing East*.
8 When the Venetian ambassador, Paolo Tiepolo, informed Gregory XIII of this treaty on 6 April 1573, the infuriated pontiff reportedly chased him through several apartments and drove him out. Stirling-Maxwell, *Don John of Austria*, 1, pp. 508–13.
9 Fróis, *Ambassade*, p. 202.
10 Boscaro, 'First Japanese Embassy', p. 16.
11 Guzman, who met the boys in Spain, notes in his *Historia*, 2, p. 294: 'Although these gentlemen appeared as children as regards their age, they were very much adults as regards judgement and discretion'.
12 Brown, 'Courtiers', pp. 896–7, points out that, on at least one occasion, in Florence, large and unruly crowds turned out not so much to see the boys, but to get a glimpse of the mural of the Virgin of the Annunciation, usually hidden from view.
13 But Valignano expresses in a private letter disappointment with the quality of some of the gifts; for example, the three sets of Mass vestments donated by Sixtus V were 'old and worn'. Valignano, *Apología*, p. 63, n. 40. Also, many of the presents received in Europe were lost in the shipwreck of the *Santiago* (on which the boys had sailed from India to Lisbon), as Valignano sadly reported from Goa. *Cartas*, 2, f. 232v.
14 Valignano believed the legation had, in fact, cost a great deal of money. Valignano, *Apología*, p. 63, n. 40. He goes on to criticize Mesquita for not having accomplished as much as might be desired in Spain and Italy because of his lack of fluency in the languages of those countries and his lack

of experience in dealing with lords and nobles. *Documenta Indica*, 14, pp. 656–57.
15 Thus, on receiving the news of papal grants for Japan in late 1583, Valignano expressed himself as delighted, only to be disappointed in later years. *Documenta Indica*, 13, pp. 406–07.
16 Schütte, *Textus*, p. 189, nn. 12 & 13.
17 Valignano, *Sumario*, p. 334, n. 4.
18 Cieslik, 'Training', p. 65. According to another source, the pope had granted an annual gift of 4,000 ducats for colleges and seminaries in Japan. *Documenta Indica*, 12, p. 697. Information about financial grants from India are found in ibid, 8, pp. 406–07 & 481, and 9, pp. 60 & 520–21. In 1603 Cerqueira reports that he has been bishop of Japan for five years, but has yet to receive any money.
19 Details of the income due from different sources are supplied in a contemporaneous document reproduced in Schütte, *Textus*, pp. 343–45.
20 Ibid, pp. 869 & 968. A wealth of information on this subject is provided in Schütte, *Cortés*, pp. 57–70.
21 Boxer, *Great Ship*, p. 67.
22 Cooper, *Rodrigues the Interpreter*, pp. 241–43.
23 Writing to Rome in 1583, Valignano lists in detail specific incidents of gifts of church goods and money destined for Japan being delayed or commandeered in Goa and Malacca. *Documenta Indica*, 12, pp. 852–56. He relates further problems in Schütte, *Textus*, p. 476.
24 Magnino, *Pontificia Nipponica*, p. 173.
25 The original Latin text of these briefs is given in Magnino, *Pontificia Nipponica*, pp. 26–27, 36–39, 64–67 & 69–71. Valignano's point of view is expressed in Valignano, *Sumario*, pp. 143–49. See Boxer, *Christian Century*, pp. 156–60, for a general account.
26 Magnino, *Pontificia Nipponica*, pp. 40–46. Valignano's changing view on this subject is reported in Moran, *Japanese*, pp. 163–65; also, Valignano, *Sumario*, pp. 138–42; Cooper, *Rodrigues the Interpreter*, pp. 106–09. The matter was discussed at a Jesuit conference held in Bungo in December 1581. Schütte, *Valignano's*, 2, pp. 220–24.
27 In a bull dated 19 February 1587, Rome appointed the Jesuit Sebastian de Moraes the first bishop of Japan. Magnino, *Pontificia Nipponica*, pp. 39–40. Negotiations concerning this appointment are given in Fróis, *Ambassade*, p. 263, n. 924.
28 The standard source of information on the Jesuit Press is Laures, *Kirishitan Bunko*; Moran, *Japanese*, pp. 145–57, also supplies much useful material.
29 The fact that no less than five members of the Japanese party (the four boys and Constantine) entered the Society of Jesus, and four persevered in their vocation (with one ending his life as a martyr), may be considered as an additional plus, although there is no way of knowing whether or not they would have entered religious life even had there been no expedition to Europe.
30 Pacheco, 'Diogo de Mesquita', p. 438.
31 In a letter to Archbishop Bragança, in *Cartas*, 2, f. 232v; the same thought is also expressed in a letter to Rome. *Documenta Indica*, 14, p. 698.
32 Scores of photos taken during this mission (24 March to 5 April 1982) and showing the boys with John Paul II, the king and queen of Spain, and

Appendix 1: The Boys' Later Careers

1. Valignano, *Sumario*, p. 174*, n. 527; Fróis, *Historia*, 3, pp. 128–30.
2. Cooper, *Rodrigues the Interpreter*, p. 82; Yūki, 'Present', p. 2.
3. Detailed information about this famous Jesuit can be found in Schütte, *Valignano's*, and Moran, *Japanese*. Valignano's different method of administering the Jesuit missions in Japan and in China is discussed in Ross, *Vision Betrayed*.
4. Pachedo, 'Diogo de Mesquita', p. 438.
5. This account of Mesquita is based on Pacheco, 'Diogo de Mesquita' and '*Cuatro Legados*'. Also, Valignano, Il Cerimoniale, pp. 118–21, and Correira, 'Father Diogo de Mesquita'.
6. Writing at the end of 1584, Valignano praises Mesquita as a virtuous and prudent man who understands the things of Japan; in time he would make a good superior, as later in fact happened. *Documenta Indica*, 14, p. 674.
7. Pacheco, 'Diogo de Mesquita', p. 433.
8. Pacheco, '*Cuatro Legados*', p. 39. Details about the treatment of Japanese Brothers at an earlier date are supplied in Moran, *Japanese*, p. 161.
9. Pacheco, 'Diogo de Mesquita', pp. 440–41.
10. Mesquita describes this unsuccessful venture in a letter dated October 1614, only a few weeks before his death. Pacheco, 'Diogo de Mesquita', p. 435.
11. Pacheco, '*Campana*', p. 19.
12. Constantine's work as printer is briefly recorded in Laures, *Kirishitan Bunko*, p. 21. In March 2004 a bronze statue, 1.3 metres in height, of Constantine, the first Japanese to use movable type, was unveiled in the city library of Isahaya, his native town.
13. Moran, *Japanese*, pp. 159–60, also recounts Dourado's career.
14. See p. 51, above. Fróis, *Ambassade*, p. 50.
15. Fróis, *Ambassade*, p. 53. Valignano, *Apología*, p. 66, n. 31, also refers to him as a Japanese.
16. Moran, 'Real Author', p. 5.
17. Schütte, *Textus*, p. 1204.
18. Valignano, *Apología*, p. 55; Schütte, *Textus*, p. 1218.
19. This account of the four boys' subsequent careers is based mainly on Pacheco, '*Cuatro Legados*'.
20. For example, letters to the Duke of Ferrara, the Doge of Venice and the Duke of Mantua. Texts are given in Berchet, *Ambasciate*, pp. 73–74, 80–81, 87, 91 & 92–93.
21. Schütte, *Textus*, p. 339. Justus did not persevere in his religious vocation and later left the Society.
22. Jesuit Archives, Rome, JapSin 12 (Ib), ff. 178–78v.
23. Cieslik, 'Training', pp. 73–74; Cooper, *Rodrigues the Interpreter*, pp. 177–8.
24. Pacheco, '*Cuatro Legados*', pp. 38–39.
25. Pacheco, '*Cuatro Legados*', pp. 39–40; Cieslik, 'Training', p. 76; Oliveira e Costa, 'Bishop', p. 114.
26. Pacheco, '*Cuatro Legados*', p. 31.
27. Another talented Japanese, Fabian Fukan, apparently embittered about this policy of discrimination, left the Jesuit order, apostatized and compiled the

polemical tract *Ha Deus* ('Against God'), in which he attacks the Christian religion and argues against its teachings.
28 Valignano, *Sumario*, p. 87, n. 75; Pachedo, *Cuatro Legados*, p. 35.
29 Farrington, *English Factory*, p. 257.
30 Pacheco, *'Cuatro Legados'*, pp. 37–38. In the town of Chijiwa, at the Tachibana Shinto shrine on the hill on which the castle of Michael's father once stood, there is a monument relating Michael's participation in the mission to Europe. The text on the bronze plaque says nothing about his subsequent career.
31 The identification of the tomb by Professor Ōishi Kazuhisa was widely reported in the Japanese press. Fr Diego Yūki, Nagasaki, kindly brought this news to my attention and added further information.
32 For an appreciation of Martin's talents, see Cieslik, *Seminariyo no Kyōshitachi*, pp. 130–32.
33 Moran, *Japanese*, p. 93.
34 Pacheco, *'Cuatro Legados'*, pp. 31, 32 & 44.
35 Jesuit Archives, Rome, JapSin 20 (1), ff. 163–63v; Cooper, 'Early Western-Style Paintings', p. 44, n. 21. This reference to Pedro the painter is of some interest, all apart from his reconciliation with the Church The extended Kano family formed the most illustrious school of painting in Japanese art history, and the screens presented to Gregory XIII in April 1585 were produced by the grand master Kano Eitoku, or at least under his direction. The Kobe Museum of Art possesses the celebrated portrait of Francis Xavier, below which appear in difficult *man'yōgana* script the name 'The Fisherman', suggesting that the work may have been executed by Pedro Kano. New evidence supporting this theory, including an unpublished letter, dated February 1603, by Kano and comments by Martin, is given in Pacheco, *'Hermandad'*, pp. 143–4.
36 Cooper, *Rodrigues the Interpreter*, p. 204.
37 Ascensión & Ribadeneira, *Relaciones*, p. 132, n. 76; Pacheco, *'Campana'*, pp. 26–27; Laures, *Kirishitan Bunko*, pp. 60–61 & 77–80.
38 Rodrigues, *Rodrigues's Account*, p. 67, n. 2
39 Pacheco, *'Cuatro Legados'*, pp. 46–7.
40 Yūki, *'Julian Nakaura'*, p. 11.
41 Valignano, *Sumario*, p. 86, n. 75.
42 Pacheco, *'Cuatro Legados'*, p. 53. The two-page letter is reproduced, together with printed text and Japanese translation, in Yūki, *'Nakaura Jurian'*. The letter is addressed to Nuno Mascarenhas, a Portuguese Jesuit in Rome; the boys had met him in Europe and also his brother Francisco, the viceroy of India, during their stay in Goa and Evora.
43 See Fig. 12.
44 As recorded by some Japanese-speaking Portuguese present at the scene. Julian's alleged statement is not so unlikely as it may at first seem, for high-ranking warriors traditionally observed the custom of *nanori*, that is, identifying themselves before battle by calling out their name and noble lineage.
45 For Ferreira, see Cieslik, 'Case'. Endō Shūsaku's novel *Chinmoku*, 1966 (*Silence*, 1969) is loosely based on this incident.
46 Pacheco, *'Cuatro Legados'*, p. 58.
47 In addition to the material contained in the preceding note, Yūki has written specifically about Julian in his *Tenshō Shōnen Shisetsu no Nakaura Jurian* and *'Julian Nakaura'*.

pp 193-196 THE JAPANESE MISSION TO EUROPE, 1582-1590

Appendix 2: The Sources

1 Further details of Fróis's life and career are found in Fróis, *Historia*, I, pp. 3-10, and Fróis, *Luis Fróis*.
2 The possibility of Fróis accompanying the expedition to Europe had in fact been discussed, but in a letter dated 25 October 1585, he explains that his age and infirmities prevented him from undertaking the journey. Fróis, *Historia*, 1, pp. 399-400. As regards the boys' notes, '[The Fathers] advised them diligently not to omit to observe, notice and commit to writing anything on this very long journey. Such was their exemplary nature and obedience towards the Fathers that they energetically copied into their notebooks whatever seemed special and worth remembering'. Valignano, *De Missione*, Preface, translated in Burnett, 'Humanism', p. 457. Other references to their diligence in note-taking are found in Guzman and Sande (see pp. 21 & 215, n. 35, above).
3 Fróis, *Ambassade*, pp. 80-82.
4 Fróis, *Ambassade*, pp. 23-29 & 204-06. The account of the first audience with Philip II, at which the boys were not present, must have come from Mesquita. Ibid, p. 75. Mesquita wrote much correspondence during the party's travels; his letters and reports are given in Japanese translation in Yūki, *Shinshiryō*, pp. 16-58. Fróis's sources are discussed in detail in Fróis, *Ambassade*, pp. xxiv-xxx, where the editors note the absence of his accustomed literary style, the unevenness evident in parts of the text, and the occasional use of the first person plural, all indicating the work was compiled from the notes taken by the travellers, letters and printed materials brought back from Europe.
5 The boys took back to Japan a printed version of the speech made by Gaspar Gonçalves during their formal audience with Gregory XIII; they also brought back books on prelates' robes and vestments, but these would hardly have been of use to Fróis when compiling his *Tratado*. Valignano, *De Missione*, pp. 235 & 237.
6 Boscaro, *Sixteenth Century*, p. 162.
7 To give just a few examples, Gualtieri's and Fróis's accounts of the boys' receptions in Florence, Mantua and Milan are practically identical. Gualtieri, *Relationi*, pp. 74-75, 130-31 & 141-45, and Fróis, *Ambassade*, pp. 127-28, 235-36 & 243-45.
8 The text in *Ambassade* was transcribed from a copy made in Macao in the 1740s and now preserved in the Biblioteca Nacional de Lisboa. Fróis, *Ambassade*, pp. xxiii-xxiv; Fróis, *Historia*, 3, p. 285, n. 27. The copying and subsequent dispersion of these Jesuit materials are studied in detail in Schütte, *Archivo*, Part 1; more briefly in Rodrigues, *Rodrigues's Account*, pp. xxviii-xxx.
9 Okamoto probably contributed a great deal, for in the following year, 1943, he published a copiously annotated Japanese translation of Fróis's text. Many of the illustrations and notes contained in Okamoto, *Kyūshū Sankō*, are also found in Fróis, *Ambassade*; the notes in the two books are not completely identical, for the former was intended for a Japanese readership, the latter for a non-Japanese. In the Acknowledgement in another work by Fróis that he edited, Okamoto pays tribute to Abranches Pinto for his meticulous transcription of the Portuguese text. Fróis, *Segunda Parte*, pp. xxv-xxvi.

10 Bernard was in fact a specialist in early Jesuit activity in China and had published scholarly books on the subject. Most, but not all, of the early *Monumenta Monographs* were published in English or German, and possibly Okamoto and Abranches Pinto did not feel sufficiently confident to edit the work in those languages, and so Bernard was chosen to translate and supplement the critical apparatus in French.
11 Quoted in Cooper, *Rodrigues the Interpreter*, p. 164; also Valignano, *Sumario*, p. 66.
12 Fróis, *Ambassade*, p. 35. These comments should not hide my admiration, even affection, for the elderly, sick, overworked and indefatigable chronicler, without whose valuable contribution our knowledge of Jesuit activity in Japan would be greatly diminished.
13 For the life and career of Eduardo de Sande, 1547–99, see Burnett, 'Humanism', pp. 427–30, where we read with regret that he experienced prejudice from some of his Portuguese confrères in India and China because his maternal grandmother had converted from Judaism.
14 Moran, 'Real Author'.
15 A Portuguese translation of *De Missione* is given in Sande, *Diálogo sobre a Missão*. Dr J. F. Moran's English translation has yet to be published.
16 Michael is the principal narrator, for the colloquia are set in Arima, far closer to Nagasaki (where the boys would disembark) than Bungo, and Michael was the representative of the Arima daimyo. Perhaps Michael was chosen as principal spokesman because Mancio's daimyo, Ōtomo Sōrin, had died at the end of June 1587, and so Mancio's role as representative was no longer so important. Of Michael's two daimyo, Ōmura Sumitada had also died less than three weeks later, but his second patron, Arima Harunobu, lived until 1612. The news of the deaths of the two daimyo reached Macao before Valignano and the party arrived there in 1588, and so could have been taken into account when the book was compiled.
17 Valignano, *De Missione*, p. 281.
18 Valignano, *Apología*, p. 55.
19 Quoted in Moran, *Japanese*, p. 47.
20 Ibid, pp. 152–53, 162 & 168. But some Japanese Jesuits who had been abroad learned the language well. Ibid, p. 168.
21 Burnett, 'Humanism', pp. 457–59 & 469.
22 Valignano in fact sent twelve copies of the text to Europe in 1592, but they were all lost in action against English ships; two years later he sent a further nine. Valignano, *Apología*, p. 53, n. 9
23 Valignano, *Apología*, p. 55. Valignano even raises the possibility of an Italian or Spanish edition. Sande also mentions in his Introduction in *De Missione* a plan to bring out a Japanese edition. The learned editor Alvarez Taladriz suggests that Valignano may have had second thoughts about publishing the work in Japanese. The Visitor asserts that the text contains only matters that would help and satisfy the Japanese and describes some of their matters in a way that could not offend them. Yet Japanese readers would hardly have been pleased by the unflattering comparison of their country in comparison with Europe; further, accounts of the abundance of weapons and heavy artillery in European armies might have been viewed with alarm. Valignano, *Apología*, p. 55, and *Adiciones*, p. 558. When discussing the contents of *De Missione*, Massarella not ineptly

pp 199–207 THE JAPANESE MISSION TO EUROPE, 1582–1590

    refers to its contents as 'Japan-bashing'. Massarella, 'Japanese Embassy', p. 221.
24 In *De Missione*, p. 412, the book's last page, Linus optimistically announces the future publication of a Japanese version of the colloquia. Two authors, Bartoli in the seventeenth century and J. C. Scheuchzer in the eighteenth, imply that a Japanese translation was in fact published, but there is no firm evidence for this assertion; neither author was ever in Japan or could read Japanese. Laures, *Kirishitan Bunko*, p. 34. Scheuchzer was certainly familiar with *De Missione* for he records a detailed summary of its contents in Kaempfer, *History*, 1, pp. lxvii–lxix.
25 A partial early English translation of this chapter is given in Hakluyt, *Principal Navigations*, 6, pp. 348–77.
26 Fróis, *Ambassasde*, p. 233, and Valignano, *De Missione*, pp. 322–24.
27 More information about the origin of *De Missione* is provided in Valignano, *Apología*, pp. 53–55, nn. 9 & 13; Moran, *Japanese*, pp. 146–48, and 'Real Author'.
28 Guzman mentions with approval the boys' piety and their obedience towards Mesquita in *Historia*, 2, p. 295.
29 Quoted in Boscaro, 'Popular Reaction', p. 4.
30 This is in marked contrast to Montaigne's text in which the less pious side of Roman life is reported in down-to-earth fashion and thus presents a more balanced account – for example, the courtesans (*Diary*, pp. 141, 155, & 239) and the gruesome public executions of murderers and robbers (Ibid, pp.128–130). In his papal audience on 28 December 1580, Montaigne followed traditional usage, genuflecting three times and then kissing the pope's foot. But he did not hesitate to report less-than-edifying behaviour of prelates, a topic never appearing in Fróis's text. Montaigne attended the pope's Christmas Mass in St Peter's, and notes: 'It seemed strange to him [Montaigne] that, both at this mass and others, the Pope and Cardinals and other prelates were seated, and, during nearly the whole mass, covered, talking and chatting together. These ceremonies appeared to him altogether to partake more of magnificence than of devotion'. *Diary*, pp. 123–24.
31 Lach, *Asia*, 1:2, pp. 688–706.

Appendix 3: Azuchi Screens and Braun's Cities

1 Cooper, *They Came*, pp. 219 & 253. The screens' ability to remain upright gave rise to a playful saying recorded in the Jesuit dictionary: 'Aqiǔdo. Merchant. Biǒbuto, Aqiǔdoroua sugunareba miga tatanu. *Proverb*. Neither byōbu nor merchants can be straight.' *Vocabulario*, f. 11.
2 With his usual foresight and attention to detail, Valignano had laid down in Goa that the screens should be carefully packed in a large box that he had bought for the purpose in Cochin. Leiria, '*Namban* Art', pp. 52–3.
3 The complete text is given in Cooper, *They Came*, p. 134.
4 *Cartas*, 2, f. 37.
5 *Cartas*, 2, ff. 39–39v. The letter is dated 15 February 1582, and was written in the name of Gaspar Coelho, the mission superior, although this excerpt was probably composed by Fróis, who was with Valignano in Azuchi as his interpreter. A similar account is found in Fróis, *Historia*, 3, pp. 261–62. For a discussion of the screen, see McKelway, 'Capitalscapes', pp. 153–60.

NOTES   pp. 207–211

6 Wheelwright, 'Visualization', provides an expert account of these works and their significance.
7 Denhaene, *'Témoignage'*, pp. 87, 89 & 120.
8 Cartari, *Imagini*, pp. 81–82; Lach, *Asia*, 2:1, p. 89, and plates 50 & 51.
9 There are three sources on the life and work of the young artist – Denhaene, *'Témoignage'*; Hoogewerff, *'Philips van Winghe'*; and Schuddeboom, *Philips van Winghe* – but none throws any light on when, where, or how he saw the screens. The talented Winghe died of malaria in Naples at the age of only thirty-two.
10 Some idea of the glory that was Azuchi can be gained from the text and illustrations in Hinago, *Japanese Castles*, pp. 17, 42–43, 85–86, 118–21 & 184–86, and Takayanagi, 'Glory.'
11 As noted earlier, one Italian correspondent referred to the screens as 'a table on which a town erected by that king of Bongo is engraved', adding that all of the gifts were 'of low value.'
12 Valignano, *De Missione*, p. 323; Fróis, *Ambassade*, p. 233, n. 815. Wieland had been appointed director of the garden in Padua in 1561; further details about his career are given on p. 231 n. 4, above.
13 Valignano, *De Missione*, p. 323.
14 In several places, Valignano, *De Missione*, for example, p. 287, mentions other books brought back to Japan, but no specific titles are recorded.
15 See, for example, the illustrations in Okamoto, *Namban Art*, figs. 2, 66, 77, 119, 121 & 123; Cortazzi, *Isles of Gold*, figs. 33 & 36; Sakamoto, *Namban Bijutsu*, figs. 5 & 24.
16 Preserved in Kobe Municipal Museum of Namban Art; Namban Bunka-kan, Osaka; and the Imperial Household Collection, Tokyo. Illustrations in Okamoto, *Namban Art*, figs. 67 & 120; Sakamoto, *Namban Bijutsu*, figs. *22 & 23*; Cooper, *Southern Barbarians*, figs. 73, 74 & 91; Tobu Museum, *Catalogue*, p. 16.
17 Other details from European engravings were reproduced in Japanese screens. Sakamoto, *Namban Bijutsu*, pp. 184–91; Tobu Museum, *Catalogue*, pp. 19, 26 & 117; Cooper, 'Western-Style Paintings', pp. 40–41. For illustrations of the Lepanto screen, see Sakamoto, *Namban Bijutsu*, figs. 1, 2 & 5; Cooper, *Southern Barbarians*, fig. 90. A general account is supplied in Grace Vlam, 'Western-Style Paintings.'
18 The more talented boys at the Jesuit school in Kyushu studied and practised Western art, and Fróis specifically mentions that they were copying 'with much skill' paintings brought back from Europe by the legation. Fróis, *Historia*, 5, p. 479.

Bibliography

Abranches Pinto. J. A., & Henri Bernard, S.J., 'Les Instructions du Père Valignano pour l'ambassade japonaise en Europe'. In Monumenta Nipponica, 6, 1943, pp. 391–403.
Acosta, José de, S.J., *The Natural and Moral History of the Indies by Father Joseph de Acosta*, ed. Clements R. Markham. Hakluyt Society, 1st series, volumes 60 & 61, London, 1880.
Ascensión, San Martín de la, & Marcelo de Ribadeneira, *Relaciones e Informaciones*, ed. José Luis Alvarez-Taladriz. Osaka, 1973.
Barsook, Eve, *Companion Guide to Florence*. Harper & Row, New York & Evanston, 1966.
Bartoli, Daniello, S.J., *Dell' Historia della Compagnia di Giesu. Il Giappone, Segunda Parte dell' Asia*. Rome, 1660.
Berchet, Guglielmo, *Le Antiche Ambasciate Giapponesi in Italia*. Venice, 1877.
Berry, Mary Elizabeth, *Hideyoshi*, Harvard University Press, 1982.
Bolitho, Harold, *Bereavement and Consolation: Testimonies from Tokugawa Japan*. Yale University Press, New Haven and London, 2003.
Borsook, Eve, *The Companion Guide to Florence*, Harper & Row, New York, 1966.
Boscaro, Adriana, 'The First Japanese Ambassadors to Europe: Political Background for a Religious Journey'. In *Kokusai Bunka Shinkokai Bulletin*, volume 103, Tokyo, August–September 1970.
———*Sixteenth Century European Printed Works of the First Japanese Mission to Europe: A Descriptive Bibliography*. E. J. Brill, Leiden, 1973.
———'Itaria ni okeru 1585-nen no Shitsetsu'. In *Spazio*, volume 13–1, Olivetti, Tokyo, 1982, pp. 25–48.
———'Popular Reaction to a Religious Visit.' Unpublished paper delivered at *Colloque International à l'occasion du 450ème anniversaire de l'arrivée des Européens au Japon*, Paris, November 1994.
Boxer, C. R., *The Christian Century in Japan, 1549–1650*, University of California Press, 1951.
Boxer, C. R., ed. & tr., *The Tragic History of the Sea, 1589–1622*. Hakluyt Society, 2nd series, volume 112, Cambridge, 1959.

BIBLIOGRAPHY

―――*The Great Ship from Amacon*. Centro de Estudos Históricos Ultramarinos, Lisbon, 1959.
British Broadcasting Corporation, 'They Went to Rome'. Radio 3, 6 & 11 October 1991.
Brito, Bernardo Gomes de, *História Trágico-Marítima*. Publicaçóes Europa-Americana, Mira-Sintra, 2 volumes, n.d.
Brockey, Liam, 'Jesuit Missionaries and the Journey to China in the Sixteenth and Seventeenth Centuries'. In *Bulletin of Portuguese/Japanese Studies*, volume 1, December 2000, Lisbon, pp. 45–72.
Brown, Judith C., 'Courtiers and Christians: The First Japanese Emissaries to Europe'. In *Renaissance Quarterly*, volume 47, 1994, pp. 872–906.
Burnett, Charles, 'Humanism and the Jesuit Mission to China: The Case of Duarte de Sande (1547–1599)'. In *Euphrosyne, Revista de Filologia Clássica*, Lisbon, 1996, pp. 425–70.
Cartari, Vicenzo, *Imagini delli dei de gl'antichi*. . . Venice, 1647.
Cartas que os padres e irmãos da Companhia de Iesus escreverão dos reynos de Iapão e China. . . . . 2 volumes, Evora, 1598. Facsimile, Tenri, 1972.
Cieslik, Hubert, S.J., 'The Training of a Japanese Clergy'. In Joseph Roggendorf, ed., *Studies in Japanese Culture: Tradition and Experiment*. Sophia University, Tokyo, 1963, pp. 41–78.
―――'*Seminariyo no Kyōshitachi*'. In *Kirishitan Kenkyū*, 11, Tokyo, 1968, pp. 27–138.
―――'The Case of Christovão Ferreira'. In *Monumenta Nipponica*, volume 29:1, 1974, pp. 1–54.
Colección de Documentos Inéditos para la Historia de España, volume 7, Madrid, 1845.
Colín, Francisco, S.J., & Pablo Pastells, S.J., *Labor evangélica, ministerios apostólicos de los obreros de la Compañía de Iesús*. . ., volume 1, Barcelona, 1900.
Columbus, Christopher, *The Voyage of Christopher Columbus: Columbus' Own Journal of Discovery Newly Restored and Translated*, tr. John Cummins. St. Martin's Press, New York, 1992.
Cooper, Michael, ed., *They Came to Japan: An Anthology of European Reports on Japan, 1543–1640*. University of California Press, 1965; Center for Japanese Studies, The University of Michigan, 1995.
―――ed., *The Southern Barbarians: The First Europeans in Japan*. Kodansha International, Tokyo, 1971.
―――'The Mechanics of the Macao-Nagasaki Silk Trade'. In *Monumenta Nipponica*, volume 27:4, 1972, pp. 423–33.
―――*Rodrigues the Interpreter: An Early Jesuit in Japan and China*. Weatherhill, New York & Tokyo, 1974.
―――'*Teatro Jesuítico*'. In *Anais* (Sophia University), 1976, pp. 139–46.
―――'Early Western-Style Paintings in Japan'. In John Breen & Mark Williams, ed., *Japan and Christianity: Impacts and Responses*, Macmillan, London, 1996, pp. 30–45.
Correia, Pedro Lage Reis, 'Alessandro Valigano Attitude towards Jesuit and Franciscan Concepts of Evangelization in Japan (1587–1597)'. In *Bulletin of Portuguese/Japanese Studies*, volume 2, June 2001, pp. 79–108.
―――'Father Diogo de Mesquita (1551–1614) and the Cultivation of Western Plants in Japan'. In *Bulletin of Portuguese/Japanese Studies*, volume 7, December 2003, pp. 73–91.

Cortazzi, Hugh, *Isles of Gold: Antique Maps of Japan*. Weatherhill, New York & Tokyo, 1983.
Crasset, Jean, S.J., *The History of the Church in Japan. Written Originally in French and now Translated into English*. 2 volumes, London, 1705–1707.
Dai-Nihon Shiryō, Tokyo Teikoku Daigaku, multiple volumes, 1922–.
Denhaene, Godelieve, 'Un témoignage de l'intérêt des humanistes flamands pour les gravures italiennes: une lettre de Philippe van Winghe à Abraham Ortelius'. In *Bulletin de l'Institut historique belge de Rome*, volume 60, 1992, pp. 69–137.
Dennistoun, James, *Memoirs of the Dukes of Urbino, illustrating the arms, arts, and literature of Italy, 1140–1630*, J. Lane, London & New York, 1909.
Dicionário de Historia de Portugal, ed. Joel Serrão. 4 volumes, Iniciatorias Editoriais, Lisbon, 1968–1971.
Dizionario Biografico degli Italiani. Istituto della Enciclopedia Italiana. 41 volumes, Rome, 1960–1992.
Documenta Indica, ed. Joseph Wicki, S.J., volumes 1–18. Monumenta Historica Soc. Iesu, Rome, 1948–1988.
Eliot, John, *Ortho-epia Gallica. Eliots Fruits for the French: Enterlaced with a double new Invention, which teacheth to speake truely, speedily and volubly the French-tongue*. John Wolfe, London, 1593.
Enciclopedia Universal Ilustrada Europea Americana, 70 volumes, Bilbao, n. d.
Ermakova, Liudmila M., '*Tenshō Ken'ō Shisetsu to Pōranda*'. In *Nihon Kenkyū*, no. 27, March 2003.
Farrington, Anthony, ed.,*The English Factory in Japan, 1613–1623*. 2 volumes, British Library, London, 1991.
Fenlon, Iain, *Music and patronage in sixteenth-century Mantua*. Volume 1, Cambridge University Press, 1980.
Figueiredo, António José, '*Primeira Embaixada de Japão à Europa*'. In *Religião e Pátria*, Macao, 1961, pp. 1–71.
Fróis, Luis, S.J., *Segunda Parte da Historia de Japam*, ed. João do Amaral Abranches Pinto & Yoshitomo Okamoto. Sociedade Luso-Japonesa, Tokyo, 1938.
———*La Première Ambassade du Japon en Europe, 1582–1592; Première Partie, La traité du Père Frois.*, ed. J. A. Abranches Pinto, Yoshitomo Okamoto, & Henri Bernard, S.J. *Monumenta Nipponica* Monograph 6, Sophia University, 1942.
———*Kyūshū Sankō Ken'ō Shisetsu Kōki. Ruisu Furoisu gencho*, tr. Okamoto Yoshitomo. Tōyōdō, Tokyo, 1943.
———*Historia de Japam*, ed. Josef Wicki, S.J. 5 volumes, Biblioteca Nacional, Lisbon, 1976–1984.
———*Luís Fróis*, Embassy of Portugal in Japan, Tokyo, 1999.
García-Diego, José A., *Juanelo Turriano, Charles V's Clockmaker: The Man and His Legend*. Monograph 26, Science History Publications, Nantucket, 1986.
Gonzaga Masses in the Conservatory Library of Milan, Fondo Santa Barbara, ed. Ottavio Beretta. Parts 1 & 3, American Institute of Musicology, Hänssler-Verlag, Neuhausen, 1997–2000.
Grande Enciclopédia Portuguesa e Brasileira. Lisbon, 40 volumes, 1936–1960.
Greene, Edward Lee, *Landmarks of Botanical History*. Stanford University Press, 1983.
Grove, *New Grove Dictionary of Music and Musicians*. Macmillan, London & New York, 20 volumes, 1992.
Gualtieri, Guido, *Relationi della Venuta degli Ambasciatori Giaponesi a Roma fino alla partita di Lisbona*. Rome, 1586. Facsimile edition, Tenri, 1972.

BIBLIOGRAPHY

Gutiérrez, Beniamino, *La Prima Ambascieria Giapponese in Italia*. Milan, 1938.
Guzman, Luis de, S.J., *Historia de las misiones que han hecho los religiosos de la compañía de Jesús* . . . . Alcalá, 2 volumes, 1601.
Hakluyt, Richard, *The Prncipal Navigations Voyages Traffiques & Discoveries of the English Nation*. 12 vols. Glasgow: James MacLehose and Sons, 1903–1905.
Hamada Kōsaku, *Tenshō Ken-ō Shisetsu Ki*. Tokyo, 1931.
Harich-Schneider, Eta, *History of Japanese Music*. Oxford University Press, 1973.
Hibbert, Christopher, *Florence: The Biography of a City*. Norton, New York & London, 1993.
Higgins, Iain Macleod, *Writing East: The 'Travels' of Sir John Mandeville*. University of Pennsylvania Press, 1997.
Hinago Motoo, *Japanese Castles*, tr. and adapted by William H. Coaldrake. Kodansha International & Shibundō, Tokyo, 1986.
Hoogewerff, G. J., *'Philips van Winghe'*. In *Mededeelingen van het Nederlandsch Historisch Instituut te Rome*, volume 7, Rome, 1927, pp. 59–82.
Immoos, Thomas, 'Japanese Themes in Swiss Baroque Drama'. In Joseph Roggendorf, ed., *Studies in Japanese Culture: Tradition and Experiment*, Sophia University, 1963, pp. 79–88.
Kaempfer, Engelbert, *The History of Japan, Together with a Description of the Kingdom of Siam, 1690–1692*, tr. J. G. Scheuchzer. John MacLehose & Sons, Glasgow, 3 volumes, 1906.
———*Kaempfer's Japan: Tokugawa Culture Observed*, tr. & ed. Beatrice M. Bodart-Bailey. University of Hawaii Press, 1999.
'Kapitan no Edo Korekushon: Orandajin no Nihon Shumi'. Tōkyō-to Edo-Tōkyō Hakubutsukan, Exhibition catalog, 3 October–3 December 2000.
Knecht, R. J., *Catherine de' Medici*. Longman, London & New York, 1998.
Kōda Shigetomo, *'Itō Manshoi no Nishokan'*. In *Shirin*, volume 16:2, April 1931, pp. 81–91.
Lach, Donald F., *Asia in the Making of Europe*. Volumes 1 & 2, University of Chicago Press, 1965–70.
Laures, Johannes, S.J., *Kirishitan Bunko: A Manual of Books and Documents on the Early Christian Mission in Japan*. Monumenta Nipponica monograph 5, Sophia University, 3rd revised edition, 1957.
Leiria, Leonor, 'Namban Art: Packing and Transportation'. In *Bulletin of Portuguese/Japanese Studies*, volume 5, December 2002, pp. 49–65.
Leti, Gregorio, *The Life of Pope Sixtus the Vth in which We have also (by pleasant Digressions) A View of the Transactions of the Romish Church and The Most Considerable Affairs of Europe In that Age*. London, 1704.
Linschoten, John Huyghen van, *The Voyage of John Huyghen van Linschoten to the East Indies*, ed. Arthur Coke Burnell and P. A. Tiele. Hakluyt Society, 1st series, volumes 70 & 71, London, 1885.
Livermore, H. V., *A History of Portugal*. Cambridge University Press, 1947.
Magnino, Leo, *Pontificia Nipponica: Le relazioni tra la Santa Sede e il Giappone attraverso i documenti pontifici*. Officium Libri Catholici, Rome, volume 1, 1947.
Mandeville, Sir John, *The Voiage and Trauaile of Syr Iohn Maundevile*. Oxford University Press, 1932. [Facsimile of the 1568 English edition]
Massarella, Derek, 'The Japanese Embassy to Europe, 1582–90, and *De Missione Legatorum Iaponensium*: Religion, Humanism, "Ecclesiastical Colonialism"?', in *Chūō Daigaku Keizai Kenkyūjo Nenpō*, 34, 2004, pp. 211–33.

Mathew, K. M., *History of the Portuguese Navigation in India (1497–1600)*. Mittal Publications, Delhi, 1988.
Matsuda Kiichi, *Tenshō Shōnen Shisetsu*. Kadokawa, Tokyo, 1965.
——— & Miura Tetsuo, '*Tenshō Ken'ō Shisetsu*'. In *Spazio*, 13:1, Olivetti, Tokyo, June 1982, pp. 7–24.
Matsuda Suihō, *Tenshō no Shōnen Shisetsu*, Komine Shoten, Tokyo, 1971.
McKelway, Matthew Philip, 'Capitalscapes: Painting and Politics in 16th-17th Century Japan', doctoral dissertation, Columbia University, 1999.
Montaigne, *The Diary of Montaigne's Journey to Italy in 1580 and 1581*, tr. E. J. Trechmann. Harcourt, Brace, New York, 1929.
Montanus, Arnoldus, *Atlas jappanensis: being remarkable addresses by way of embassy from the East-India company of the United Provinces, to the emperor of Japan*. London, 1670.
Moran, J. F., *The Japanese and the Jesuits: Alessandro Valignano in sixteenth-century Japan*. Routledge, London & New York, 1993.
———'The Real Author of the *De Missione Legatorum Iapanensium ad Romanam Curiam . . . Dialogus*: A Reconsideration'. In *Bulletin of Portuguese/Japanese Studies*, volume 2, 2001, pp. 7–21.
Mundy, Peter, *The Travels of Peter Mundy, in Europe and Asia, 1608–1667*. Volume 3:2, *Travels in Achin, Mauritius, Madagascar, and St. Helena, 1638*, ed. Richard Carnac Temple. Hakluyt Society, 2nd series, volume 46, London, 1919.
Murakami Naojirō, '*Ōtomo Ōmura Arima Sanke Shisetsu no Kanjōkan*'. In *Shigaku Zasshi*, volume 12:4, 1901, pp. 496–505.
New Catholic Encyclopedia. McGraw-Hill, New York, 19 volumes, 1967–1979.
Okamoto Yoshitomo, *The Namban Art of Japan*, tr. Ronald K. Jones. Weatherhill/Heibonsha, New York & Tokyo, 1972.
Oliveira e Costa, João Paulo, 'Bishop D. Luís Cerqueira (1552–1614) and the Faith of the Japanese Christians'. In *St. Francis Xavier: An Apostle of the East*, volume 2, Sophia University Press, 2000, pp. 105–21.
Oxford English Dictionary. 2nd edition, 20 volumes, Oxford, 1989.
Pacheco, Diego, S.J., 'Diogo de Mesquita, S.J., and the Jesuit Mission Press'. In *Monumenta Nipponica*, volume 26:3–4, 1971, pp. 431–43.
———'*La Campana del "Hospital Santiago" de Nagasaki*'. In *Boletín de la Associación Española de Orientalistas*, volume 7, Madrid, 1971, pp. 11–29.
———'*Los Cuatro Legados Japoneses de los Daimyos de Kyushu despues de Regresar a Japón*'. In *Boletín de la Asociación Española de Orientalistas*, Madrid, 1973, pp. 19–58.
———*Os Quatro Legados dos Dáimios de Quiuxu após Regressarem ao Japão*. Instituto Cultural de Macau, 1990. [Portuguese and Japanese translations of the previous work.]
———'*La Hermandad del Santísimo Sacramento y la Rebelión de Shimabara*'. In *Boletín de Bellas Artes*, Seville, 2002, pp. 133–51.
Other works by Diego Pacheco are listed under his Japanese name, Yūki Ryōgo.
Parker, Geoffrey, *Philip II*. Open Court, Chicago & La Salle, Illinois, 3rd edition, 1995.
Pastor, Ludwig von, *The History of the Popes from the Close of the Middle Ages*, ed. Ralph Francis Kerr, London: Kegan Paul, Trench, Trubner & Co., volumes 20 & 21, 1930–1932.
Peyrefitte, Roger, *The Prince's Person*, tr. Peter Fryer. Farrar, Straus & Giroux, New York, 1965.

BIBLIOGRAPHY

Polo, Marco, *The Book of Ser Marco Polo the Venetian Concerning the Kingdoms and Marvels of the East*, ed. Henry Yule. John Murray, London, 2 volumes, 3rd edition, 1929.
Purchas, Samuel, ed., *Hakluytus Posthumus or Purchas His Pilgrimes, Contayning a History of the World in Sea Voyages and Lande Travells by Englishmen and others*. James MacLehose & Sons, Glasgow, 20 volumes, 1905–1907.
———*Purchas His Pilgrimes in Japan*, ed. Cyril Wild. J. L. Thompson and Kegan Paul, Kobe & London, 1939.
Pyrard, François, *The Voyage of François Pyrard of Laval*, tr. Albert Gray. Hakluyt Society, 1st series, volume 77, London, 1888.
Rajagopalan, S., *Old Goa*, New Delhi, 1975.
Ridolfi, Carlo, *The Life of Tintoretto and of his children Domenico and Marietta*, tr. Catherine & Robert Enggass. Pennsylvania State University Press, 1984.
Rodrigues, João, S.J., *João Rodrigues's Account of Sixteenth-Century Japan*, ed. & tr. Michael Cooper, Hakluyt Society, London, 2001.
Ross, Andrew, C., *A Vision Betrayed: The Jesuits in Japan and China, 1542–1742*, Orbis Books, Maryknoll, N.Y., 1994.
Russell-Wood, A. J. R., *A World on the Move: The Portuguese in Africa, Asia, and America, 1415–1808*. St. Martin's Press, New York, 1993.
Sakamoto Mitsuru, ed., *Namban Bijutsu to Yōfūga. Genshoku Nihon no Bijutsu*, volume 25, Shogakukan, Tokyo, 1970.
Sande, Duarte de, S.J., *Diálogo sobre a Missão dos Embaixadores Japoneses à Cúria Romana*, tr. Américo da Costa Ramalho, Fundação Oriente, Macao, 1997.
San Gerónimo, Fray Juan de, 'Memorias de Fray Juan de San Gerónimo. Monge . . . del Escorial sobre varios sucesos del Reinado de Felipe II'. In *Colección de Documentos Inéditos*, volume 7, pp. 5–442.
Satow, E. M., 'The Origin of Spanish and Portuguese Rivalry in Japan'. In *Transactions of the Asiatic Society of Japan*, volume 18, 1890, pp. 133–56.
Schuddeboom, Cornelis, *Philips van Winghe (1560–1592) en het onstaan van de christelijke archeologie*. Geldermalsen, Haren, 1996.
Schurhammer, Georg, S.J., *Orientalia*, Rome & Lisbon, 1963.
———'Die erste Japanische Gesandtschaftsreise nach Europa (1582–1590)'. In Schurhammer, *Orientalia*, pp. 731–41.
———'Uma obra raríssima impressa em Goa no ano 1588: A Oratio Habita a Fara D. Martino'. In Schurhammer, *Orientalia*, pp. 743–53.
———*Francis Xavier: His Life, His Times*, tr. M. Joseph Costelloe, S.J., volume 4, Jesuit Historical Institute, Rome, 1982.
Schütte, Josef Franz, S.J., *Documentos sobre el Japón conservados en la Colección <Cortes> de la Real Academia de la Historia*. Madrid, 1961.
———'Ignacio Moreira of Lisbon, Cartographer in Japan 1590–1592', In *Imago Mundi*, volume 16, 1962, pp. 116–28.
———*El Archivo del Japón: Vicisitudes del Archivo Jesuítico del Extremo Oriente*. Real Academia de la Historia, Madrid, 1964.
———*Introductio ad Historiam Societatis Jesu in Japonia, 1549–1650*. Institutum Historicum Soc. Jesu, Rome, 1968.
———*Textus Catalogorum Japoniae*. Monumenta Historica Soc. Iesu, Rome, 1975.
———*Valignano's Mission Principles for Japan*. Institute for Jesuit Sources, St. Louis, 2 volumes, 1980–1985.
Shōwa Shōnen Shisetsudan (Shōwa Young Envoys' Mission 1982). Nagasaki, 1983.

251

Simon, Kate, *A Renaissance Tapestry: The Gonzagas of Mantua*. Harper Row, New York, 1988.
Steegmann, Mary G., *Bianca Capello*. Constable, London, 1913.
Stirling-Maxwell, William, *Don John of Austria*. Longman, London, 2 volumes, 1883.
Takayanagi, Shun'ichi, 'The Glory That Was Azuchi'. In *Monumenta Nipponica*, volume 32:4, 1977, pp. 515–24.
Teixeira, Manuel, *Macau no Sec. XVI*. Macau, 1979.
Tietze, Hans, *Tintoretto, The Paintings and Drawings*. Phaidon, New York, 1948.
Tobu Museum of Art, *Catalogue: St. Francis Xavier – His Life and Times*. Tobu Museum of Art, Tokyo, 1999.
Toby, Ronald P., 'Carnival of the Aliens: Korean Embassies in Edo-Period Art and Popular Culture'. In *Monumenta Nipponica*, volume 41:4, 1986, pp. 415–56.
Tsuboi Kumazō, 'Ōtomo Ōmura Arima Sanke Shisetsu Venechia Seifu e Teiseshi Kanjōkan'. In *Shigaku Zasshi*, volume 12:5, 1901, pp. 616–30.
Tucci, Giuseppe, 'Japanese Ambassadors as Roman Patricians'. In *East and West*, volume 2, 1952, pp. 65–71.
Valignano, Alessandro, S.J., *De Missione Legatorum Iaponensium ad Romanam curiam, rebusq; in Europa, ac toto itinere animadversis dialogus ex ephemeride ipsorum legatorum collectus, & in sermonem latinum versus ab Eduardo de Sande Sacerdote Societatis IESV*. Macao, 1590. Facsimile edition, Tōyō Bunkō, Tokyo, 1935.
———*Historia del Principio y Progresso de la Compañía de Jesús en las Indias Orientales*, ed. Josef Wicki, S.J. Institutum Historicum S.I., Rome, 1944.
———*Il Cerimoniale per i Missionari del Giappone*, ed. Giuseppe Fr. Schütte, S.J., Storia e Letteratura, Rome, 1946.
———*Sumario de las Cosas de Japon (1583), Adiciones del Sumario de Japon (1592)*, ed. José Luis Alvarez-Taladriz, Sophia University, Tokyo, 1954.
———*Apología de la Compañía de Jesús de Japón y China (1598)*, ed. José Luis Alvarez-Taladriz. Osaka, 1998.
Vasiljevová, Zdeńka, 'An Unknown Sixteenth Century Czech Print on the Japanese Mission to Rome of 1585'. In *Asian and African Studies*, volume 24, 1989, pp. 125–35.
Verwilghen, Albert-Felix, 'Christian Music in Japan from 1549 till 1614'. In *Kokusai Bunka Shinkōkai Bulletin*, volume 95, Tokyo, April–May 1969, pp. 1–13.
Vlam, Grace, 'Western-Style Secular Painting in Momoyama Japan', University of Michigan, 1976.
Vocabulario da Lingoa de Iapam. . .. Nagasaki, 1603. Facsimile edition, Benseisha, Tokyo, 1973.
Voltaire, *Essai sur les mœurs et l'esprit des nations et sur les principaux faits de l'histoire depuis Charlemagne jusqu'à Louis XIII*, volume 2. Classique Garnier, Paris, 1990.
Waterhouse, David, 'The Earliest Japanese Contacts with Western Music'. In *Review of Culture*, 1996, Macao, pp. 36–47.
———'Southern Barbarian Music in Japan'. In Salwa El-Shawan Castelo-Branco, ed., *Portugal and the World: The Encounter of Cultures in Music*, Publicações Dom Quixote, Lisbon, 1997, pp. 351–77.
Wheelwright, Carolyn, 'A Visualization of Eitoku's Lost Paintings at Azuchi Castle'. In George Elison & Bardwell L. Smith, ed., *Warlords, Artists and Commoners: Japan in the Sixteenth Century*, University of Hawaii Press, 1981.
Young, G. F., *The Medici*. The Modern Library, New York, 1930.

BIBLIOGRAPHY

Yūki Ryōgo, S.J., *Tenshō Shōnen Shisetsu no Nakaura Jurian*. Nihon Nijūroku Seijin Kinenkan, Nagasaki, 1981.

——— *Roma wo Mita: Tenshō Shōnen Shisetsu, 1582–1982*. Nihon Nijūroku Seijin Shiryōkan, Nagasaki, 1982.

———'*Nakaura Jurian no Tegami*'. Pamphlet, Nihon Nijūroku Seijin Kinenkan, Nagasaki, 1982.

———'*Atarashiku Hakken shita Itō Mancio no Nitsū no Tegami*'. In *Nagasaki Dansō*, 1983, pp. 9–26.

———'*Shinshiryō Tenshō Shōnen Shisetsu*'. In *Kirishitan Kenkyū*, volume 29, Nansōsha, Tokyo, 1990.

———'A Present of Arabian Horses,' tr. Fumiko F. Earns. In *Crossroads*, Nagasaki, volume 2, 1994.

———'*Julian Nakaura, Legado, Jesuita, Martir, 1568–1633*'. Nagasaki, 1997.

Other works by Yūki Ryōgo are listed under his Spanish name, Diego Pacheco.

Index

Abranches Pinto, João do Amaral, ix, 196
Acosta, José de, 221 n. 25
Acquaviva, Claudio, 84–5, 99, 224 nn. 29, 31
Albert, Cardinal, 45–7, 48, 132, 133, 137, 203
Alcalá, 70–1
Alessandrino, Cardinal, 226, n. 12
Alexander the Great, 146
Alicante, 74, 77
allegiance ceremony, 56–9
Almeida, João de, 28
Almeida, Jorge, 46
Altemps, Marquis, vii, 99, 102, 226 n. 6
Alvarez-Taladriz, José Luis, 216 n. 15
ambassadors, European: vii, 58, 65, 69, 86, 91,93, 97, 99, 100, 102, 107, 113, 114, 117,123, 128, 201, 225 n. 3, 238 n. 8
Ancona, 109
Arima Harunobu, 13, 63, 152, 153,159
Armoury and Treasury, Royal, 68
Asano Nagamasa, 153
Assisi, 108
Augsburg print, 125, 232 n. 23
Augustine, 21, coach accident, 71; 184,

Azuchi Castle, 147
 description, 205
 destroyed, 207; 245 n. 10
Azuchi screens, 94, 203–7, 225–6

Barcelona, 130–1
Bartoli, Daniello, quoted 85; 201, 244 n. 24
Belmonte, 71–2
Benacci, Alessandro, quoted, 110, 228 n. 17
Berchet, Guglielmo, *Antiche Ambasciate Giapponesi*, 202
Bernard, 213 n. 1
Bernard, Henri, ix, 196, 218 n. 23, 243 n. 10
Boccapaduli, Antonio, 90
Bologna, 109–10
Boncompagni, Giacomo—*see* Sora, duke of
Borja, Juan de, 65
Borja, St Francis, 221 n. 20
Boscaro, Adriana, x, 202
boys, the
 'boys', 14
 chaperoned 19, 37–8, 217 n. 14
 companions, 14
 described, 60, 110, 117, 126–7, 226 n. 8
 entry into novitiate, 184–5, 227 n. 1
 fluency 61,126, 237 n. 17

254

INDEX

lack of individuality 17–18, 192
legates selected, 13; 14
lessons, 27, 28
low-key legation, 16, 17, 129
marvel, 61, 126, 218 n. 21
music, 27, 33, 49–50, 51, 81, 127, 132, 150–1, 158
note-taking, 21, 51, 53, 54, 66, 81, 124–5, 215 n. 35
obedience, 223 n. 22
piety, 73, 166
recreation, 27, 39, 141
student dress, 38
'unrecognized' by families, 152–3
very young 18
well-mannered, 126
Bragança, Catarina, and family, 50–1, 132, 219 n. 11
Bragança, João de, 55, 133
Bragança, Theotonio de (archbishop of Evora), 6, 38, 48–50, 132; 217 n. 15; minor orders for George Loyola, 133
Braun, Georg, 209
Brunswick, duchess of, 128
byōbu, 204, 244 n. 1

cañas, 219 n. 12
Capello, Bianca – *see* Tuscany, archduchess of
Carletti, Francesco, quoted, 204
carracks, 25, 216 nn. 1, 2, 4
Castelo Branco, Afonso de, 133, 135
Catarina, Princess, 58, 61
Cerqueira, Luis de, 175, 188, 239 n. 18
certificates of Rome senate, 226 n. 11
chaperoning, 19, 37–8, 217 n. 14
Chijiwa, Michael – *see* Michael
Chinese boy, 64; coach accident, 71
Chioggia, 113, 168
Christianity
  Crown grants to churches in India, 212 n. 9
  financial problems, 6–7
  friars, 9–11
  gift-giving, 6, 212 n. 8
  introduced into Japan, 4
  need to be better known in Europe, 7

number of converts, 4, 6, 7, 148
schools, 5
cities screens, 245 n. 16
Civitates Orbis Terrarum, 118, 153, 209, 210
cities copied, 210
regional costumes, 211
clavicembalo, 81, 132, 223 n. 16
clock, astronomical, 55, 129 n. 3
Cochin, 33–4, 39
Cocks, Richard, quoted 15–16, 186
Coelho, Gaspar, 18, 149
Coimbra, 133–6
convents, 135
student plays, 136
student welcome, 134
university, 135–6
Collona, Ascanio, 233 n. 4
Columbus, Christopher, 3–4
Córdoba, Diego de, 63, 64, 65
Corpus Christi procession, 110
Cremona, 122
Crichton ('The Admirable'), James, 231 n. 9

daimyo, Christian, 13, 155; 154, 156
David, 223 n. 14
De Missione Legatorum: translated by Sande, 198
content, 199–200
34 Dialogues, 198
difficult style, 198
George Loyola as translator, 199
Japanese editions, 243 nn. 23, 24
Japanese translation planned, 199
Michael chief narrator, 243 n. 16
Valignano quoted, 198
Dias, Álvaro, 21
Divina Bonitas, 171
Doglioni, Nicolò, 230 n. 10
Dourado, Constantine, 21
account of Vila Viçosa, 51
also of Toledo, Escorial? 54–5
biography, 183–4
coach accident, 71; 147; 176; 236 n. 23; 240 n. 12
name, 184
Drake, Francis, 234 n. 5
Dum ad uberes fructus, 173

empress (sister of Philip II), 58, 64, 132, 220 n. 8
Escorial, 59, 65–8
Evora, 48–50
   archbishop – *see* Bragança, Theotonio de
   cathedral organ, 49–50
Ex pastorali officio, 173

Farnese, Alessandro, 83
Ferrara, 110–11
Fiamma, Gabriel, 113
Florence 80–2
   Palazzo Vecchio, 81
   Santissima Annunziata, 82
   statues, 81, 222 n. 14, 223 n. 15
Fonseca, Vincente de, 36, 217 n. 4
fountains, 81, 84, 218 n. 5
Franciscans, 10–11 ; oppose legation, 15
Fróis, Luis
   author *of Tratado*, 193–5
   based on boys' notes, 51, 54, 66, 124
   career, 193–4
   compiles *Tratado*, 195–6
   literary style, 196–7, 242 n. 4
   quoted, 8
   similarities with Gaultieri's *Relationi*, 195
   Tratado text published, 196
Fukan, Fabian, 240 n. 27

Gama, Miguel da, 13
Genoa, 128–9
geographical knowledge, Japanese, 209–10
gifts presented, 46, 61–2, 203, 218 n. 1, 223 n. 18, 225 n. 6, 245 n. 11
   Japanese robes as gifts 111, 114, 121–2
gifts 111, 114, 121–2
Goa, 35–7, 145–8
   Martin's Latin speech, 145–7
Gómez, Pedro, 28, 187
Gonçalves, Gaspar, speech, 89–90, 167
Gonzaga, Guglielmo, 231 nn. 7, 9, 11, 12
Gonzaga, Muzio, 120
Gonzaga, Scipione, 231 n. 10

Gonzaga, Vicenzo, 231 n. 9
Good Hope, Cape of, 39, 141, 235 n. 8
Granada, Luis de, 47
Granvelle, Antoine Perrenot de, 58, 220 n. 9
Gregorian calendar, 34, 216 n. 16, 224 n. 24
Gregory XIII
   Antonio Boccapaduli's speech, 90
   biography, 224 n. 24
   boys accompany him to Santa Maria sopra Minerva, 92–3
   commemorative medal, 94
   funeral and burial, 97
   Gaspar Gonçalves's speech, 89–90
   illness and death, vii, 95
   Mancio and Michael read letters, 89
   military alert in Rome, 96
   Montaigne's description, 224 n. 1
   Ōtomo Sōrin's letter, 89
   private audiences with boys, 91, 94–5
   procession, 87–8
   provides new robes, 92
   receives gift of Azuchi screens, 94
   sends military escort, 83
   solemn audience, 88–91
   urges haste, 83
Grillo, Angelo, 232 n. 14
Guadalupe shrine, 53, 219 n. 1
Gualtieri, Guido, 195, 242 n. 7
Guzman, Luis de, 71–3
   Historia de las Misiones, 200
   met boys at Belmonte, 200; 215 n. 35
   quoted, 238 n. 11

Hara, Martin – *see* Martin
Hasekura Tsunenaga, 215 n. 36, 227 n. 11
   portraits, 230 n. 14
Henry III of France, 132, 228 n. 20
Henry VIII of England, 233 n. 30
Hideyoshi – *see* Toyotomi Hideyoshi
Hieronymites, 218 n. 3
Hogenberg, Franz, 209
Holbein the Younger, Hans, 233 n. 30
horses 137, 145, 148, 153, 155, 158, 234 n. 13, 235 n. 12, 236 n. 7, 237 nn. 8, 11
   Japanese, 237 n. 11

INDEX

Isabella, Princess, 58, 61
Itō, Jerome, 13
Itō, Justus, 185, 240 n. 21
Itō, Mancio – see Mancio
Iwakura Tomomi, 216 n. 36

Japan
  Christianity, 4–8
  Europeans arrive, 4
  Japanese opinion of selves, 8–9; of Europeans, 8–9, 213 n. 16
  Japanese Mission to Europe
    assessment, 163–78
    Europe to India, 141–8
    Hideyoshi audience in Kyoto, 155–8
    India to Europe, 39–41
    India to Macao, 148–51
    Italy, 77–129
    Macao to India, 30–8
    Macao to Nagasaki, 151–4
    Nagasaki to Macao, 25–30
    papal audience in Rome, 86–91
    Philip II audience in Madrid, 60–3
    Portugal, 45–52, 132–7, 132–7
    preparation, 12–22
    purpose, 3–11
    reenactment, 178–9
    Return journey: Spain, 130–32
    sources, 193–202
    Spain, 53–74
    subsequent careers, 180–92
  Jesuit Press, 147, 151, 175–6, 188
  Jesuits: and friars 9–11, 15, 213 n. 21
    monopoly in Japan, 9–11, 173–4, 213 n. 25
    theatre, 233 n. 11
Julian
  dance, 80
  family, 14,19, 215 n. 26
  Knight of St Peter, 102;
  martyrdom, 191–2
  meets pope, 86, 7;
  Mesquita, 163, 177;
  'not recognized', 152
  ordination, 175
  Roman Patrician, 101–102
  sick, 18, 86–7, 94, 96, 99, 111, 124, 130
  subsequent career, 189–92
Jurakutei palace, 155, 156, 158

Kano Eitoku, 207
Kano, Pedro, 188, 241 n. 35
Konishi Yukinaga (Augustine), 155, 187
Kuroda Nagamasa, 154
Kuroda Yoshitaka, 153
Kyoto, 155–8

Lach, Donald, quoted viii, 164; 202
Lateran, St John, procession, 101
  figure 9
  mural, 101
Leghorn, 77–8
Lepanto, Battle of (screen), 211
Lima, Ignacio de, 22
Linschoten, John, quoted, 31, 218 n. 17, 236 nn. 6, 8
Lisbon, 41–8, 133, 137
Loreto, 108–109
Lorraine, duchess of, 128, 233 n. 30
Loyola, George, 20–1
  biography, 184
  death, 151, 215 n. 30
  Escorial, 67
  minor orders, 133
  near-accident, 50
  Philip II, 62
  printing, 147, 176
  speech, 135

Macao, 27–30
  allegiance to new king, 29, 149–151
  silk trade, 7, 27–8
Madrid, 56–70
  allegiance ceremony, 56–9
  audience with Philip II, 61–3
  Escorial, 65–8
  Royal Armoury and Treasury, 68; 132
Malacca, 31, 149
Mallorca, 77
Mancio, Ōtomo Sōrin,13
  archduke of Tuscany, 78–9
  audience, 94
  baptism, 120
  Cardinal Albert, 45
  coronation ceremony, 100
  dance, 79
  death, 177

257

Mancio, Ōtomo Sōrin (cont.)
  duke of Terranova, 123
  family, 19, 214 n. 4, 215 n. 26
  Hideyoshi, 157–58
  ill, 31
  Knight of St Peter, 102
  kaō, 127
  letters, 149
  Mandeville, John, 238 n. 7
  mentioned in letters, 63, 70, 89
  Mesquita, 163, 169
  Milan portraits, 125
  music, 151
  'not recognized', 152
  official legate, 17; 18,
  ordained, 175
  organ, 49–50
  Ōtomo Yoshimune, 155
  papal audience, 87–9
  Philip II, 61, 62
  portrait of archduchess, 80, 223 n. 20
  Roman Patrician, 101–102
  Rome procession, 87
  Santa Maria sopra Minerva, 93
  Sixtus V, 99
  subsequent career, 184–6
  Tintoretto, 116
  viceroy, 35
Mantua, 120–2
  firework display, 121
  gifts received, 121
  'The Test', 232 n. 16
  Vicenzo Gonzaga, 231 n. 9
Mantua, duke of, 119
Mark, St, festival, 115, 229 n. 9
Martin
  'Campo', 214 n. 4
  companion, 14
  dance 79
  Knight of St Peter, 102
  later career, 187–9
  Latin speeches, 39, 145–7
  Mesquita 177
  'not recognized', 152
  oldest boy? 18
  ordained, 175
  papal audiences, 88, 94
  Roman Patrician, 101–102
  Rome procession, 87
  sick, 56, 65; 70
  talent, 217 n. 16
  translation work, 188
Martins, Pedro, 175, 217 n. 4
Mascarenhas, Francisco de, 34, 36, 38, 132
Mata, Gil de la, 215 n. 32
Medici, Eleanora de', 232 n. 16
Medici, Isabella de' 222 n. 8
Medici, Pietro de', 78, 222 nn. 2, 5
Mendoza, Francisco de, 55
Meneses, Duarte de, 235 n. 11
Meneses, Jorge de, 143, 147
Mesquita, Diogo de
  appointed to legation, 20
  biography, 181–3
  Cardinal Albert, 45–6
  carriage accident, 71
  dance, 79
  Doge, 114
  gives lessons, 27, 28
  ill, 31
  Kyoto procession, 156
  letter, 39
  Milan portraits, 116, 125
  Naples visit, 108
  papal audience, 89
  Philip II, 56–7, 61–2, 64, 65, 69, 70
  private audience, 95
  quoted, 163, 177
  Rome procession, 81
  sails from Lisbon, 137
  translation, 127
  Tratado, 194, 242n. 4
  trek in India, 33
  Valignano, 217 n. 9, 238 n. 14, 240 n. 6
  Valignano's instructions, 37–8
Michael
  age, 125
  audience, 94
  Augsburg print, 232 n. 23
  dance, 79
  description of city, 124–5
  family, 13, 19, 214 n. 4, 237 nn. 20, 26, 45
  fortress, 124
  Hideyoshi ,158
  illness, 55, 56, 73, 152
  Knight of St Peter, 102

INDEX

later career, 186–7
legate, 17
Milan, 123–5
'not recognized', 152
organ, 49–50
papal audience, 88–91
Philip II, 61–2
plaque, 241 n. 30
quoted, 130, 233 n. 29
Roman Patrician, 101–102
Rome procession, 87
Santa Maria sopra Minerva, 93
tomb, 241 n. 31
Milan, 123–5:
description of city, 124–5
fortress, 124
Urbano Monte and portraits, 124–5
military escorts, 82
Minerva, Santa Maria sopra, 92–3, 225 n. 2
Mirabilia Dei, 171
mission, reenactment of, 178–9, 239 n. 32
Molino, Constantino, 114
Montaigne, quoted, 221 n. 1, 222 n. 4, 224 n. 1, 225 n. 2, 227 n. 4, 229 n. 21, 230 n. 1, 244 n. 30
style, 244 n. 30
Montalto, Felice, 226 n. 1. *See* Sixtus V
Montanus, Arnoldus, quoted, 40
Monte, Urbano, 125, 126–7, 218 n. 21, 232 n. 22
Montserrat abbey, 131
Monzón, 131
Moraes, Sebastian de, 175, 239 n. 27
Moran, J. F., ix, x
Moreira, Cristóvão, 21
Mōri Terumoto, 154
Moura, Cristóbal de, 57, 59, 63, 220 n. 7
Mozambique, 142, 143–4
Mundy, Peter, quoted, 36, 40–1
Murcia, 73–4
Muro, 154
musical concerts, 150–1, 158
musical instruments, 81, 132, 150–1, 223 n. 16, 236 n. 21

Nagasaki, 4, departure, 22; return, 151
Nakaura, Julian – *see* Julian

nanbanjin, 213 n. 16
Naples, visit cancelled, 107–108; 227 n. 3

Oda Nobunaga, screens, 38, 147
death, 207
letters, 50, 206
Okamoto Yoshitomo, ix, 196, 242 n. 9
Olivares, count of, 86, 93, 95, 97, 221 n. 2
Philip II's letter, 69–70
Ōmura Sumitada, 13, 63; death, 149, 152
Ōmura Yoshiaki, 159, 236 n. 1
Orihuela, 74
Orsini, Paulo Giordano, 93, 222 n. 8, 228 n. 12
Ortelius, 153, 208
Osaka Castle, 149
Ōtomo Sōrin (Francis of Bungo)
death, 149, 152
legation, 13
letter 62–3
quoted, 5
Ōtomo Yoshimune (Constantine), 154–5
and Mancio, 155

Padua, 118
Orto Botanico, 118,
Wieland's gift of books, 118
Palladio, Andrea, 231 n. 5
papal conclave, 97–8
Pavia, 127–8
Peretti, Felice, 226 n. 1. *See* Sixtus V
Perpinhão, Luis, 55, 217 n. 13
Perugia, 108
Pesaro, 109
Philip II
ascends Portuguese throne, 10, 56, 59
audiences, 61–3, 131
personal life 220 n. 17
Philip, Prince, 58, 61
Pietro, Medici de', 222 n. 5
Polirone, San Benedetto di, monastery, 121
Polo, Marco, quoted, 3, 212 n. 1
Ponce de Leon, Francisca, 71–2
Ponte, Nicolò da, 114–15, 229 n. 6

printing press 219 n. 7
Priuli, Lorenzo, 93
protests canopy bearers, 99–100; 117
quoted, 201, 226 n. 8; 227 n. 13
Pyrard, François de, quoted, 36

Quiroga, Gaspar de, 65, 221 n. 21

Ramón, Pedro, 16, 188
relics, 65, 67, 68, 88, 134, 142, 144
Riano, Marquis, vii, 99
Ricci, Matteo, 28
Rodrigues, João, 156, 213 n. 13, 238 n. 7
Rodrigues, Nuno, 7, 37, 84, 107, 133, 137, 217 nn. 10,12
Rome, 84–107
　audience, 88–91
　coronation, 99–100
　death of pope, 95–6
　election of Sixtus V, 98
　funeral, 97
　Knights of St Peter, 102
　papal conclave, 97–8
　Patricians of Rome, 101
　private audiences, 94–5, 101
　procession, 87–8
　St John Lateran, 100–101
　Santa Maria sopra Minerva, 92–3
　senate, 101
　seven churches, 95, 96

Sá, Leonardo de, 28
sakazuki, 46,157, 218 n. 2
Sala Regia, 88
Sánchez, Alonso, 29
Sande, Eduardo de, quoted, 21; 243 n. 13
San Gerónimo, Juan de, 67–8
San Sisto, Cardinal, 91, 96
Santa Barbara, church, 120
Santiago (ship), 39,142, 143, 148
　wrecked, 234 n. 3
São Felipe (ship), 137, 141, 142, 143
　captured, 234 n. 5
São Lourenço (ship), 143
Saragossa, 131–2
Scheuchzer, J. G. , quoted, viii; 244 n. 24

sea voyages, dangers of, 25–6, 29–30, 215 n. 29
Sfondrati, Niccolò, 122, 232 n. 17
ships – *see* carracks
Siena, 82–3
silk trade, 7, 27–8
Sintra, 47
Sixtus V
　boys' visits, 9
　canopy bearers, 99–100
　character, 98–9
　coronation, vii, 99–100
　elected pope, 98
　gifts 102–103
　Knights of St Peter 102
　with boys to St John Lateran, 100–101
Sofala, 234 n. 2
Sora, duke of, vii, 83, 87, 94, 96, 99; 'nephew', 225 n. 8
Sō Yoshitomo, 154
Spinola, Cardinal, 108
　family, 227 n. 8
St Helena, 39–40
Sumario de las Cosas de Japon, 34

Takayama Hide no kami (Darius), 155
Takayama Ukon (Justus), 155
Teatro Olimpico, 119, 231 n. 5
Tenshō Ken'ō Shisetsu, 22
Tenshō Shōnen Shisetsu, 22
Terranova, duke of, 122, 123; gifts, 127
Theatrum Orbis Terrarum, 118, 209
theological debate, 71
Tiepolo, Paolo, 238 n. 8
Tintoretto, 116
Toledo 54–5
　cathedral, 54–5
　Gianello Turriano's clock, 55, 219 n. 3
Toledo, Eleanora de, 222 nn. 5, 8
Toyotomi Hidetsugu, 156, 237 n. 16
Toyotomi Hideyori, 156
Toyotomi Hideyoshi, 147
　allegiance 220 n. 12
　audience, 156–8
　expulsion edict, 149
　Hideyoshi's gifts, 157
　invites Mancio, 157
　musical recital, 158

INDEX

questions Michael, 158
speaks with boys, 157
viceroy's letter and gifts, 155, 156–7
volte-face, 150, 250 n. 20
with Mancio and João Rodrigues, 158
Tratado dos Embaixadores Iapões – *see* Fróis, Luis
Turriano, Gianello, 55, 219 n. 3
Tuscany, archduchess of (Bianca Capello)
 dance, 79–80
 portrait, 82, 153, 222 nn. 4, 5; 223 n. 20
Tuscany, archduke of (Francesco de' Medici), 77–8, 221 n. 1

Urbino, duchess of, 229 n. 21
Urbino, duke of, 109, 228 n. 12

Valignano, Alessandro
 adaptation, 5
 anxiety about boys, 144, 235 n. 7
 arrival in Japan, 5
 audience with Hideyoshi, 155–8
 biography, 180–1
 early history, 4–5
 friars, 9–11
 Hideyoshi, 153
 Historia del Principio, 220 n. 6
 letters to Evora, 6–7, 148
 loss of gifts, 239 n. 23
 low-key legation, 16–17
 Mesquita, 217 n. 9, 238 n. 14, 240 n. 6
 mission finances, 6–8
 moral responsibility, 19–20
 nurses boys 27, 31
 organizes legation, 12–13
 quoted 6, 7, 8–9, 11, 14, 15, 16, 153
 remains in India, instructions, 37–8
 returns to Japan, 151
 reunited, 145; Martin's speech, 145–7
 Sumario de las Cosas de Japon, 34
 'the boys' 14
 to Kyoto, 154–5
 Viceroy's ambassador, 148, 150
Venice, 113–17
 Doge, 114–15
 gifts received, 116–17, 230 n. 16.
 Grand Canal, St Mark's Square, 114
 procession, 115, 230 n. 1
 proposed portraits, 116
 sightseeing, 115
Verona, 119
Vicenza, 119; Teatro Olimpico, 119
Vila Viçosa, 50–2, 132
Villa Pratolino, 81, 222 n. 11
Vilela, Gaspar, quoted, 204
Visconte, Gaspar, 123
Viterbo, 83
Vizcaino, Sebastian, 236 n. 5
voyages, sea, 25–6, 216 nn. 1, 4
 becalming, 142, 144
 deaths, 41
 drinking water, 31
 storms, 27, 29–30, 30–1, 141, 144

Wieland, Melchior, 118, 209, 231 n. 4, 245 n. 12
Winghe, Philips van, 208
world maps, 245 n. 15

Xavier, Francis, 4, 35; quoted, 8, 196

Yūki Ryōgo, x, 202, 212 n. 2

Zipangu, 3, 4, 17

261

The façade of the church of São Paolo, Macao, behind which are buried Martin Hara and Alessandro Valignano. The rest of the church was destroyed by fire in 1835.